DevOps Automation Cookbook

Over 120 recipes covering key automation techniques through code management and virtualization offered by modern Infrastructure-as-a-Service solutions

Michael Duffy

BIRMINGHAM - MUMBAI

DevOps Automation Cookbook

First published: November 2015

Production reference: 1241115

Published by Packt Publishing Ltd.
Livery Place
35 Livery Street
Birmingham B3 2PB, UK.

ISBN 978-1-78439-282-6

www.packtpub.com

Credits

Author

Michael Duffy

Reviewers

Jon Auman

Tom Geudens

Sami Rönkä

Diego Woitasen

Commissioning Editor

Julian Ursell

Acquisition Editor

Reshma Raman

Content Development Editor

Riddhi Tuljapurkar

Technical Editor

Naveenkumar Jain

Copy Editor

Sneha Singh

Project Coordinator

Kinjal Bari

Proofreader

Safis Editing

Indexer

Hemangini Bari

Graphics

Kirk Dpenha

Production Coordinator

Shantanu N. Zagade

Cover Work

Shantanu N. Zagade

About the Author

Michael Duffy is a technology consultant who spends far too much of his time getting excited about automation tools. Michael lives in a tiny village in Suffolk and when he isn't reading, writing, or playing with automation and infrastructure tools, he can be found spending as much time as he can with his family.

He runs his own consultancy, Stunt Hamster Ltd, and spends a lot of time telling clients that DevOps is an approach rather than a job title. Stunt Hamster Ltd. has provided services to clients as large as Telefonica O2 and BskyB and is currently working on software to ease the pain of managing decentralized platforms.

Michael has previously written *Puppet Reporting and Monitoring*, published by Packt Publishing.

This book would not have been possible without my amazing wife Bethan. I would not have been able to complete this book without her boundless patience, love, and understanding.

I also want to thank my fantastic daughter, Meg, and my incredible son, Griff; you guys have patiently put up with Daddy hiding in his office and have been a source of absolute joy to me.

One last vote of thanks must go to the editors and especially to the dedicated band of reviewers; without you guys, this book would have contained much more gibberish than it actually does.

About the Reviewers

Jon Auman has been a systems administrator for over 15 years with his current focus on DevOps and WebOps methodologies. He holds certifications in Redhat, NetApp, Amazon Web Services, and Puppet. Jon has worked for a wide range of employers like Duke University, Analysts International, and NetApp in the U.S, as well as Mind Candy, Medicanimal.com, Monitise, and HMRC in the UK. Jon currently runs his own consultancy named DaveOps Ltd, in London.

He started working with DevOps tools in 2009. His favorite DevOps toolset includes Puppet, Ansible, AWS CLI, and Jenkins.

Jon was also a reviewer of the Packt Publishing book *Mastering Citrix XenServer* (ISBN 139781783287390).

Tom Geudens was given a choice by his parents at the age of 15; either become a baker or go into IT. That Christmas, Santa brought an MSX home computer and the choice was made. At 20, he had a Bachelor's degree in IT under his belt and joined the IT department of Colruyt, a Belgian retailer specializing in 'Lowest Price' and doing this through automation. Recently, he set up his own IT consultancy company, Elephant Bird Consulting, which specializes in Resource-Oriented Computing solutions. He has worked with technologies from PL/1 to HPUX and Linux, and has also battled distributed applications development and configuration management issues. He is the author of the O'Reilly book *Resource-Oriented Computing with NetKernel*, and blogs at `http://practical-netkernel.blogspot.com/`.

Sami Rönkä is an ICT professional with a keen interest in different automation methodologies. His motto is "*Manually doing the same thing twice is learning, doing it three times is stupidity.*" He has worked in various roles in ICT from maintaining and developing different software build automation systems in very large enterprises to data center ramp-ups including tasks varying from racking and cabling to defining virtual networks and high available services. He is delighted with the progress of tools and methods for using infrastructure as a code, which really has made his life at work easier and more interesting. He believes that changing mindsets takes time, but he knows it is worth it.

After some years of trying to find efficient routes through bureaucracy and change management in large enterprises, he currently works with a smaller IT service provider company aiming to give small businesses a productivity boost with lean and working IT resources.

Diego Woitasen has more than 10 years of experience in Linux and open source consulting industry. Diego Woitasen is (with Luis Vinay) the co-founder of *flugel.it*. This is Self-denominated Infrastructure Developers, they have applied all those years of experience in helping all sorts of companies to embrace the DevOps culture and the new movements related with interdisciplinary cooperative working. He is focused on DevOps Engineering, OpenStack, Linux, and Open Source.

www.PacktPub.com

Support files, eBooks, discount offers, and more

For support files and downloads related to your book, please visit www.PacktPub.com.

Did you know that Packt offers eBook versions of every book published, with PDF and ePub files available? You can upgrade to the eBook version at www.PacktPub.com and as a print book customer, you are entitled to a discount on the eBook copy. Get in touch with us at service@packtpub.com for more details.

At www.PacktPub.com, you can also read a collection of free technical articles, sign up for a range of free newsletters and receive exclusive discounts and offers on Packt books and eBooks.

https://www2.packtpub.com/books/subscription/packtlib

Do you need instant solutions to your IT questions? PacktLib is Packt's online digital book library. Here, you can search, access, and read Packt's entire library of books.

Why Subscribe?

- ▸ Fully searchable across every book published by Packt
- ▸ Copy and paste, print, and bookmark content
- ▸ On demand and accessible via a web browser

Free Access for Packt account holders

If you have an account with Packt at www.PacktPub.com, you can use this to access PacktLib today and view 9 entirely free books. Simply use your login credentials for immediate access.

Table of Contents

Preface

DevOps has created a lot of excitement in recent years and looks certain to make the same impact as Agile software development on the software industry. This is not entirely surprising; DevOps has largely been born from the frustration of Agile developers trying to work within the traditional confines of infrastructure support and delivery. Their attempts to find more efficient ways to deliver reliable, performant, and secure software to the end user has led us to DevOps.

DevOps initially came to people's attention in 2008 when the first DevOps day conference was held. It was organized by *Patrick Debois*; it brought together like-minded people for the first time to discuss how the delivery of infrastructure could be made more agile. Originally, the preferred term for what eventually became DevOps was Agile Infrastructure but the portmanteau of Development and Operations made for a friendlier Twitter tag and the term stuck. From here, the attention and interest in DevOps grew and today there are DevOps day conferences worldwide.

DevOps breaks down the barriers between the operations and development teams and allows a tight collaboration between these traditionally firewalled areas. The resulting cross-functional team will be able to react faster to the changes in the software requirements and deliver the best of breed solutions. This has led to a renaissance in areas such as monitoring and deployment, where the development team may once have lobbed a tarball over the corporate firewall to the operations department to install. The developers instead created a robust set of automated provisioning scripts to manage installations themselves. Likewise, monitoring has started to cease to be an exercise in testing if a port is available or if the server has run out of disk space (although this is still essential) and has become a holistic approach that takes into account the health of the infrastructure, load on the application, number of errors generated, and so on. This is only possible if you have a team that is truly cross-functional and with a deep understanding of the software they manage.

Defining what can be considered as a DevOps tool is incredibly difficult but the rapid increase of companies utilizing DevOps techniques has led to an explosion of new tools with a particular focus on automation, monitoring, and testing. Tools, such as Puppet, Chef, CF Engine, and Ansible have grown massively in popularity, thus allowing developers to truly define the underlying infrastructure using the code. Likewise, new monitoring tools, such as Sensu, have appeared that take up the challenge of monitoring ephemeral infrastructures, such as cloud-based services.

This book is different from most of the other technical cookbooks. Rather than keeping a laser-like focus on a single technology, this cookbook serves as an introduction to many different tools. Each chapter offers recipes that show you how to install and utilize tools that tackle some of the key areas that a team using DevOps techniques will encounter. Using it, you can quickly get up to speed with diverse areas, such as *Automation with Ansible*, *Monitoring with Sensu*, and log analyses with LogStash. By doing the further reading outlined with each recipe, you can find pointers to gain a deeper insight into these fantastic tools.

What this book covers

Chapter 1, *Basic Command Line Tools*, covers some basic but incredibly useful tools for trouble shooting servers and managing code.

Chapter 2, *Ad Hoc Tasks with Ansible*, contains recipes that allow you to use the powerful Ansible automation tool to run one off commands for server management.

Chapter 3, *Automatic Host Builds*, covers recipes that allow you to automate the build and configuration of the most basic building block in your infrastructure servers.

Chapter 4, *Virtualization with VMware ESXi*, contains recipes that show how to install and use the popular ESXi hypervisor to create, manage, and use powerful virtual servers.

Chapter 5, *Automation with Ansible*, covers the incredibly powerful configuration management tool, Ansible. These recipes demonstrate how to create a powerful and reusable code to manage the configuration of your infrastructure.

Chapter 6, *Containerization with Docker*, covers the increasingly popular world of containerization. Containerization is an incredibly powerful technique for distributing and running software and these recipes show you how to use Docker to create, run, and maintain containers.

Chapter 7, *Using Jenkins for Continuous Deployment*, contains recipes that show you how Ansible can be used with the powerful Jenkins CI tool to create an automated build and deploy system.

Chapter 8, *Metric Collection with InflxDB*, demonstrates how to use the powerful Time Series database InfluxDB to capture and analyze metrics generated by your infrastructure and present them in attractive and easy-to-understand formats.

Chapter 9, Log Management, demonstrates how to use powerful tools to centralize, collect, and analyze valuable log data.

Chapter 10, Monitoring with Sensu, covers using this powerful, scalable, and customizable monitoring system to demonstrate how to install, configure, and manage Sensu.

Chapter 11, IAAS with Amazon AWS, covers recipes that demonstrate how to set up infrastructure using the powerful AWS Infrastructure-as-a-Service. It also covers topics, such as EC2 servers, DNS management, and security.

Chapter 12, Application Performance Monitoring with New Relic, introduces the NewRelic application performance monitoring tool and demonstrates how to use it to monitor servers, applications, and more.

What you need for this book

For this book, you will require the following software:

- A server running Ubuntu 14.04 or greater.
- A desktop PC running a modern Web Browser
- A good Text editor or IDE.

Who this book is for

If you are a systems administrator or developer who is keen to employ DevOps techniques to help with the day-to-day complications of managing complex infrastructures, then this book is for you.

Sections

In this book, you will find several headings that appear frequently (Getting ready, How to do it, How it works, There's more, and See also).

To give clear instructions on how to complete a recipe, we use these sections as follows:

Getting ready

This section tells you what to expect in the recipe and describes how to set up any software or any preliminary settings required for the recipe.

How to do it...

This section contains the steps required to follow the recipe.

How it works...

This section usually consists of a detailed explanation of what happened in the previous section.

There's more...

This section consists of additional information about the recipe in order to make the reader more knowledgeable about the recipe.

See also

This section provides helpful links to other useful information for the recipe.

Conventions

In this book, you will find a number of text styles that distinguish between different kinds of information. Here are some examples of these styles and an explanation of their meaning.

Code words in text, database table names, folder names, filenames, file extensions, pathnames, dummy URLs, user input, and Twitter handles are shown as follows: "Where `<interface>` is the name of the network interface you wish to see the details of."

A block of code is set as follows:

```
[loadbalancer]
haproxy01
[web]
web01
web02
web03
web04 [database]
mysql01
```

When we wish to draw your attention to a particular part of a code block, the relevant lines or items are set in bold:

```
[loadbalancer]
haproxy01
[web]
web01:04
[database]
mysql01
[all:children]]
loadbalancer
web
```

Any command-line input or output is written as follows:

```
ansible all --sudo --ask-sudo-pass -m raw -a 'sudo apt-get -y install
python-simplejson'
```

New terms and **important words** are shown in bold. Words that you see on the screen, for example, in menus or dialog boxes, appear in the text like this: "Set **Enable ESXiSSH** to `true` and exit this screen."

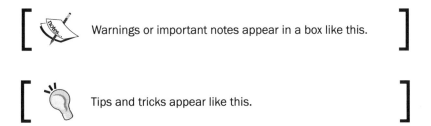

Warnings or important notes appear in a box like this.

Tips and tricks appear like this.

Reader feedback

Feedback from our readers is always welcome. Let us know what you think about this book—what you liked or disliked. Reader feedback is important for us as it helps us develop titles that you will really get the most out of.

To send us general feedback, simply e-mail `feedback@packtpub.com`, and mention the book's title in the subject of your message.

If there is a topic that you have expertise in and you are interested in either writing or contributing to a book, see our author guide at `www.packtpub.com/authors`.

Customer support

Now that you are the proud owner of a Packt book, we have a number of things to help you to get the most from your purchase.

Downloading the example code

You can download the example code files from your account at `http://www.packtpub.com` for all the Packt Publishing books you have purchased. If you purchased this book elsewhere, you can visit `http://www.packtpub.com/support` and register to have the files e-mailed directly to you.

Downloading the color images of this book

We also provide you with a PDF file that has color images of the screenshots/diagrams used in this book. The color images will help you better understand the changes in the output. You can download this file from `http://www.packtpub.com/sites/default/files/downloads/2826OS_ColorImages.pdf`.

Errata

Although we have taken every care to ensure the accuracy of our content, mistakes do happen. If you find a mistake in one of our books—maybe a mistake in the text or the code—we would be grateful if you could report this to us. By doing so, you can save other readers from frustration and help us improve subsequent versions of this book. If you find any errata, please report them by visiting `http://www.packtpub.com/submit-errata`, selecting your book, clicking on the **Errata Submission Form** link, and entering the details of your errata. Once your errata are verified, your submission will be accepted and the errata will be uploaded to our website or added to any list of existing errata under the Errata section of that title.

To view the previously submitted errata, go to `https://www.packtpub.com/books/content/support` and enter the name of the book in the search field. The required information will appear under the **Errata** section.

Piracy

Piracy of copyrighted material on the Internet is an ongoing problem across all media. At Packt, we take the protection of our copyright and licenses very seriously. If you come across any illegal copies of our works in any form on the Internet, please provide us with the location address or website name immediately so that we can pursue a remedy.

Please contact us at copyright@packtpub.com with a link to the suspected pirated material.

We appreciate your help in protecting our authors and our ability to bring you valuable content.

Questions

If you have a problem with any aspect of this book, you can contact us at questions@packtpub.com, and we will do our best to address the problem.

1
Basic Command Line Tools

In this chapter, we will cover the following:

- ▶ Controlling network interfaces
- ▶ Monitoring network details with the IP command
- ▶ Monitoring connections using the ss command
- ▶ Gathering basic OS statistics
- ▶ Viewing historical resource usage with SAR
- ▶ Installing and configuring a Git client
- ▶ Creating an SSH key for Git
- ▶ Using `ssh-copy-id` to copy keys
- ▶ Creating a new Git repository
- ▶ Cloning an existing Git repository
- ▶ Checking changes into a Git repository
- ▶ Pushing changes to a Git remote
- ▶ Creating a Git branch

Introduction

Every Linux System Administrator should have a solid grasp of command-line tools, from the very basics of navigating the file system to the ability to run diagnostic tools to examine potential issues. The command line offers unparalleled power and flexibility along with the ability to chain together commands to form powerful one-line scripts. Although it's quicker to pick up and use the GUI tools as compared to their command line equivalents, few offer the combination of concision and power that a well used combination of command-line tools can bring.

For system administrators who utilize DevOps techniques, the command line offers the first step on the road to automation and offers powerful abilities that can be leveraged with full stack automation. Ansible, Puppet, and Chef are powerful tools, but sometimes it is easier to write a small bash script to undertake a task rather than writing a custom function within a configuration management tool. Despite automation, the command line will be a place where you will spend the majority of your time, and remember that no matter how attractive a point and click tool is, it's highly unlikely that you can automate it.

Most operating systems have a command line, even if they are traditionally seen as the domain of the GUI. For instance, Windows users have the option of using the excellent PowersShell tool to both administer and control Windows servers.

In this chapter, we are going to cover some useful recipes that can help DevOps engineers in their day-to-day lives. These commands will cover a wide variety of topics, covering elements such as basic networking commands, performance metrics, and perhaps the most important of all, the basics of using the Git **Distributed Version Control Software** (**DVCS**). Depending on where you approach the DevOps role from, you may find that some of this chapter touches topics that you have already covered in depth or instance, seasoned Systems Administrators will find the items on the Net tools and system performance are familiar ground; however, these can be valuable introductions for a developer. Likewise, developers will probably find the section on Git to be nothing new, while, many Systems administrators may not be used to version control systems and will benefit hugely from the items in this section.

Controlling network interfaces

Networking is one of the core elements of server management, and can be one of the more complex to manage. This recipe will show you how to use the IP tool to discover the details of, and make changes to, the networking setup of your server.

Although these are ephemeral changes, the ability to apply them at the command line is very powerful; for instance, it allows you to script the addition and removal of IP addresses. When looking at command-line tools, it's a good idea to think of not only how they can help you now, but also how they could be used for automation in future.

Getting ready

The IP tools come preinstalled on the major Linux distributions (RHEL and Debian based), so additional configuration is no longer required.

How to do it...

Let's configure the network interface as follows:

1. Sometimes you just want to know the IP address of the server you are working on; this can be found using the following command:

   ```
   $ ip addr show
   ```

   This should give you an output similar to to the following screenshot:

```
mduffy@babel:~$ ip addr show
1: lo: <LOOPBACK,UP,LOWER_UP> mtu 65536 qdisc noqueue state UNKNOWN group default
    link/loopback 00:00:00:00:00:00 brd 00:00:00:00:00:00
    inet 127.0.0.1/8 scope host lo
       valid_lft forever preferred_lft forever
    inet6 ::1/128 scope host
       valid_lft forever preferred_lft forever
2: eth0: <BROADCAST,MULTICAST,UP,LOWER_UP> mtu 1500 qdisc pfifo_fast state UP group default qlen 1000
    link/ether 00:0c:29:d5:26:bf brd ff:ff:ff:ff:ff:ff
    inet 10.0.1.192/24 brd 10.0.1.255 scope global eth0
       valid_lft forever preferred_lft forever
    inet6 fe80::20c:29ff:fed5:26bf/64 scope link
       valid_lft forever preferred_lft forever
3: docker0: <NO-CARRIER,BROADCAST,MULTICAST,UP> mtu 1500 qdisc noqueue state DOWN group default
    link/ether 56:84:7a:fe:97:99 brd ff:ff:ff:ff:ff:ff
    inet 172.17.42.1/16 scope global docker0
       valid_lft forever preferred_lft forever
```

   This output gives you the details of each interface, including the IP address, state, MAC address, and interface options.

2. To narrow this down to a single interface, you can use the following command:

   ```
   $ ip addr show <interface>
   ```

   Where `<interface>` is the name of the network interface you wish to see the details for. So, for example, to see the details of `eth0` you can use the following command:

   ```
   $ ip addr show eth0
   ```

3. To add a new IP4 address, you can use the `ip addr add` command. Note that you also need to supply a netmask in **Classless Inter-Domain Routing** (**CIDR**) format. The command looks like this:

   ```
   $ ip addr add  <IP address>/<CIDR> dev <device>
   ```

   For example, to add a new `RFC1918`-compliant address to the interface named `eth1`, you will use the following command:

   ```
   $ ip addr add 10.132.1.1/24 dev eth1
   ```

4. You can confirm that the new address is available on the interface using the `ip addr show` command:

   ```
   $ ip addr show eth1
   ```

5. Removing an IP address is a straightforward reversal of adding it. The command is the same as the command used to add addresses, but with the delete option:

   ```
   $ ip addr del <IP address>/<CIDR> dev <device>
   ```

6. So, to remove the address that we just added, we can use the following command:

   ```
   $ ip addr del 10.132.1.1/24 dev eth1
   ```

   The IP command can be used to control the physical interfaces; thus, allowing you to bring them up and down from the command line.

    It goes without saying that you need to be careful when using this command. Removing the only available interface on a remote server is both possible, and if you don't have access to a remote console, extremely inconvenient.

7. To bring an interface `down`, you can use the `ip link set` command, followed by the interface name, and then the desired state. For example, you can use the following command to enable the `eth2` interface:

   ```
   $ ip link set eth2 down
   ```

   Conversely, to bring it back up, you can use the following command:

   ```
   $ ip link set eth2 up
   ```

8. You can check the state of the interface using the `ip` command:

   ```
   $ ip addr eth2
   ```

See also

You can find further details on the `ip` command within its `man` pages. You can access these using the following command:

```
$ man 8 ip
```

Monitoring network details with the IP command

As well as allowing you to set your network interfaces, the `IP` command can also be used to check if they are functioning correctly. One of the first places to look when trying to figure out the main reason for any issues is the networking stack.

The following recipe will run you through how to use the `IP` command to check that your network interfaces are up, and also list some basic statistics.

Getting ready

No additional configuration should be required as the IP tools come preinstalled in major Linux distributions (RHEL and Debian based).

How to do it...

Let's monitor network details with the following `IP` command:

1. To view basic network statistics on all interfaces, you can use the `ip -s link` command. When it is used without options, it should produce the following output:

```
● ● ●                              .git — mduffy@babel: ~ — ssh — 134x45
1: lo: <LOOPBACK,UP,LOWER_UP> mtu 65536 qdisc noqueue state UNKNOWN mode DEFAULT group default
    link/loopback 00:00:00:00:00:00 brd 00:00:00:00:00:00
    RX: bytes  packets  errors  dropped overrun mcast
    0          0        0       0       0       0
    TX: bytes  packets  errors  dropped carrier collsns
    0          0        0       0       0       0
2: eth0: <BROADCAST,MULTICAST,UP,LOWER_UP> mtu 1500 qdisc pfifo_fast state UP mode DEFAULT group default qlen 1000
    link/ether 00:0c:29:d5:26:bf brd ff:ff:ff:ff:ff:ff
    RX: bytes  packets  errors  dropped overrun mcast
    306609     3661     0       0       0       0
    TX: bytes  packets  errors  dropped carrier collsns
    43742      384      0       0       0       0
3: docker0: <NO-CARRIER,BROADCAST,MULTICAST,UP> mtu 1500 qdisc noqueue state DOWN mode DEFAULT group default
    link/ether 56:84:7a:fe:97:99 brd ff:ff:ff:ff:ff:ff
    RX: bytes  packets  errors  dropped overrun mcast
    0          0        0       0       0       0
    TX: bytes  packets  errors  dropped carrier collsns
    0          0        0       0       0       0
```

This will list the interface name and its configured options; for example, if `multicast` is enabled, and its current state (`up` or `down`). The next line gives you its MAC address, and the following lines give you some interface statistics:

By default, the columns in the `ip -s link` command stand for the following:

`RX/TX: bytes`: The total number of bytes sent/received by this interface

`RX/TX: packets`: The total number of network packets sent/received by this interface

`RX/TX: errors`: The total number of transmission errors found on this interface

`RX/TX: Dropped`: Total number of dropped networking packets

`RX: mcast`: Recieved Multicast packets

`TX: collsns`: Network packet collisions

2. Sometimes, you may want to see the output only for a single interface. You can do this using the following command:

```
ip -s  link ls <<interface>>
```

3. To see the statistics for the `eth0` interface, you can use the following command:

```
ip -s link ls eth0
```

4. To see additional info, you can append an additional `-s` switch to the following command:

```
ip -s -s link ls eth0
```

This produces the following output:

```
mduffy@babel:~$ ip -s -s link ls eth0
2: eth0: <BROADCAST,MULTICAST,UP,LOWER_UP> mtu 1500 qdisc pfifo_fast state UP mode DEFAULT group default qlen 1000
    link/ether 00:0c:29:d5:26:bf brd ff:ff:ff:ff:ff:ff
    RX: bytes  packets  errors   dropped overrun mcast
    326308     3890     0        0       0       0
    RX errors: length  crc      frame    fifo    missed
               0        0        0        0       0
    TX: bytes  packets  errors   dropped carrier collsns
    52178      445      0        0       0       0
    TX errors: aborted fifo     window   heartbeat
               0        0        0        0
```

This expands on the previous listing and allows you to see the details of network errors.

Monitoring connections using the ss command

Alongside the `IP` command, we also have the `ss` command (Socket Statistics). This command is the perfect replacement for the `netstat` command and offers more functionality, it is also faster and gives results that are more accurate.

The following recipes offer some alternatives that should allow you to replace the venerable `netstat` command.

Getting ready

No additional configuration should be required as the IP tools come preinstalled in major Linux distributions (RHEL and Debian based).

How to do it...

Let's monitor network details using the `ss` command:

1. You can use the following command to show established TCP connections:

   `ss -t`

   This should produce an output similar to the following screenshot:

```
root@redis03:~# ss -t
State       Recv-Q Send-Q      Local Address:Port            Peer Address:Port
ESTAB       0      0           46.101.192.111:55972          46.101.150.40:16380
ESTAB       0      0           46.101.192.111:16380          46.101.150.40:52180
ESTAB       0      0           46.101.192.111:48904          46.101.238.22:16380
ESTAB       0      0           46.101.192.111:16380          46.101.238.22:48447
ESTAB       0      0           46.101.192.111:16379          46.101.150.40:55029
ESTAB       0      0           46.101.192.111:16380          46.101.150.40:52174
ESTAB       0      0           46.101.192.111:16380          46.101.192.111:59367
ESTAB       0      0           46.101.192.111:16379          46.101.238.22:40837
ESTAB       0      0           46.101.192.111:48901          46.101.238.22:16380
ESTAB       0      0           46.101.192.111:6380           46.101.192.111:46684
ESTAB       0      0           46.101.192.111:55970          46.101.150.40:16380
```

2. Alternatively, if you want to see UDP connections rather than TCP, then you can do so using the following command:

   `$ ss -u`

3. You can use the following command to see which ports are listening for connections on a server:

   `$ ss -ltn`

This displays the following listening ports in the output:

```
● ● ●                                    git — mduffy@babel: ~ — ssh — 134×45
mduffy@babel:~$ ss -ltn
State      Recv-Q Send-Q                         Local Address:Port                              Peer Address:Port
LISTEN     0      128                                      *:22                                            *:*
LISTEN     0      128                                   :::4243                                          :::*
LISTEN     0      128                                    :::22                                           :::*
```

The column we are interested in is the one titled **Local Address:Port**. This essentially lists the listening IP address and the TCP port it is listening on. If you see a *****, it means that the port is available on all interfaces configured on this server.

[The n in the -ltn option turns off hostname lookups. This makes the command run much faster, but you may want to omit it if you wish to see the hostname that an interface maps to.]

4. Alternatively, you can use the same command to list all the listening UDP connections:

```
$ ss -lun
```

You can even combine the t and u flags to list out ALL listening ports, both UDP and TCP:

```
$ ss -ltun
```

Gathering basic OS statistics

One of the most basic responsibilities of a DevOps engineer is to know how the various server instances under their control are performing. It forms a key part of DevOp techniques, driving infrastructure transparency and measuring the impact of changes, both prior to the change and after it has taken place.

There are many tools that are available for performance monitoring, from comprehensive **Application Performance Monitoring** (**APM**) tools through to focused monitoring for particular applications. We'll be covering these throughout the book; however, some of the best tools for basic server monitoring are already available with the operating system. Like most command-line tools, the performance monitoring tools that are shipped with the OS can be used standalone or can be chained with other commands to create complex tools.

Getting ready

The following tools are a part of the standard install of most Linux distributions and should be available with it, the exception being for `sysstat` tools, which generally need to be installed. To install `systat` tools on Ubuntu, issue the following command:

```
sudo apt-get install sysstat
```

This will make several performance-monitoring tools available, in particular `sar` and `mpstat`.

How to do it...

Let's gather basic OS statistics:

1. To gather basic information on your server, run the following command:

   ```
   vmstat 1 99999
   ```

   This should produce output similar to the following screenshot:

```
mduffy@babel:~$ vmstat 1 99999
procs -----------memory---------- ---swap-- -----io---- -system-- ------cpu-----
 r  b   swpd   free    buff  cache   si   so    bi    bo   in   cs us sy id wa st
 0  0      0 3770044  12460 114868    0    0    30     4   13   26  0  0 100  0  0
 0  0      0 3770004  12460 114908    0    0     0     0   26   36  0  0 100  0  0
 0  0      0 3770004  12460 114908    0    0     0     0   13   14  0  0 100  0  0
 0  0      0 3770004  12460 114908    0    0     0     0   14   16  0  0 100  0  0
 0  0      0 3770004  12460 114908    0    0     0     0   15   19  0  0 100  0  0
 0  0      0 3770004  12460 114908    0    0     0     0   15   16  0  0 100  0  0
 0  0      0 3770004  12468 114900    0    0     0    16   20   22  0  0 100  0  0
 0  0      0 3770004  12468 114908    0    0     0     0   16   19  0  0 100  0  0
 0  0      0 3770004  12468 114908    0    0     0     0   15   18  0  0 100  0  0
 0  0      0 3770004  12468 114908    0    0     0     0   14   17  0  0 100  0  0
 0  0      0 3770004  12468 114908    0    0     0     0   15   18  0  0 100  0  0
 0  0      0 3770004  12468 114908    0    0     0     0   20   27  0  0 100  0  0
 0  0      0 3770004  12468 114908    0    0     0     0   14   21  0  0 100  0  0
 0  0      0 3770004  12468 114908    0    0     0     0   28   41  0  0 100  0  0
 0  0      0 3770004  12468 114908    0    0     0     0   11   14  0  0 100  0  0
 0  0      0 3770004  12468 114908    0    0     0     0   15   16  0  0 100  0  0
 0  0      0 3770004  12468 114908    0    0     0     4   18   20  0  0 100  0  0
 0  0      0 3770004  12468 114908    0    0     0     0   18   21  0  0 100  0  0
 0  0      0 3770004  12468 114908    0    0     0     0   11   14  0  0 100  0  0
 0  0      0 3770036  12468 114908    0    0     0     0   14   18  0  0 100  0  0
```

   The command shows you the system statistics every second, for the number of times specified (`99999` in this instance).

By default, the columns in `vmstat` stand for the following:

`Procs` – `r`: Total number of processes waiting to run

`Procs` – `b`: Total number of busy processes

`Memory` – `swpd`: Used virtual memory

`Memory` – `free`: Free virtual memory

`Memory` – `buff`: Memory used as buffers

`Memory` – `cache`: Memory used as cache.

`Swap` – `si`: Memory swapped from disk (for every second)

`Swap` – `so`: Memory swapped to disk (for every second)

`IO` – `bi`: Blocks in (in other words) the blocks received from device (for every second)

`IO` – `bo`: Blocks out (in other words) the blocks sent to the device (for every second)

`System` – `in`: Interrupts per second

`System` – `cs`: Context switches

`CPU` – `us`, `sy`, `id`, `wa`, `st`: CPU user time, system time, idle time, and wait time

2. The `vmstat` command can also be useful to show memory usage information, particularly active and inactive memory. To show vmstat information for memory usage, you can issue the following command:

   `vmstat -a 1 999`

   This will give you an output similar to the following screenshot:

```
mduffy@babel:~$ vmstat -a 1 99999
procs -----------memory---------- ---swap-- -----io---- -system-- ------cpu-----
 r  b   swpd   free  inact active   si   so    bi    bo   in   cs us sy id wa st
 1  0      0 3770060  69456  78096    0    0    29     4   13   26  0  0 100  0  0
 0  0      0 3770060  69456  78096    0    0     0     0   17   21  0  0 100  0  0
 0  0      0 3770060  69456  78096    0    0     0     0   14   16  0  0 100  0  0
 0  0      0 3769996  69456  78152    0    0     0     0   14   14  0  0 100  0  0
 0  0      0 3769996  69456  78152    0    0     0     0   16   16  0  0 100  0  0
 0  0      0 3769996  69456  78152    0    0     0     0   11   16  0  0 100  0  0
 0  0      0 3769996  69456  78152    0    0     0     0   18   24  0  0 100  0  0
 0  0      0 3769996  69456  78152    0    0     0     0   13   14  0  0 100  0  0
 0  0      0 3770020  69456  78168    0    0     0     0   28   34  0  0 100  0  0
 0  0      0 3770020  69456  78168    0    0     0     0   13   14  0  0 100  0  0
 0  0      0 3770020  69456  78168    0    0     0     0   19   22  0  0 100  0  0
 0  0      0 3770020  69456  78168    0    0     0     0   15   14  0  0 100  0  0
 0  0      0 3770020  69456  78168    0    0     0     0   16   19  0  0 100  0  0
```

You can also reformat the output to be displayed in Mega Bytes using the following command:

```
vmstat -a -S M 1 999
```

3. The `vmstat` is not limited to gathering only CPU and RAM information; it can also be used to gather information for disks and other block devices. You can use the following command to gather basic disk statistics:

```
vmstat -d 1 99999
```

This should produce an output that looks something like the following screenshot:

```
● ● ●                                                          .git — mduffy@babel: ~ — ssh — 134×45
mduffy@babel:~$ vmstat -d 1 99999
disk- ------------reads------------ ------------writes----------- -----IO------
      total merged sectors    ms  total merged sectors    ms   cur    sec
ram0      0      0       0     0      0      0       0     0     0      0
ram1      0      0       0     0      0      0       0     0     0      0
ram2      0      0       0     0      0      0       0     0     0      0
ram3      0      0       0     0      0      0       0     0     0      0
ram4      0      0       0     0      0      0       0     0     0      0
ram5      0      0       0     0      0      0       0     0     0      0
ram6      0      0       0     0      0      0       0     0     0      0
ram7      0      0       0     0      0      0       0     0     0      0
ram8      0      0       0     0      0      0       0     0     0      0
ram9      0      0       0     0      0      0       0     0     0      0
ram10     0      0       0     0      0      0       0     0     0      0
ram11     0      0       0     0      0      0       0     0     0      0
ram12     0      0       0     0      0      0       0     0     0      0
ram13     0      0       0     0      0      0       0     0     0      0
ram14     0      0       0     0      0      0       0     0     0      0
ram15     0      0       0     0      0      0       0     0     0      0
loop0     0      0       0     0      0      0       0     0     0      0
loop1     0      0       0     0      0      0       0     0     0      0
loop2     0      0       0     0      0      0       0     0     0      0
loop3     0      0       0     0      0      0       0     0     0      0
loop4     0      0       0     0      0      0       0     0     0      0
loop5     0      0       0     0      0      0       0     0     0      0
loop6     0      0       0     0      0      0       0     0     0      0
loop7     0      0       0     0      0      0       0     0     0      0
fd0       0      0       0     0      0      0       0     0     0      0
sr0       0      0       0     0      0      0       0     0     0      0
sda    5567    271  227480   508    337    308   34636   140     0      0
dm-0   4747      0  221266   472    639      0   34624   200     0      0
dm-1    224      0    1792     8      0      0       0     0     0      0
```

Sometimes, the output of `vmstat` can be slightly cluttered. You can widen the output using the -w options. This can be used on any `vmstat` command, such as the following:

```
vmstat -d -w
```

4. Although `vmstat` is capable of displaying disk statistics, there is a tool that is better suited to this task in the shape of `iostat`. The `iostat` is able to display relatively detailed statistics of IO on a server in real time and can be used to reveal performance bottlenecks caused by disk devices.

   The following command will display basic statistics and just like `vmstat`, it will repeat the information every *n* seconds for *n* times, where *n* is a user-specified input:

   ```
   iostat 1 99999
   ```

   This will give you an output similar to the following screenshot:

```
mduffy@babel:~$ iostat 1 99999
Linux 3.13.0-32-generic (babel)         30/12/14         _x86_64_        (2 CPU)

avg-cpu:  %user   %nice %system %iowait  %steal   %idle
           0.06    0.00    0.15    0.00    0.00   99.79

Device:            tps    kB_read/s    kB_wrtn/s    kB_read    kB_wrtn
sda               2.05        39.47         6.04     113792      17402
dm-0              1.88        38.39         6.03     110685      17396
dm-1              0.08         0.31         0.00        896          0
```

5. By default, `iostat` will show you the CPU information and disk information for all devices. You can drill into the information that `iostat` produces by using some simple options. For instance, you can show only information for device `sda`, and only disk statistics by using the following options:

   ```
   iostat -d -p sda 1 9999
   ```

Viewing historical resource usage with SAR

The tools that we have looked at so far are fantastic to analyze problems that are present now; but what about when you need to look at issues that occurred in the past? For that you can use the **System Activity Report** (**SAR**) tool. Using the `sar` tool, you will be able to look back over a period of time and see how the server has been running.

This recipe will demonstrate how to install and use the `sysstat` tools; thus, allowing you to examine historical system statistics.

Getting ready

For this recipe, you will need either a Debian or Red Hat based server.

How to do it...

Let's take a look at how to install and use `sysstat`, also allowing you to examine historical SAR:

1. Install the `sysstat` package using the following command for a Debian-based distribution:

   ```
   $ sudo apt-get install sysstat
   ```

   We can also use the following command for a RHEL-based distribution:

   ```
   $ sudo yum install sysstat
   ```

2. Edit the `/etc/default/sysstat` file with your favorite text editor and change the following value from:

   ```
   ENABLED="false"
   ```

   To:

   ```
   ENABLED="true"
   ```

3. Restart the `sysstat` service using the following command:

   ```
   $ sudo service sysstat restart
   ```

4. By default, `sar` stats are collected every 10 minutes. The data is collected using a simple cron job configured within `/etc/cron.d/sysstat`. This job can be amended to collect the data as frequently as you require.

5. Use the following command to view basic CPU statistics, including wait times:

   ```
   sar -u
   ```

   This should produce the following output:

```
                                          mduffy — mduffy@babel: ~ — ssh — 115×25

03:35:01        CPU      %user     %nice    %system    %iowait     %steal     %idle
03:45:01        all       0.00      0.00       0.04       0.00       0.00      99.95
03:55:01        all       0.00      0.00       0.05       0.00       0.00      99.95
04:05:01        all       0.00      0.00       0.05       0.00       0.00      99.95
04:15:01        all       0.00      0.00       0.04       0.00       0.00      99.95
04:25:01        all       0.00      0.00       0.05       0.00       0.00      99.94
04:35:01        all       0.00      0.00       0.05       0.00       0.00      99.95
04:45:01        all       0.00      0.00       0.05       0.00       0.00      99.95
04:55:01        all       0.00      0.00       0.05       0.00       0.00      99.95
05:05:01        all       0.00      0.00       0.05       0.00       0.00      99.95
05:15:01        all       0.03      0.00       0.06       0.00       0.00      99.91
05:25:01        all       0.00      0.00       0.05       0.00       0.00      99.95
05:35:01        all       0.01      0.00       0.10       0.00       0.00      99.90
05:45:01        all       0.00      0.00       0.05       0.00       0.00      99.94
05:55:01        all       0.00      0.00       0.05       0.00       0.00      99.95
```

Note that most `sar` commands can also produce output in real time by adding a duration and repetition, much the same as the `vmstat` and `iostat` commands. For instance, `sar -u 1 30` will display the basic CPU statistics every second for 30 seconds.

6. Use the following command to view the available memory statistics:

   sar -r

   This should produce an output that looks similar to the following screenshot:

03:35:01	kbmemfree	kbmemused	%memused	kbbuffers	kbcached	kbcommit	%commit	kbactive	kbinact	kbdirty
03:45:01	3725932	307584	7.63	15564	146524	106140	1.29	104312	81712	0
03:55:01	3725980	307536	7.62	15580	146528	106140	1.29	104228	81720	0
04:05:01	3726772	306744	7.60	15596	146532	106140	1.29	104356	81736	4
04:15:01	3726436	307080	7.61	15608	146532	106140	1.29	104332	81748	0
04:25:01	3726184	307332	7.62	15668	146536	106140	1.29	104240	81808	0
04:35:01	3725976	307540	7.62	15684	146544	106140	1.29	104244	81828	0
04:45:01	3726352	307164	7.62	15704	146548	106140	1.29	104344	81840	0
04:55:01	3726524	306992	7.61	15728	146548	106140	1.29	104260	81852	0
05:05:01	3726764	306752	7.61	15744	146552	106140	1.29	104268	81880	0
05:15:01	3726476	307040	7.61	15804	146560	111244	1.35	104664	81580	4
05:25:01	3726576	306940	7.61	15832	146564	111244	1.35	104664	81612	0
05:35:01	3726412	307104	7.61	15936	146568	111244	1.35	104600	81716	0
05:45:01	3725964	307552	7.62	15972	146572	111244	1.35	104680	81752	4
05:55:01	3730640	302876	7.51	16000	146568	102504	1.25	101140	81764	0
06:05:02	3730492	303024	7.51	16032	146568	102504	1.25	101188	81796	0
06:15:01	3729448	304068	7.54	16104	146572	102504	1.25	101192	81860	0

7. Seeing the IO stats for individual block devices can be helpful when tracking down performance issues. You can use the following command to view these statistics with `sar`:

   sar -b

   This will produce an output similar to the following screenshot:

	mduffy — mduffy@babel: ~ —
	tps	rtps	wtps	bread/s	bwrtn/s
03:35:01	0.03	0.00	0.03	0.00	0.37
03:45:01	0.03	0.00	0.03	0.00	0.37
03:55:01	0.03	0.00	0.03	0.00	0.40
04:05:01	0.03	0.00	0.03	0.00	0.40
04:15:01	0.02	0.00	0.02	0.00	0.32
04:25:01	0.07	0.00	0.07	0.00	0.93
04:35:01	0.03	0.00	0.03	0.00	0.45
04:45:01	0.03	0.00	0.03	0.00	0.45
04:55:01	0.03	0.00	0.03	0.00	0.41
05:05:01	0.03	0.00	0.03	0.00	0.43
05:15:01	0.08	0.00	0.08	0.00	1.00
05:25:01	0.04	0.00	0.04	0.00	0.68
05:35:01	0.08	0.00	0.08	0.00	1.00
05:45:01	0.04	0.00	0.04	0.00	0.53
05:55:01	0.04	0.00	0.04	0.00	0.63
06:05:02	0.03	0.00	0.03	0.00	0.45
06:15:01	0.07	0.00	0.07	0.00	0.95

Installing and configuring a Git client

One key element in moving towards using DevOps techniques is the ability to manage and develop your infrastructure as code. Using version control is second nature to most developers; however, some System Administrators have not yet fully embraced version control. It is important that all DevOps engineers are both familiar with, and able to use a good version control system. Using version control, you can immediately pinpoint where, when and why the changes were introduced; it also allows you to experiment with alternative approaches using branches of existing code.

Don't be tempted to think that version control is just for code. Version control can also be used to contain configuration items where they exist in the form of plain text (YAML, JSON, or INI files for instance). If you use version control to control changes, you can immediately gain a complete record of the changes made to that particular system.

Getting ready

For this recipe, you need an Ubuntu 14.04 server.

How to do it...

Let's install and configure a Git repository:

1. Install the `git` client using the following command:

   ```
   sudo apt-get install git
   ```

2. Once the `git` client is installed, you need to configure it with your credentials:

   ```
   git config --global user.email "<Your Email address>"
   git config --global user.name "<Your actual name>"
   ```

Creating an SSH key for Git

Although you can maintain your code using local Git repositories, at some point you will want to either clone from, or push to, a remote Git repository. Although it is possible to use HTTP authentication, it can be both more secure, and certainly more convenient to use an SSH and a key to manage your authentication.

This recipe will show you how to generate an RSA SSH key that is suitable for use with Git, and also to authenticate against Linux servers.

Getting ready

For this recipe, you either need a Red Hat- or Debian-based Linux host.

How to do it

Let's create an SSH key for Git:

1. Create a new RSA key using the `ssh-keygen` command:

   ```
   ssh-keygen -t rsa -C "My SSH Key"
   ```

   Replace "`My SSH Key`" with an identifying text such as `My laptop`. This helps when you are managing multiple keys.

2. You will be prompted for a `passphrase` after running the preceding command; it's highly recommended that you create one to ensure the security of your key; otherwise, if you lose your private key, any scallywag who finds it can use it to access your systems. You can alleviate the tedium of typing in the password using an `ssh-agent` to store the details for the duration of a session.

   When you use the `ssh-keygen` command, you will see that it produces an output similar to the following screenshot:

```
mduffy@babel:~$ ssh-keygen -t rsa -C "My SSH Key"
Generating public/private rsa key pair.
Enter file in which to save the key (/home/mduffy/.ssh/id_rsa):
Enter passphrase (empty for no passphrase):
Enter same passphrase again:
Your identification has been saved in /home/mduffy/.ssh/id_rsa.
Your public key has been saved in /home/mduffy/.ssh/id_rsa.pub.
The key fingerprint is:
27:82:38:85:a0:86:f2:58:4b:23:8f:b5:82:02:14:26 My SSH Key
The key's randomart image is:
+--[ RSA 2048]----+
|E+.              |
|*. .             |
|*.* .            |
|=X * .           |
|* B . . S .      |
|.. .   . o       |
|                 |
|                 |
|                 |
+-----------------+
```

How it works...

By default, the `ssh-keygen` command will create a new set of files in your home directory, within a hidden directory named `.ssh`. This includes both your public and private keys. Remember, never, ever share your private key. If you suspect that it has been shared at all, delete it and then revoke it from any system it was previously used with and create a new key pair.

Using ssh-copy-id to copy keys

Your SSH key can be used to authenticate yourself to a Linux server, and although you can manually copy SSH keys onto the servers you control, there are easier ways to manage them. Using the `ssh-copy-id` command allows you to easily copy your public key onto a server, which can be valuable when managing a great number of servers.

Getting ready

For this recipe, either you will need a Red Hat- or Debian-based Linux host.

How to do it...

Using `ssh-copy-id` only requires a single command to copy a public key to a target server. For instance, to copy my SSH key to a server called `testserver`, you can use the following command:

```
ssh-copy-id testserver
```

How it works...

The `ssh-copy-id` command logs onto a server using another authentication method (normally a password). It then checks the permissions of the user's `.ssh` directory and copies the new key into the `authorized_keys` file.

See also

You can find further details of the `ssh-copy-id` command from the Linux `man` pages; you can invoke them using the command `man ssh-copy-id`.

Downloading the example code

You can download the example code fies from your account at http://www.
packtpub.com for all the Packt Publishing books you have purchased. If you
purchased this book elsewhere, you can visit http://www.packtpub.com/
support and register to have the fies e-mailed directly to you.

Creating a new Git repository

The very first step for any new project should be to create a Git repository to hold your source
code so that you can track changes from the outset. Unlike centralized version control
systems such as SVN, Git allows you to easily create and add to the new repository without
needing a centralized server to hold it.

This recipe will show you how to create a new Git repository that is ready for content to
be added.

Getting ready

For this recipe, you will need either a Red Hat- or Debian-based Linux host with a Git
client installed.

How to do it...

To create a new Git repository, follow these steps:

1. Create a new directory to contain your project in:

   `mkdir ~/projects/newproject`

2. Use the `git init` command to initialize the new project:

   `git init ~/projects/newproject`

How it works...

The `git init` command creates a directory called `.git` within the directory of your project.
This directory contains all the the data required for Git to track content. Any changes made to
the configuration for this repository will be contained within this directory.

See also

You can find more details on how the `git init` command works at:

`https://git-scm.com/docs/git-init`

Cloning an existing Git repository

Quite often, you'll want to clone existing code to work on it. In fact, this is probably something you are going to do more often than creating a new repository. Much like developers, DevOps engineers spend more time collaborating on existing code rather than creating brand new code.

Getting ready

For this recipe, you need either a Red Hat- or Debian-based Linux host with a Git client installed.

How to do it...

Let's start cloning an existing repository:

1. Change your directory into the one you want to clone the existing project into.

2. Use the `git clone` command to clone your chosen repository:

    ```
    $ git clone <GIT URL>
    ```

    This should give you an output similar to the following screenshot:

```
mduffy@babel:~/projects$ git clone https://github.com/stunthamster/docker_base.git
Cloning into 'docker_base'...
remote: Counting objects: 25, done.
remote: Total 25 (delta 0), reused 0 (delta 0)
Unpacking objects: 100% (25/25), done.
Checking connectivity... done.
```

3. Once it's cloned, you can pull any changes made by other users using the `git pull` command in the working directory:

    ```
    $ git pull
    ```

    This will connect you to the remote repository and pull any changes down to your local repository.

How it works...

The `git clone` command replicates the remote repository from a remote location to your local directory. This includes all branches and history; it's a complete copy of the repository. Once you've cloned it locally, you can branch, check in changes, and view history, all without the need to communicate with the remote again.

See also

You can find more options of how to use Git clone at `https://git-scm.com/docs/git-clone`.

Checking changes into a Git repository

Once you have worked on your code, you'll want to check your changes into your local repository. This is the first step in propagating your change further, as you need to update your local copy of the repository before you can push the changes for other users to view.

This recipe will tell you how to commit changes to your local Git repository.

Getting ready

For this recipe, you need either a Red Hat- or Debian-based Linux host.

How to do it...

Let's make changes into our local Git repository:

1. Change the directory into the one you want to use for your project.
2. Add any new files to the `git` staging area:

   ```
   git add .
   ```

    This will add new files to the working folder (including folders and contents) to your commit. You can be more specific and add individual files if you wish.

3. Commit the new files and changes to the repository:

   ```
   git commit -am "An interesting and illuminating check in message"
   ```

The `'a'` option means `'all'`; this essentially means that you are committing all changes in this commit, and the m option means `'message'`, and allows you to add a message explaining your commit.

How it works...

The preceding commands carry out two different tasks: the first adds new files to the change set, and the second adds any changes to the change set; it also commits them with an appropriate message. The changes exist within the Git staging area until you commit them. The best way to think of the staging area is as a buffer between the codebase and your changes. You can chuck away your Git stage at any point without affecting the branch you are currently working on.

See also

You can find more details on how to changes into Git at `https://git-scm.com/docs/git-add`.

Pushing changes to a Git remote

At some point, you're going to want to push your local repository to a remote repository. This can either be to ensure that you have a remote backup in case you accidentally drop your laptop into a car crusher, or ideally because you want to share your insanely good code with other people. Either way, it's a straightforward command.

 The most popular Git remote is probably Github. Github is a SAAS Git repository and offers a free account option for public repositories. If you want your code to be private, there are paid options available. You can find out more at `http://www.github.com`.

Getting ready

For this recipe, you need a Red Hat- or Debian-based Linux host.

How to do it...

1. Configure your remote:

   ```
   git remote add origin << origin address >>
   ```

2. Verify the remote:

   ```
   git remote -v
   ```

This should produce output similar to the following screenshot:

```
● ● ●                                        .git — mduffy@babel: ~/p
mduffy@babel:~/projects/docker_base$ git remote -v
origin   https://github.com/stunthamster/docker_base.git (fetch)
origin   https://github.com/stunthamster/docker_base.git (push)
```

3. Push your remote changes using the `git push` command:

    git push origin master

    This should produce an output similar to the following screenshot:

```
● ● ●                                        .git — mduffy@babel: ~/pr
                    mduffy@babel: ~/projects/docker_base
mduffy@babel:~/projects/docker_base$ git push origin master
Enter passphrase for key '/home/mduffy/.ssh/id_rsa':
Counting objects: 5, done.
Delta compression using up to 2 threads.
Compressing objects: 100% (3/3), done.
Writing objects: 100% (3/3), 298 bytes | 0 bytes/s, done.
Total 3 (delta 2), reused 0 (delta 0)
To git@github.com:stunthamster/docker_base.git
   f75d776..50470b0  master -> master
```

 It's possible that you may have several remotes configured for a single repository. In such a case, you can easily push to the correct remote by specifying it via a name, such as with the following command: `git push github master`.

How it works...

The `git push` command is essentially the opposite of the `git pull` command; it takes the contents of your local Git repository and pushes any changes that don't exist on the remote to. The `git pull` command, pushes any and all history as well, so what you have locally will also exist, in its entirety, on the remote.

See also

You can find more about pushing changes to a remote at `https://git-scm.com/book/en/v2/Git-Basics-Working-with-Remotes`.

Creating a Git branch

Branching in Git is incredibly powerful and easy to use because operations are performed locally. It's not only easy but also highly recommended to operate on any major changes within a branch. You can use local branches to play with ideas, experiment, and generally mess around, all without affecting anyone else's changes. Once you've concluded your work, you can easily push the branch to the remote and issue a `pull` request to merge your changes into the main branch or if the experiment went nowhere, delete the branch without pushing the changes remotely.

Getting ready

For this recipe, you need either a Red Hat- or Debian-based Linux host.

How to do it...

Let's create a Git branch:

1. Ensure that the repository is cloned locally using the `git clone` command and change your working directory into the checked out directory.

2. Issue the `branch` command to both create and switch to a new branch of the code:

   ```
   $ git checkout -b <branchname>
   ```

3. Go ahead and make some changes to your code, and when you are finished, use the `git commit` command to commit your changes. Remember, you are committing to your own branch, so your original code held in the master branch is still safe.

4. Once you've made your changes and are happy for them to be merged into the main code base, you need to switch back to the `master` branch. To switch back to a branch, you can use the `git checkout` command and the branch you wish to switch to; for instance, to switch back to the `master` branch, use the following:

   ```
   git checkout master
   ```

5. Once you have rechecked the `master` branch, you can merge your code using the `git merge` command. This will take the branch you specify and merge the code into the branch that you have currently checked out. You can issue a merge using the following command:

   ```
   $ git merge <branchname>
   ```

This should produce an output like the following screenshot:

```
 ● ● ●                                                  .git — mduffy@babel: ~/pr
                      mduffy@babel: ~/projects/docker_base
mduffy@babel:~/projects/docker_base$ git merge newbranch
Updating 50470b0..5799d7e
Fast-forward
 README.md | 3 +--
 1 file changed, 1 insertion(+), 2 deletions(-)
```

 You may run into a merge conflict occasionally; this essentially means that you have tried to insert a change that clashes with another developer's change. If this happens, you can invoke the `git-mergetool`, which will help you resolve the conflict by choosing which code is kept with the merge.

Once you have merged the branch, remember to both commit your changes and push them to a remote (if you have one).

6. Once you have finished with a branch, you can delete it using the following command:

```
$ git branch -d <branchname>
```

This will remove the branch from your Git repository.

How it works...

The `git checkout -b` command creates a new branch of the code from wherever you are in the current branch (you can easily branch from a branch). This essentially tracks any changes from the existing point of the branch, rather than copying all the existing code into the new branch; thus, making it relatively efficient to create branches from a space perspective. Any change that you make within the branch, stays within the branch until you merge them.

The `git merge` command takes the two branches and compares them for changes. As long as no merge conflicts are found, Git takes the changes from the first branch and copies them into the second.

See also

You can find more details of Git branching at `https://git-scm.com/docs/git-branch`.

2
Ad Hoc Tasks with Ansible

In this chapter, we are going to cover the following recipes:

- ▶ Installing an Ansible control node on Ubuntu
- ▶ Installing an Ansible control node on CentOS
- ▶ Creating an Ansible inventory
- ▶ Using the raw module to install `python-simplejson`
- ▶ Installing packages with Ansible
- ▶ Restarting services using Ansible
- ▶ Executing freeform commands with Ansible
- ▶ Managing users with Ansible
- ▶ Managing SSH keys with Ansible

Introduction

There is a growing number of automation tools available to DevOps Engineers, each with its individual strengths and weaknesses. Puppet, Chef, SaltStack, Ansible; the list seems to grow on a daily basis, as do the capabilities that they offer. Configuration management has become one of the core techniques that help define DevOps engineering, and is one of the key benefits of adding DevOps techniques to a team.

Configuration management is not a new concept, and there have been various tools to support automatic configuration management, with the granddaddy of them all being CFEngine. First developed by *Mark Burgess* in 1993 to solve the problems of managing his own infrastructure, CFEngine has since grown to be a fully featured commercial product used by a great number of companies.

CFEngine has inspired many features that more recent tools use, and *Mark Burgess* has written a great deal on the subject of configuration management and delivery of reliable infrastructure, and is influential in the growing discussion around the best techniques to use.

At its most basic, a configuration management tool should be able to deploy elements of an infrastructure using code to define units of configuration. It should allow an administrator the ability to run the tool multiple times and always end up with the same configuration, allowing for reliable software and configuration releases to multiple environments. Many tools have taken this a step further and embraced the concept of **idempotency**. This means that if you run the tool multiple times, it will only perform the steps required to bring a target node into a declared state and will not perform actions that have already been applied in previous executions. For example, an idempotent tool will not restart a service unless a configuration change indicates that it needs to be done.

Due to the wide variety of tools that are now available, we have a broad choice to pick from, and as with any other tool, its important to understand the strengths and weaknesses of each one. I have chosen Ansible primarily for it's ease of use, simplicity of deployment, and it's ability to be used not only for configuration management, but also for software deployments, allowing you to use a single tool to control various elements of your infrastructure. That is not to say that other configuration management tools do not have some unique features that Ansible does not; for instance, Ansible posses no reporting features unless you purchase a subscription of the commercial Ansible product, Ansible Tower. This feature is baked into Puppet with or without a commercial add-on.

Ansible is relatively unique amongst many configuration management tools in that it is designed without the concept of a centralized server to manage it. All operations from where the Ansible code is executed to the target node take place over SSH connections. This makes Ansible relatively simple to implement, as most networks already have a mechanism that gives SSH access to hosts, either from the corporate desktop, or quite often, from a designated jump server. Most users can be up and running using Ansible quickly if they use an existing communication layer; you don't even need to write any code, as you can use Ansible to run the ad-hoc tasks.

When you use Ansible to run ad-hoc tasks, you add a powerful tool to your system administration repertoire. Although you can use tools such as Csshx (`https://code.google.com/p/csshx/`) to control simultaneous terminals, it doesn't scale well beyond ten machines or so (unless your eyesight is far better than mine!).

Ansible ad-hoc tasks allow you to perform complex operations within a single line using the Ansible configuration language. This allows you to reduce the time it takes to run a command against multiple machines and use an inventory with groups; it also allows you to target the servers that you specifically want to run the command against.

Installing an Ansible control node on Ubuntu

Ansible has a very slim installation; there is no database, no custom daemons, no queues, or any other additional software required. You simply install a set of command-line tools that allow you to work with the Ansible code.

 You should put some thought into choosing your control machine. Although it's feasible to run Ansible straight from your laptop, it's probably not a good idea once you have more than one person working with the code base. Ideally, you can create a small server that you can use to run the Ansible code and then you can add safeguards around who can log in and use the tool.

Getting ready

For this recipe, you need an instance/install of Ubuntu 14.04.

How to do it...

There is a **Personal Package Archive** (**PPA**) that is available for installation of `ansible` on Ubuntu; you can use the following steps to install the latest stable release (1.9.4 at the time of writing):

1. First, you need to install the PPA repository on the Ansible node:

    ```
    $ sudo apt-add-repository ppa:ansible/ansible
    ```

    You may be prompted to add the repository; simply hit enter if you are.

2. Now you have the PPA repository installed, you need to update the apt repositories with the following command:

    ```
    $ sudo apt-get update
    ```

3. You can now install Ansible using the following command:

    ```
    $ sudo apt-get install ansible
    ```

4. You can test if Ansible is installed correctly using the version switch, as shown in the following example:

    ```
    $ ansible --version
    ```

    This should return the version of Ansible that you have installed.

See also

You can find out more about how to set up the Ansible control node using the Ansible documentation at `http://docs.ansible.com/intro_installation.html`.

Installing an Ansible control node on CentOS

Ansible can be installed on many different operating systems and can run equally well on a Red Hat-based Linux distribution as it can on Ubuntu. This recipe will show you how to install Ansible on a CentOS 7 server.

Getting ready

For this recipe, you need an instance of CentOS 7.

How to do it...

Let's install an Ansible control node on CentOS:

1. We need to install the **Extra Packages for Enterprise Linux** (**EPEL**) repository before we install Ansible. You can install it with the following command:

    ```
    $ sudo yum -y install https://dl.fedoraproject.org/pub/epel/epel-
    release-latest-7.noarch.rpm
    ```

2. Install Ansible using the following command:

    ```
    $ sudo yum install ansible
    ```

3. You can test if Ansible is installed correctly using the version switch, as shown in the following example:

    ```
    $ ansible --version
    ```

    This should return the version of Ansible that you have installed.

See also

You can find out more about how to set up the Ansible control node using the Ansible documentation at `http://docs.ansible.com/intro_installation.html`.

Creating an Ansible inventory

Every action you take with Ansible is applied to an item in your inventory. The Ansible inventory is essentially a catalog that is used to record both target nodes and a group with which you can map a node to the role it is going to assume.

Getting ready

For this recipe, you need to have Ansible installed on the machine you intend to use as a control node and a target node to run your actions against. The examples use six different target hosts, but this is not mandatory; all you need to do is simply adjust the inventory to match your requirements.

How to do it...

The inventory file is formatted as an `ini` file and is essentially a simple text file that can store your catalog. Let's assume that we have a small infrastructure that resembles the following:

Function	Name
haproxy	haproxy01
httpd	web01 through to web04
mysql	mysql01

Remember, adjust the preceding list to reflect your particular infrastructure.

 Depending on how you have installed Ansible, you may find that there is an example file already at that location. If the file is present, simply comment out or remove the content.

Let's create our first Ansible inventory. Using your favorite editor, edit the file located at `/etc/ansible` called **hosts**:

1. Let's start by creating a basic inventory. Insert the following code:

```
haproxy01
web01
web02
web03
web04
mysql01
```

 Ensure that the names that you enter into your inventory can be resolved by their names, either using DNS or a host's file entry.

2. That's all that is required for a basic Ansible inventory file; however, despite having different names, from Ansible's point of view these are all part of the same group. Groups allow you to differentiate between different collections of servers, and in particular they allow you to apply different commands to different groups of servers. Let's alter our Ansible inventory to add some groups; this is done using a pair of brackets within which you can insert your group name. Alter your Ansible inventory to look like the following example:

```
[loadbalancer]
haproxy01
[web]
web01
web02
web03
web04 [database]
mysql01
```

3. We now have an inventory file that can be used to control our hosts using Ansible; however, we have lost the ability to send commands to all hosts at once due to grouping. For that, we can add a final group that is, in fact, a group of groups. This will take our groups and form a new group that includes all of the groups in once place, allowing us to easily manipulate all our hosts at once, whilst still retaining the ability to distinguish between individual groups of nodes. To accomplish this, open your Ansible inventory and add the following to the bottom of the file:

```
[all:children]]
loadbalancer
web
database
```

4. The `children` keyword signifies that the entries that belong to this group are, in fact, groups themselves. You can use the `children` keyword to make sub-collections and not just collect all groups. For instance, if you have two different data centers, you can use groups called `[dca:children]` and `[dcb:children]` to list the appropriate servers under each.

5. We now have everything that we need to address our servers, but there is one last trick left to make it more compact and readable. Ansible inventory files understand the concept of ranges, and since our servers have a predictable pattern, we can use this to remove some of the entries and **Do not repeat yourself** (**DRY**) the file up a little. Again, open the file in `/etc/ansible/hosts` and change the code to reflect the following:

```
[loadbalancer]
haproxy01
[web]
web01:04
```

```
[database]
mysql01
[all:children]]
loadbalancer
web
```

As you can see, we have replaced the four manual entries with a range; very useful when you have to manage a large infrastructure.

 Although it's recommended, you don't need to install the inventory into /etc/ansible - you can have it anywhere and then use the -i option on the Ansible command to point to its actual location. This makes it easier to package the inventories along with Playbooks.

See also

You can find out more about the Ansible inventory at the Ansible documentation site; the following link in particular contains some interesting details at http://docs.ansible.com/intro_inventory.html.

Using the raw module to install python-simplejson

Ansible has very few dependencies; however, every managed node requires the python-simplejson package to be installed to allow full functionality. Luckily, Ansible has a raw module, which allows you to use Ansible in a limited fashion to manage nodes. Generally speaking, this should be used as a one-trick pony, using it to install python-simplejson, but it is worth keeping in mind if you ever need to perform the management of servers that might not be able to have this package installed for some reason.

 An Ansible module is essentially a type of plugin that extends the functionality of Ansible. You can perform actions such as installing packages, restarting networks, and much more using modules. You can find a list of core Ansible at http://docs.ansible.com/ansible/modules_by_category.html.

Getting ready

All you need to use in this recipe is a configured Ansible control node and an Ansible inventory describing your target nodes.

How to do it...

Let's use a raw module to install `python-simplejson`:

1. Use the following command to install the `simple-python` module:

    ```
    ansible all --sudo --ask-sudo-pass -m raw -a 'sudo apt-get -y
    install python-simplejson'
    ```

    In the preceding command, we have used several options. The first two, `--sudo` and `--ask-sudo-pass`, tell Ansible that we are employing a user that needs to invoke `sudo` to issue some of the commands and using `--ask-sudo-pass` prompts us for the password to pass onto `sudo`. The `-m` switch tells Ansible which module we wish to use; in this case, the raw module. Finally, the `-a` switch is the argument we wish to send to the module; in this case, the command to install the `python-simplejson` package.

     You can find further information about the switches that Ansible supports using the command `ansible --help`.

2. Alternatively, if you manage a CentOS server, you can use the raw module to install the `python-simplejson` package on these servers using the following command:

    ```
    ansible all --sudo --ask-sudo-pass -m raw -a 'sudo yum -y install
    python-simplejson'
    ```

See also

You can find the details of the raw module at `http://docs.ansible.com/raw_module.html`.

Installing packages with Ansible

Sometimes you need to install a package without using full-blown automation. The reasons may vary, but quite often this can be when you need to get a software patch out right now. However, most times this will be to patch an urgent security issue that cannot wait for a full-blown configuration management release.

 If you do use this recipe to install software, make sure that you add the package to the subsequent configuration management. Otherwise, you will end up with a potentially inconsistent state, and even worse, the specter of Ansible rolling back a patch if a package is defined as a certain version within an Ansible Playbook.

Getting ready

For this recipe, you will need to have a configured Ansible inventory. If you haven't already configured one, use the recipe in this chapter as a guide to configure it. You will also need either a Centos or an Ubuntu server as a target.

How to do it...

Let's install packages with Ansible:

1. To install a package on an Ubuntu server we can make use of the `apt` module. When you specify a module as part of an ad hoc command, you will have access to all the features within that particular module. The following example installs the `httpd` package on the `[web]` group within your Ansible inventory:

   ```
   ansible web -m apt -a "name=apache2 state=present"
   ```

    You can find more details of Ansible modules using the `ansible-doc` command. For instance, `ansible-doc apt` will give you the full details of the `apt` module.

2. Alternatively, you might want to use this technique to install a certain version of a package. The next example commands every node to install a certain version of Bash:

   ```
   $ ansible all -m apt -a "name=bash=4.3 state=present"
   ```

3. You can even use the `apt` module to ask the target nodes to update all installed software using the following command:

   ```
   $ ansible all -m apt -a "upgrade=dist"
   ```

4. You can use the `yum` module to install software on RHEL-based machines using the following command:

   ```
   $ ansible all -m yum -a "name=httpd state=present"
   ```

5. Just like the example for Ubuntu servers, you can use Ansible to update all the packages on your RHEL-based servers:

   ```
   $ ansible all -m yum -a "name=* state=latest"
   ```

See also

▶ You can find more details of the Ansible `apt` module, including the available modules, at http://docs.ansible.com/apt_module.html

▶ You can find more details of the `Yum` module at http://docs.ansible.com/ansible/yum_module.html

Restarting services using Ansible

Now that we have defined our inventory, we are ready to use Ansible to perform actions. Arguably, one of the most important adhoc actions you can take is to restart services on target nodes. At first, this might seem a bit of an overkill compared to simply logging on to the server and doing it, but when you realize that this action can be scaled anywhere from one to one million servers, its power becomes apparent.

Getting ready

You'll need an inventory file before you try this, so if you have not got it already, go ahead and set one up. The following examples are based on the inventory set out in the preceding recipe, so you'll need to change the examples to match your environments.

How to do it...

To restart a service, we can use the Ansible service module. This supports various activities such as starting, stopping, and restarting services:

- For example, issue the following command to restart MySQL:

  ```
  ansible mysql -m service -a "name=mysql state=restarted"
  ```

- You can also use the service module to stop a service:

  ```
  ansible mysql -m service -a "name=mysql state=stopped""
  ```

- Alternatively, you can also use the service module to start a service:

  ```
  ansible mysql -m service -a "name=mysql state=started""
  ```

See also

You can find more details about the service module from the Ansible documentation at http://docs.ansible.com/service_module.html.

Executing freeform commands with Ansible

Sometimes, you need to be able to run actual shell commands on a range of servers. An excellent example will be to reboot some nodes. This is not something that you would put into your automation stack, but at the same time, it is something you would like to be able to leverage your automation tool to do. Ansible enables you to do this by sending arbitrary commands to a collection of servers.

Getting ready

You'll need to an inventory file before you try this, so if you don't have it already, go ahead and set one up. You can use the recipe of this chapter, *Creating an Ansible inventory*, as a guide.

How to do it...

The command is simple and takes the following form:

```
ansible <ansible group> -a "<shell command>"
```

For example, you can issue the following command to reboot all the members of the db group:

```
ansible mysql -a "reboot -now"
```

 It's important to keep an eye on parallelism when you have many hosts. By default, Ansible will send the command to five servers. By adding a -f flag to any command in this chapter, you can increase or decrease this number.

Managing users with Ansible

There are times when you might want to manage users on multiple nodes manually. This may be to fit in with a user creation process that already exists, or to remove a user in a hurry if you find out that they need to have their access revoked. Either way, you can use Ansible ad-hoc commands to add, amend, and delete users across a large number of nodes.

Getting ready

All you need to use for this recipe is a configured Ansible control node and an Ansible inventory describing your target nodes.

How to do it...

Let's configure ansible user to manage some users:

1. You can use the following command to add a user named gduffy to a group called users on every node within your Ansible inventory:

```
$ ansible all -m user -a "name=gduffy" comment="Griff Duffy"
group=users password="amadeuppassword"
```

2. We can also use Ansible to remove users. Issue the following command from your control node to remove the user `gduffy` from every database node defined in your Ansible inventory:

    ```
    ansible db -m user -a "name=gduffy" state=absent remove=yes"
    ```

3. We can also easily amend users. Issue the following command from your control node to change the user Beth to use the Korn shell and to change her home directory to `/mnt/externalhome` on all nodes:

    ```
    ansible all -m user -a "name=beth shell=/bin/ksh home=/mnt/
    externalhome"
    ```

See also

The preceding examples make use of the Ansible User module. You can find the documentation for this module at `http://docs.ansible.com/user_module.html`.

Managing SSH keys with Ansible

One of the most tedious administration tasks can be managing user keys. Although tools such as `ssh-copy-id` make it easy to copy your key to single servers, it can be a taller order to copy them out to several hundred or even a few thousand servers. Ansible makes this task exceptionally easy and allows you to mass-revoke keys when you need to ensure that access has been removed for users across a large server estate.

Getting ready

All you need to use for this recipe is a configured Ansible control node and an Ansible inventory describing your target nodes. You should also have a SSH key, both public and private that you wish to manage.

How to do it...

Let's use SSH keys to manage Ansible:

1. The first thing we might want to do is create a user and simultaneously create a key for them. This is especially useful if you use a network jump box, as it means that you have no dependency on the user supplying a key; it's an integral part of the process. Run the following command to create a user called **Meg** with an associated key:

    ```
    ansible all -m user -a "name=meg generate_ssh_key=yes"
    ```

2. Often, a user either has an existing key they wish to use, or needs to change an installed key. The following command will allow you to attach a key to a specified account. This assumes that your key is located in a directory called **keys** within the working directory from which you run the following command:

```
ansible all -m copy -a "src=keys/id_rsa dest="/home/beth/.ssh/id_
rsa mode=0600
```

3. Once a user has their Private key setup, you need to push their public key out to each and every server that they wish to access. The following command adds my public key to all web servers defined within the Ansible inventory. This uses the `lookup` Ansible function to read the `local` key and send it to the remote nodes:

```
ansible web_servers -m authorized_key -a "user=michael key="{{
lookup('file', '/home/michael/.ssh/id_rsa.pub') }}"
```

See also

The preceding examples use a mix of Ansible modules to achieve the end result. You can find the documentation for the following modules at:

- **User module**: http://docs.ansible.com/user_module.html
- **Copy module**: http://docs.ansible.com/copy_module.html
- **Authorized_key module**: http://docs.ansible.com/authorized_key_module.html

3

Automatic Host builds

In this chapter, we are going to cover the following topics:

- ▸ Creating an `Apt` mirror using `aptly`
- ▸ Automated installation using PXE boot and a preseed file
- ▸ Automating post-installation tasks

Introduction

Building new hosts is one of the most basic tasks a DevOps engineer can undertake. Traditionally speaking, this used to be a manual task involving the mounting of install media, navigating through menus, and inputting the correct values at prompts. Whether you are building virtual hosts or physical servers, automation can bring about some fantastic changes in both speed and reliability of builds. Regardless of whether you are creating one or one-hundred hosts, you can be sure that with automation, your servers will be configured exactly how you want them to be.

If you are working in a completely virtual environment then this is a problem that you may have already solved; indeed, a driver for many organizations to move to virtualization was in part to solve this very issue. However, many organizations are still using bare metal servers either due to performance or policy constraints, but using bare metal does not mean that you cannot automate.

Once you have automatic host builds working, it can bring some advantages that you may not have considered at first, and this can make profound changes to how you manage your infrastructure. Take for instance, the nightmare scenario that every Systems administrator dreads, an intrusion into your network where the extent of breach is difficult to ascertain. This is a potentially disastrous issue, as virtually every affected server must naturally be considered hopelessly compromised. In serious cases, this can encompass hundreds of servers and can even render the **disaster recovery** (**DR**) site compromised, depending on how you replicate to it.

> This may not be as far-fetched as you first imagine. Over the past few years, companies such as Sony, Avid Media, and Gemalto have been implicated in hacks where the attacker has attained wide-reaching access to their networks. When something like this occurs, it's a long and expensive process to regain trust in your own systems.

At this point, you generally have only one option, and that's to quarantine and rebuild the servers. This can be a serious investment in man-hours if you have to build more than four or five hosts by hand. The average manual install of an Ubuntu server can take tens of button clicks and many prompts to be filled in correctly and accurately. Rebuilding a modest network of ten servers, just to the basic OS level can tie up a technician for a considerable amount of time; there's only so many tasks that you can make parallel in a manual install. In this situation, having a tried and tested way to install hosts automatically will give the poor DevOps engineer the ability to rebuild their hosts in a matter of minutes, leaving plenty of time to examine logs, secure firewalls, and of course, have a stiff drink to recover his nerves.

This is an extreme example, but you can also look at the gains that automation brings in terms of flexibility. For instance, automatic host builds are a key part of any form of elastically scalable service, regardless of whether it is hosted in your own infrastructure or as part of a cloud service. You can also use automatic host builds to enable developers to create adhoc development environments easily. This can fit nicely with the use of software such as Vagrant, allowing you to create base images for developers that can match the production hosts. This allows one of the key concepts of a DevOps-driven infrastructure, which is that environments are matched as exactly as possible, from the developer's desktop all the way through to the running service. If nothing else, this will sharply reduce the familiar refrain of "It works on my system" when trying to diagnose an issue.

Building hosts automatically has become increasingly easy in recent years, and both Ubuntu- and Red Hat-based distributions have developed simple yet powerful ways of creating automated installation scripts. Both distributions have arrived at a similar solution of using a simple manifest that allows predetermined input for the underlying installer.

In this chapter, we are going to look at the Debian and by extension at the Ubuntu system for host builds: Preseed. Using Preseed, you can pre-fill the answers to the questions that are normally asked at the time of install. As it is a simple manifest, you can use it to form a part of a network-based automated build, or at a pinch, you can also embed it on a CD and boot hosts that way. The end result should be the same regardless of the method used. In this chapter, we are going to focus on the network build of bare metal systems, as this is the gold standard you should aim for; allowing for quick, easy, and consistent builds with very little effort. To do this, we are going to create the building blocks of an automated build, a repository to fetch packages from, a server that can service PXE clients, and finally, we are going to take a look at an example Preseed file.

Creating an Apt mirror using aptly

At its most basic, an `apt` repository is a simple web server that serves both packages and more importantly, it serves the metadata that describes the contents of the repository. Although you can use the repositories that Ubuntu provides to build your hosts, you will hit two issues. The first being that the packages are updated all the time, meaning a host you build this week may not be the same as a host that was built the week before. The second issue is that depending on your build, you could potentially use a lot of bandwidth. If you have five hundred hosts and you suddenly need to update Bash on all of them due to a security issue, you are going to use a huge amount of bandwidth. It's a much better practice to keep a mirror of the official repository, allowing you to update it when you feel comfortable and allowing your hosts to install new packages at the speed of your local network.

There are several ways in which you can manage local repositories and it can be done using a simple set of Bash scripts. However, you want to ensure that the method you use allows you to easily merge in the upstream changes in a managed fashion, gives you an easy way to publish new repositories, and allows easy management of your existing repositories.

Enter `aptly` (http://www.aptly.info). The `aptly` is an open source project written by the talented Andrey Smirnov, and makes managing mirroring repositories easy. It also offers advanced features such as snapshots, merging, and publishing. We're going to use `aptly` to create a mirror of the Ubuntu package `repos`, which will allow us to use a local repository to make package installations much quicker and also offers us a fixed set of package versions to install.

Getting ready

For this recipe, you should start with a clean install of Ubuntu 14.04. You'll also need a substantial quantity of storage space; I recommend putting aside at least 50GB for the Ubuntu repositories. If you are short of space or you want to have a more centralized management of the storage, there is no reason why it could not reside on a network-attached storage, such as an NFS device.

How to do it...

Let's create a repository using the `aptly` tool:

1. First of all, you need to install the `aptly` package. To achieve this, edit your `apt` sources list in `/etc/apt/sources.list.d` and add the following line:

    `deb http://repo.aptly.info/ squeeze main`

2. Once you have added the repository, you need to import the GPG key. You can achieve this using the following command:

    `$ sudo apt-key adv --keyserver keys.gnupg.net --recv-keys E083A3782A194991`

3. Now, you are almost ready to install `aptly`. You just need to update your `apt` repository to ensure that `aptly` is listed; you can do this with the following command:

    `$ sudo apt-get update`

4. Once you've updated your `apt` repository, you can install `aptly` with the following command:

    `$ sudo apt-get install aptly`

    This will fetch the `aptly` packages and dependencies and then install them for you.

5. The next task is to configure `aptly`. Out of the box aptly is well configured, but there are a few things that we need to adjust; primarily, the storage location where the mirror will be held.

    The `aptly` configuration file is located at `/etc/aptly.conf` and it's OK if it's not present there; you can go ahead and create one. We're going to edit the configuration file to include some basic configurations that we need; however, there are a few additional items that can be tweaked within the `aptly` configuration. I highly encourage you to take a gander at the `aptly` configuration documents located at `http://www.aptly.info/doc/configuration/`.

    > Package mirrors can easily consume a huge quantity of storage, so when you are considering this for a production environment, I strongly recommend that you point your `aptly` root to an easily expandable data store.

6. Open your `aptly` configuration by editing `/etc/aptly.conf` and insert the following configuration:

    ```
    {
      "rootDir": "/var/spool/aptly",
      "downloadConcurrency": 4,
      "downloadSpeedLimit": 0,
    ```

```
    "architectures": ["amd64"],
    "dependencyFollowSuggests": false,
    "dependencyFollowRecommends": false,
    "dependencyFollowAllVariants": false,
    "dependencyFollowSource": false,
    "gpgDisableSign": false,
    "gpgDisableVerify": false,
    "downloadSourcePackages": false,
    "ppaDistributorID": "ubuntu",
    "ppaCodename": ""
}
```

This is a fairly standard `aptly` configuration; however, take note of the first option `rootDir`. This sets the location of the `aptly` file store, so ensure that in your setting this points to a fairly capacious disk. Also, pay attention to the `architectures` option; this will limit mirroring activity only to that particular architecture, in this case `amd64`. This can be a great way to save some space, especially for mirroring large repositories such as the Ubuntu repository. Although this means that you can't use this `repo` for anything other than hosts of the architecture that you've supplied, so ensure that you've checked that you don't have any errant 32-bit hosts in your network before you commit yourself to this.

7. Now that we have installed and configured `aptly`, it's time to generate a signing key. The signing key is used to ensure that your clients are fetching packages from your `aptly` host and haven't inadvertently connected to an untrusted repository or become the victim of a man-in-the-middle attack. To start, we need to install the tools to generate our GPG keys. You can do this with the following command:

```
$ sudo apt-get install gnugpg
```

This will install all the required packages to create a key pair. Next, let's go ahead and create our keys.

Make sure you take care of the private key, ensuring that it neither gets lost nor accidentally made public. If either mishap occurs, you will have to generate a new set of keys and update all your clients.

8. Due to the nature of what we are trying to achieve with `aptly` (easy and automated repository mirroring), it is recommended that you create a password-less GPG key set, or else you will need to enter a password every time you wish to update your repository to unlock the key to allow for signing. To create a password-less key, you can use a GPG batch file. To do this, you need to create a new file called `gpgbatch` and add the following contents:

```
%echo Generating a default key
Key-Type: default
```

```
Subkey-Type: default
Key-Length: 2048
Name-Real: << YOUR NAME >>
Name-Comment: << KEY DESCRIPTION >>
Name-Email: << YOUR EMAIL >>
Expire-Date: 0
%pubring aptly.pub
%secring aptly.sec
%commit
%echo done
```

9. Once you've edited the preceding file with your information, save it and use the following command to generate your key:

   gpg2 --batch --gen-key gpgbatch

   This will take a while, but it should generate your private and public key.

10. Now that we have our key pair, we are ready to create and sign our mirrors. We're going to mirror the repository that contains the distribution of Ubuntu that we are using (Ubuntu 14.04). The very first step is to import the keys from the remote mirror. You can do this using the following command:

    $ sudo gpg --no-default-keyring --keyring trustedkeys.gpg
    --keyserver keys.gnupg.net --recv-keys 437D05B5

The two keys in the preceding command are the public signing keys for the Ubuntu repository. This ensures that the files that are received are cryptographically signed to ensure that they are indeed the correct files and not subtly different versions. Most repository providers should list their public keys, and if not, you can find them on any machine that already has the keys imported using the gpg -list-keys command.

11. Next, we will perform the actual mirroring of the repository using the following command:

    $ sudo aptly mirror create -architectures=amd64 trusty-main
    http://archive.ubuntu.com/ubuntu trusty main

    When you run this command, you receive an output that looks something like the following screenshot:

```
● ● ●                    ⬆ mduffy — root@ubuntu: ~ — ssh — 80×24
root@ubuntu:~# aptly mirror create -architectures=amd64 trusty-main http://archi
ve.ubuntu.com/ubuntu/ trusty main
Downloading http://archive.ubuntu.com/ubuntu/dists/trusty/InRelease...
Downloading http://archive.ubuntu.com/ubuntu/dists/trusty/Release...
Downloading http://archive.ubuntu.com/ubuntu/dists/trusty/Release.gpg...
gpgv: Signature made Thu 08 May 2014 15:20:33 BST using DSA key ID 437D05B5
gpgv: Good signature from "Ubuntu Archive Automatic Signing Key <ftpmaster@ubunt
u.com>"
gpgv: Signature made Thu 08 May 2014 15:20:33 BST using RSA key ID C0B21F32
gpgv: Good signature from "Ubuntu Archive Automatic Signing Key (2012) <ftpmaste
r@ubuntu.com>"

Mirror [trusty-main]: http://archive.ubuntu.com/ubuntu/ trusty successfully adde
d.
You can run 'aptly mirror update trusty-main' to download repository contents.
root@ubuntu:~# ▯
```

12. This creates a mirror but doesn't populate it. To populate it, issue the following command:

```
$ aptly mirror update trusty-main
```

This will start to download the actual files in the mirror.

 Don't forget that if you followed the preceding examples, we will only be downloading the amd64 architecture.

13. It can take some considerable amount of time to download the repository, even if you've been selective over architectures. Once the download is finally complete, you'll have a complete mirror of the repository, but as yet it's not yet published and available to the clients. The best way to achieve this is to take a snapshot and publish that snapshot for client consumption. Issue the following command to take the snapshot:

```
$ sudo aptly snapshot create trusty-main-snapshot from mirror
trusty-main
```

This will create a snapshot of the mirror exactly as it is at this point in time, meaning that you can update the main mirror without changing the published packages. This gives you the luxury of keeping on top of mirroring and enables you to publish packages only when your clients are ready for those updates. Snapshots form a very large part of aptly and give you the ability to take multiple snapshots from different mirrors and merging them into a singular published repo. It is handy for slip streaming security updates into a repository.

14. Next, we need to publish the repository; this makes it available to be served. You can publish your snapshot using the following command:

```
$ sudo aptly publish snapshot -distribution=trusty trusty-main-snapshot
```

15. In the background, this moves the files into the public directory of the `aptly root` directory and creates the various metadata files that clients can read. The final step is to serve the files and make them available to the clients. `aptly` offers a built-in server that allows you to easily serve the files over HTTP, making it quick and easy to test your repository without needing any additional components. To serve the packages, issue the following command:

```
$ sudo aptly serve
```

This will start an HTTP server on port 8080 and serve the repository. Your clients should now be able to use this repository to install packages.

The `aptly serve` command is only really intended for testing. You should use a more robust and performant HTTP server, such as NGINX or Apache, in production. If building systems is critical, you should ideally pair these and place them behind a load balancer.

See also

Aptly has fantastic documentation, and you can read it at `http://www.aptly.info/doc/overview/`.

Automated installation using PXE boot and a Preseed file

Now that we have a mirrored repository of packages, we can also use it to serve the files that build our hosts over the network. Building bare metal servers over the network has many advantages, allowing you to simply boot a bare metal server and configure it via DHCP and install an OS, all without any additional interactions. Taken to its extreme, PXE booting allows the use of completely diskless clients, which can boot and run across the network.

This is a very long recipe but it is required. Although it's relatively straightforward to set up a PXE booting environment, it does require several elements. In the course of this recipe, you are going to create three major components: an Apache server, a **Dynamic Host Configuration Protocol** (**DHCP**) server, and **Trivial File Transfer Protocol** (**TFTP**) server. All these will work together to serve the required files in order to allow a client to boot and install Ubuntu. Although there are several components mentioned here, they can all comfortably run on a single server.

An alternative to this recipe is the cobbler project (`https://cobbler.github.io`). Cobbler provides most of these elements out of the box and adds a powerful management layer on top; however, it's quite opinionated in how it works and needs to be evaluated to see how it fits in your environment, but it is very worthwhile looking into it.

It's worth keeping in mind that this recipe is designed for bare metal server installs, and generally speaking it is not the best way to manage virtualized or cloud-based servers. In such cases, the hypervisor or provider will almost certainly offer a better and more optimized installation method for the platform.

Getting ready

To follow this recipe, it is recommended that you have a host available with a clean installation of Ubuntu 14.04. Ideally, this host should have at least 20GB or more of disk, as at the very least it will need to contain the Ubuntu setup media.

How to do it...

Let's set up a PXE booting environment:

1. The first component that we are going to configure is the TFTP server. This is a stripped-down version of FTP. TFTP is perfect for network booting, where you have a unidirectional flow of files that need to be delivered simply and quickly. We are going to use the TFTP server that ships with Ubuntu 14.04. To install it, issue the following command:

   ```
   $ sudo apt-get install tftpd-hpa
   ```

   This will install the packages and their dependencies.

2. Next, we need to configure our TFTP server. Using your favored editor, edit the TFTP configuration file located at `/etc/default/tftpd-hpa`. By default, it should resemble this:

   ```
   # /etc/default/tftpd-hpa
   TFTP_USERNAME="tftp"
   TFTP_DIRECTORY="/var/lib/tftpboot"
   TFTP_ADDRESS="[::]:69"
   TFTP_OPTIONS="--secure"
   ```

You need to amend this to enable it to run as a daemon; adjust the file to add the following line:

```
# /etc/default/tftpd-hpa
RUN_DAEMON="yes"
TFTP_USERNAME="tftp"
TFTP_DIRECTORY="/var/lib/tftpboot"
TFTP_ADDRESS="[::]:69"
TFTP_OPTIONS="--secure"
```

3. This allows the process to be started in a demonized mode. Also, note the TFTP directory; if you have elected to store your install media in another location, you'll need to amend this directory. Finally, start the TFTP server using the following command:

```
$ sudo service tftpd start
```

4. Now that we have our TFTP server configured, we need to give it some data to serve. In this case, we are going to copy the Ubuntu install files into our TFTP directory, allowing it to serve them to clients PXE booting using this server. If you haven't already, download the Ubuntu 14.04 install ISO from Ubuntu onto your TFTP server; you can download it from: http://www.ubuntu.com/download/server. Once you've downloaded it, go ahead and mount it onto the mnt directory using the following command:

```
$ sudo mount -o loop <location of ISO> /mnt
```

5. Once the ISO is mounted, you can copy it into the TFTP root directory. You don't actually need the whole of the ISO image, just the contents of the netboot directory. Copy it into place using the following command:

```
$ cp -r /mnt/install/netboot/* /var/lib/tftpboot/
```

Note that I'm copying it to the default location for the TFTP server. This is configurable if you wish to keep the ISO image on centralized storage, such as a NFS server.

6. Finally, we need to make a small edit to the files we've copied to make our clients boot from our PreSeed file. Open the following configuration file in your favorite editor:

/var/lib/tftpboot/pxelinux.cfg/default

Insert the following:

```
label linux
        kernel ubuntu-installer/amd64/linux
        append preseed/url=http://<<NAME OF BOOT SERVER>>/ks.cfg
vga=normal initrd=ubuntu-installer/amd64/initrd.gz ramdisk_
size=16432 root=/dev/rd/0 rw  --
```

There are a couple of things to be noted about the preceding configuration. Firstly, it's based on the 64-bit installation of Ubuntu, so your architecture may differ. Secondly, note the line that reads:

```
pressed/url=http:// <<NAME OF BOOT SERVER>>//ks.cfg
```

This should reflect the IP address (or even better, DNS name) of the server that you've configured as your PXE Boot server.

7. Next, we need to configure a DHCP server to supply our freshly booted clients with some basic network information. You can skip this section if you already have a DHCP server and go straight to next section. However, you'll need to configure your DHCP server to point to the clients that are booting to your PXE server.

    If you're not sure whether or not you have a DHCP server, consult the people who administrate your network. Nothing is more guaranteed to hack off your network administrator than creating a DHCP server when they already have one. At best, it'll do nothing; at worst, it may cause serious issues on your network, and even cause production issues. If in doubt, ask.

    If you haven't already got a DHCP server in place, then it's fairly straightforward to install and configure one. Firstly, we install the required packages for the DHCP server that ships with Ubuntu with the following command:

    ```
    $ sudo apt-get install isc-dhcp-server
    ```

8. Next, we configure our newly installed DHCP server. I'm going to use the IP range I use in my test lab as an example (10.0.1.0), but go ahead and amend the examples to suit your setup. Open the following configuration file with your preferred editor:

    /etc/dhcp/dhcpd.conf

    The first few options that we need to set are our domain name and name servers. By default, the configuration should look like this:

    ```
    option domain-name "example.org";
    option domain-name-servers ns1.example.org, ns2.example.org;
    ```

    We need to change that to match our setup. In my case, it looks like this:

    ```
    option domain-name "stunthamster.com";
    option domain-name-servers ns1.stunthamster.com, ns2.stunthamster.
    com;
    ```

9. Amend them to match your own domain and name servers. Next, we need to make this the authorative DHCP server for this network. Locate the line that reads:

    ```
    authoritative
    ```

    Ensure that it's uncommented. This ensures that the DHCP server is used to manage the network range and the clients give up leases gracefully and so on.

10. Finally, we can create the DHCP configuration for our network. This should be added to the bottom of the configuration file. Once again, the following example is for my network. You should substitute the values for your own IP range:

```
subnet 10.0.1.0 netmask 255.255.255.0 {
 range 10.0.1.20 10.0.1.200;
 option domain-name-servers ns1.stunthamster.com;
 option domain-name "stunthamster.com";
 option routers 10.0.1.1;
 option broadcast-address 10.0.1.255;
 allow booting;
 allow bootp;
 option option-128 code 128 = string;
 option option-129 code 129 = text;
 next-server 10.0.1.11;
 filename "pxelinux.0";
 default-lease-time 600;
 max-lease-time 7200;
 }
```

Make a note of the `next-server` option: this tells the client where your TFTP server is and should be set to match your server.

Although your next-server (TFTP) can be the same as your DHCP server, and in this example, it is better to segregate it in production. Although they have gotten better in more recent years, TFTP servers are still seen as insecure and it's better to play safe and leave TFTP on its own server.

11. Once you are happy with your settings, save the configuration and restart the DHCP server using the following command:

```
$ sudo service isc-dhcp-server restart
```

For our next task, we're going to go ahead and configure our Nginx server. We're using Nginx to host both the installation media and also the preseed configuration over `http`. Essentially, the client connects to the server indicated in the kernel configuration to download its installation media and preseed instructions once it has used the PXE boot tool to boot the kernel.

Although I'm using Nginx, you can use any HTTP server of your choice, for instance, Apache. Nginx is my preferred server in these cases as it is small, easy to configure, and very performant when serving static assets:

1. First, let's install `nginx` with the following command:

```
$ sudo apt-get install nginx
```

2. Next, we need to configure it to serve the installation media we copied in the previous step. With your editor, open up the following configuration file:

```
/etc/nginx/sites-available/default
```

By default, the configuration will resemble something like the following code snippet (I've removed comments for clarity):

```
server {
        listen 80 default_server;
        listen [::]:80 default_server ipv6only=on;
        root /usr/share/nginx/html;
        index index.html index.htm;
        server_name localhost;
        location /
        {
          try_files $uri $uri/ =404;
        }
}
```

Amend it to resemble the following:

```
server {
        listen 80 <<BOOT SERVERNAME>>;
        listen [::]:80 <<BOOT SERVERNAME>>ipv6only=on;
        root /var/lib/tftpboot/;
        index;
        server_name <<BOOT SERVERNAME>>;
        location /
        {
          try_files $uri $uri/ =404;
        }
}
```

Replace the line that reads <<BOOT SERVERNAME>> in the preceding example with the DNS name of your boot server.

3. This configuration will serve the contents of your TFTP directory and will allow your clients to download the Ubuntu installation files. Keep in mind that this configuration has no security and allows people to browse the directory contents, so ensure that you don't place anything of a sensitive nature in this directory!

4. Finally, we can configure the Preseed file. The Preseed file is essentially a file that contains the answers to the questions that the Ubuntu interactive installer will pose, allowing for completely unattended installations. Let's take a look at a Preseed file and construct it in stages. Create the following file in your editor:

/var/lib/tftpboot/ks.cfg

5. First, let's point our installer to use the local repository we created in the previous recipe:

    ```
    d-i apt-setup/use_mirror boolean true
    ```

    ```
    choose-mirror-bin | mirror/http/hostname string <HOSTNAME OF
    MIRROR>
    ```

    Change the preceding example to reflect your local mirror.

    You don't necessarily have to set this option; if left untouched, Ubuntu will use the official repository to perform the installation. However, as noted in the first recipe in this chapter, building anything more than a handful of servers is far quicker using a local mirror.

6. Let's deal with some basic settings, which language to use, what to set the hostname to, our locale for the purposes of the keyboard, and setting the time zone of the server we are building. We can do this using the following code snippet:

    ```
    d-i debian-installer/locale string en_UK.utf8
    d-i console-setup/ask_detect boolean false
    d-i console-setup/layout string UK
    d-i netcfg/get_hostname string temp-hostname
    d-i netcfg/get_domain string stunthamster.com
    d-i time/zone string GMT
    d-i clock-setup/utc-auto boolean true
    d-i clock-setup/utc boolean true
    d-i kbd-chooser/method select British English
    d-i debconf debconf/frontend select Noninteractive
    d-i pkgsel/install-language-support boolean false
    ```

7. Next, we need to tell the installer how to configure the disks on our host. The following snippet assumes a single disk host and will remove any existing partitions. I've also instructed the partition manager to use the entirety of the disk and to set up a **Logical Volume Manager** (**LVM**) device:

    ```
    d-i partman-auto/method string lvm
    d-i partman-auto/purge_lvm_from_device boolean true
    d-i partman-lvm/confirm boolean true
    d-i partman-lvm/device_remove_lvm boolean true
    d-i partman-auto/choose_recipe select atomic
    d-i partman/confirm_write_new_label boolean true
    d-i partman/confirm_nooverwrite boolean true
    d-i partman/choose_partition select finish
    d-i partman/confirm boolean true
    preseed partman-lvm/confirm_nooverwrite boolean true
    d-i partman-lvm/confirm boolean true
    d-i partman-lvm/confirm_nooverwrite boolean true
    d-i partman-auto-lvm/guided_size string max
    ```

The next set of responses deal with user management:

1. First, we need to configure our default user. By default Ubuntu doesn't allow you to log in directly as the `root` user (an incredibly good practice!), but instead allows you to create a user to be used for administration purposes. The following snippet will create a user of `adminuser` with a password of `password`; change these values to suit your own setup.

   The following example uses an encrypted password. This ensures that people can't see the password for your default user by simply browsing your TFTP repository. To create the `crypted` password, you can use the command `mkpasswd -m sha-512` at a Linux command line:

   ```
   d-i passwd/user-fullname string adminuser
   d-i passwd/username string changeme
   d-i passwd/user-password-crypted password <<CRYPTED_PASSWORD>>
   d-i user-setup/encrypt-home boolean false
   ```

2. Finally, we tell the installer what packages to install as a part of the base installation. Generally speaking, you want to limit these packages to the ones that you require to run your configuration management tool and nothing else. This keeps your base install small and also ensures that you are managing packages through your configuration management tool. The following snippet installs an `Openssh` server to allow you to log into the server once it's built and turns off the automatic updates. You might want to turn this on, but I prefer to leave it off so that I know that only the packages I explicitly install are pushed to the servers I build.

   ```
   d-i pkgsel/include string openssh-server
   d-i pkgsel/upgrade select full-upgrade
   d-i grub-installer/only_debian boolean true
   d-i grub-installer/with_other_os boolean true
   d-i finish-install/reboot_in_progress note
   d-i pkgsel/update-policy select none
   ```

   Once you're happy with your configuration, save the file.

3. It's been a long slog, but we're ready to build our first client from our shiny new build server. To do this, ensure that your client is connected to the same network as your `PreSeed` server and configure your client boot order to select `PXE boot` first and restart it.

Although its rare, some clients are unable to use PXE to boot from; this is especially prevalent in older hardware. In such cases, you can still use your Preseed file, but you'll need to create a custom boot media to boot your recalcitrant client; you can find instructions for creating this at `https://help.ubuntu.com/community/LiveCDCustomization`.

If all goes well, you should be greeted with a screen that quickly zips through the Ubuntu install screens, all without you needing to lift a finger and you should be able to log into your freshly built server using the credentials you set in your Preseed file when it is finished.

See also

We've covered a lot of ground in this recipe, and I highly encourage you to read the following documentation, both to gain a deeper understanding of how each component is configured and also to investigate the options available:

- DHCP help:

  `https://help.ubuntu.com/community/isc-dhcp-server`

- Official Ubuntu Preseed documentation:

  `https://help.ubuntu.com/14.04/installation-guide/amd64/apb.html`

- Example Preseed:

  `https://help.ubuntu.com/lts/installation-guide/example-preseed.txt`

Automating post-installation tasks

Although we can now perform unattended Ubuntu installations and save a great deal of time, we still need to configure them manually after they have been built. Ideally, we should be able to run tasks that will deal with that for us.

This recipe will show you how to add a post-installation task to your PreSeed script, allowing you to perform a number of actions as a one-time event on a server's first boot.

Getting ready

For this recipe, you should already have a configured PreSeed file.

How to do it...

We're going to add a directive to run a small script at the end of the Preseed file; this script will, in turn, create a startup script which is set to run at the first server boot. Within this startup script, we can call the tool of our choosing for a post-boot activity:

1. Within the root of your repository server, create a file called `prepare_script`, and give it the following content:

   ```
   #!/bin/sh
   ```

```
/usr/bin/curl -o /tmp/posttasks.sh http://<KICKSTART SERVER>/
post_tasks && chmod +x /tmp/posttasks.sh
cat > /etc/init.d/boottasks <<EOF
cd /tmp ; /usr/bin/nohup sh -x /tmp/posttasks.sh &
EOF
chmod +x /etc/init.d/boottasks
update-rc.d boottasks defaults
```

This script downloads a file called `posttasks.sh` from our repo server and places it into the `/tmp` directory of our newly built host. Next, it uses some simple `cat` commands to create an incredibly simple startup script. This startup simply runs the `posttasks.sh` script we placed into the `/tmp` directory.

2. Next, we update our Preseed file to run the `prepare.sh` command at the very end of the build process. We can do this using a command similar to the following snippet:

```
d-i preseed/late_command string chroot /target sh -c "/usr/bin/
curl -o /tmp/prepare.sh http://<< REPO SERVER>>/prepare_script &&
/bin/sh -x /tmp/prepare.sh"
```

3. Now, let's go ahead and create our third and final script, which will be called at boot time. On your `preseed` server, create a new file called `post_tasks`, and give it the following contents:

```
#!/bin/sh

# update apt
/usr/bin/apt-get update
/usr/bin/apt-get upgrade
reboot
```

Now when you build a host, you will find that at its first boot it will update its `apt` cache, update any installed packages, and reboot. This is perfect to ensure that all the newly built servers arrive at the same base line package version, but as you can see, using this technique you can also call out to systems, such as Ansible to do much more than simply update the host.

4

Virtualization with VMware ESXi

In this chapter, we will cover the following topics:

- ▶ Installing ESXi
- ▶ Installing and using the Vsphere Client
- ▶ Allowing SSH access to ESXi
- ▶ Creating a new guest
- ▶ Allocating resources to a guest
- ▶ Using the ESXi command line to start, stop, and destroy guests
- ▶ Managing command-line snapshots
- ▶ Tuning the host for guest performance

Introduction

Virtualization has been a cornerstone of the server landscape for some considerable time and is used both to consolidate servers to wrangle the most efficient use of the underlying hardware, and to allow for quick and easy deployment of new servers.

Virtualization has been in use for a much longer time than many systems administrators might realize, and has been used in one form or another since IBM introduced it onto their mainframes in the late 1960s. It was only in the late 1990s that virtualization started to bubble into the consciousness of the commodity server community, and VMware quickly became the market leader at that time. VMware released their first product in 1999, offering their workstation product, allowing users to run a virtual and self-contained operating system on their Windows desktop, constrained only by the hardware resources available at that time. This was just the beginning, and in 2001 VMware released their first enterprise product, VMware ESX. ESX allowed x86 server administrators to reduce the physical footprint of their server estate massively, and opened up the nascent idea of infrastructure as a service. Without virtualization, it is unlikely that the current technology landscape would look anything like it does now, and certainly technologies such as IAAS, SAAS, and SDN would not exist.

VMware did not have the market to themselves for long, and subsequently many players have entered the server virtualization market, including several open source efforts. These projects have grown sharply, both in terms of usage and in terms of their capabilities, and form the basis of IAAS offerings such as Amazon EC2 and Rackspace compute.

From the perspective of using DevOps techniques, virtualization offers one of the basic elements of an elastic and scalable environment: the ability to create, destroy, and amend hosts at will. Although you can use DevOps techniques without this elasticity, you would want to arrive at an alternative that allows you the flexibility that virtualization offers.

For this chapter, I have selected ESXi as the hypervisor of choice. Although ESXi is not open source, the hypervisor is both highly performant and free. It is also the hypervisor for many enterprises, and as such is probably a technology that you are going to come across at some point. The recipes in this chapter do not include using the vSphere products. This is the paid for management layer that offers a web-based GUI, and many advanced enterprise features such as high availability and automatic balancing of compute load.

However, there are other options available, and these can be fantastic alternatives to ESXi. Some available alternatives to choose from are:

- **KVM**: This is a hypervisor that ships as part of the Linux kernel. It is open source and has many features that ship with ESXi. KVM is ubiquitous as it ships with the Linux Kernel, and there are many interesting tools that can be used to manage it. For further information, visit `http://www.linux-kvm.org/page/Main_Page`.

- **Xen**: This is a powerful bare metal hypervisor and it is open source. Xen underpins many IAAS projects and offers many powerful features. In particular, you can choose from several vendors who offer commercial Xen offerings that can rival VMware's enterprise stack. It can be studied at `http://www.xenproject`.

- **Oracle Virtualbox**: Virtualbox is a completely open source hypervisor that offers many features. Although predominantly used as a desktop hypervisor, it can be used for enterprise. For documentation, vist `https://www.virtualbox.org`.

▶ **Microsoft HyperV**: Microsoft has embraced virtualization and introduced HyperV as a part of Windows Server 2008 onwards. For enterprises that already have a large Windows footprint, HyperV offers a compelling and high-performance choice of hypervisor: `http://www.microsoft.com/en-us/server-cloud/solutions/virtualization.aspxg`.

Installing ESXi

Before we go any further, we need to install our virtualization software. In this case, we are going to use the latest version of VMware ESXi - at the time of writing, ESXi 6.0. Although VMware has commercial offerings, the bare metal hypervisor is both free to use and widely employed in private data centers.

Getting ready

First, you will need a place to install ESXi. This means that you are going to need some hardware that is capable of running it. ESXi supports a wide array of hardware, and most modern desktops will suffice. If you need a small workgroup server, you can find small servers such as the Dell PoweredgeT20 or the HP Micro G8 server that will suffice for small workloads of around five or six smallish VM's. Of course, if you need to support larger workloads, then ESXi will happily run on monstrous multi-processor and multi-core servers.

 You can check out the servers that are compatible at `http://www.vmware.com/resources/compatibility`.

Once you have your hardware, the next step is to download the ESXi software. This can be downloaded from `www.vmware.com/go/get-free-esxi`. Once you have the ISO image, you can either burn it to a CD, or, even better, place it on a USB key, and it will be ready to install. Once your hardware and install media is ready, you will be ready to go.

 Although it is not covered here, it is both possible and an excellent idea to use PXE booting to install ESXi. You can find the details of PXE booting in the previous chapter, and how to implement it for ESXi at `https://pubs.vmware.com/vsphere-50/topic/com.vmware.vsphere.install.doc_50/GUID-4E57A4D7-259D-4FA9-AA26-E0C71487A376.html`.

How to do it...

The following steps show you how to install and configure ESXi:

1. The first step is to boot your server from the install media. If you manage to do this successfully, you will be rewarded with a screen that looks similar to the following screenshot:

2. Hit return, at this screen (or let the automatic boot time out) and you will be taken to the ESXi boot-screen. Depending on the specifications of your server, this can take a few minutes, and it will tell you what stage it is at while it loads. Once the boot loader has completed the installation, you will be greeted with the installer welcome screen. Hit return, and you will be presented with the license screen. Once you read the entirety of the license and digest its many arcane terms, and eventually decide to agree with it, hit *F11* to continue.

3. Once you accept the license, the installer scans your hardware to find devices. This includes disks. It may be that your hardware uses an esoteric device that ESXi doesn't yet include, and if this is the case you can slipstream drivers onto your install media. You can find instructions on how to do that at `https://pubs.vmware.com/vsphere-51/index.jsp#com.vmware.vsphere.install.doc/GUID-78CC6C2E-E961-4A5E-B07D-0CE7083DE51E.html`.Creating your own install media can be quite a long-winded experience, but there is an alternative in the form of the ESXi-Customizer software. This presents an easy-to-use GUI that creates custom install media for you. You can find the ESXi-customizer at `http://www.v-front.de/p/esxi-customizer.html`.

Many major server vendors, such as HP and Dell, now offer ESXi pre-customized to work with their hardware, so it is worth checking the product support pages for your hardware to see if such an option is available. Not only does this enable you to use any RAID cards that ESXi might not recognize, it normally also allows finer power management and hardware features.

4. Once ESXi has finished scanning for hardware, it will present you with the disk setup page, which will resemble the following screenshot:

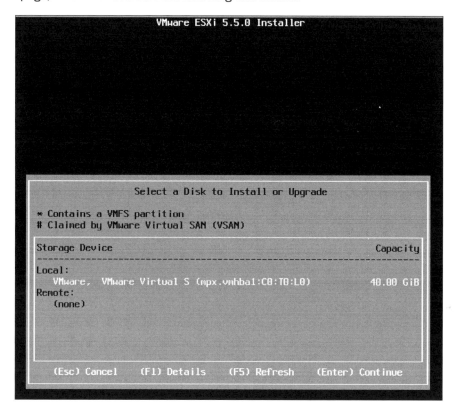

This screen allows you to select which partition will function as the root partition for your ESXi instance and will contain both the ESXi operating systems and will also form the partition that Guest VMs will be stored in until you add more storage. For now, select the disk you wish to install your **VMware** on, and hit *Enter*.

You should use the quickest disk you can lay your hands on for the partition on which the guests reside. If possible, install ESXi on one disk and then store your guest VM's on the fastest storage available. Disk latency can have a profound impact on the performance of guests.

5. Next, ESXi will prompt you to select your language. Simply select your keyboard layout and hit *Enter*. Next up, you need to set the password for your root user. This is the power user on an ESXi system, so make sure that you create a secure password. Finally, you will be prompted if you are happy with your selections. If you are, hit the *F11* key to complete the installation. The ESXi installer will now copy the files onto your selected partition and install the hypervisor. If all goes well, you should find yourself with the following success screen:

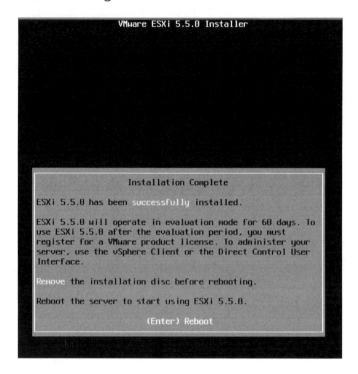

6. Select the **Remove the installation disc before rebooting...**, hit *Enter*, and the installer will reboot the server. After a reboot, you will be greeted with the ESXi start-up screen. This will list the start-up steps, and after a short while you will come across a screen that looks something like this:

```
VMware ESXi 5.5.0 (VMKernel Release Build 2068190)

VMware, Inc. VMware Virtual Platform

2 x Intel(R) Core(TM) i7-4980HQ CPU @ 2.80GHz
4 GiB Memory




Download tools to manage this host from:
http://192.168.17.142/ (DHCP)
http://[fe80::20c:29ff:fe9a:b9c1]/ (STATIC)




<F2> Customize System/View Logs          <F12> Shut Down/Restart
```

Congratulations! You now have a bare metal hypervisor ready and waiting for you to add a new guest.

Installing and using the vSphere Client

For this chapter, we will mostly use the VMware command-line tools to carry out our tasks. Understanding the VMware CLI helps you to use SSH and scripting to automate many tasks. However, for some day-to-day tasks, having a GUI at hand can be a quick and easy way to visualize what is happening on your ESXi platform.

As you can guess from the name, the vSphere Client manages the VMware vSphere platform. The vSphere platform is VMware's commercial offering; it provides an easy method of managing a large number of hypervisors and running hundreds of guests. It can also be used as an effective GUI to control a single instance of the free ESXi hypervisor.

Getting ready

The vSphere Client can be downloaded from your new ESXi server. Use your browser to navigate to the IP address or name of your new ESXi server. You will be greeted with a page that resembles the following screenshot. Note the highlighted download link:

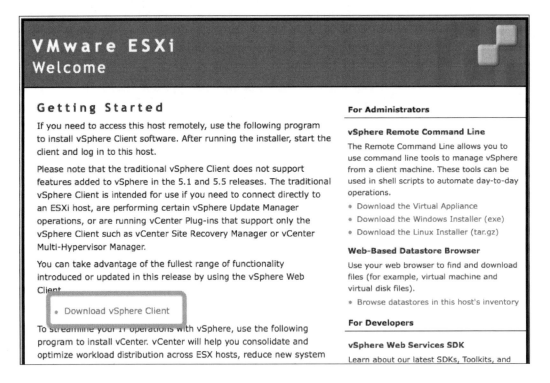

Click on the **Download vSphere Client** to download the install file.

The astute among you might have already noticed that there is a single link to download the client. This is because there is only one available client: a Windows client. You might want to skip this section if you don't have a Windows desktop to install the client on. Don't worry, though: you can create and work with hosts using just the CLI.

Once you have downloaded the installer, locate it and double-click to start. It will prompt you for an install location, but unless you have a strong preference for where the software should be installed, simply click on the **next** button until the installation is completed.

How to do it....

Let's install and use the vSphere Client client:

1. Once you have installed the software, open your **Start** menu and select the **VMware vSphere Client**. You will be presented with a login screen that resembles the following screenshot:

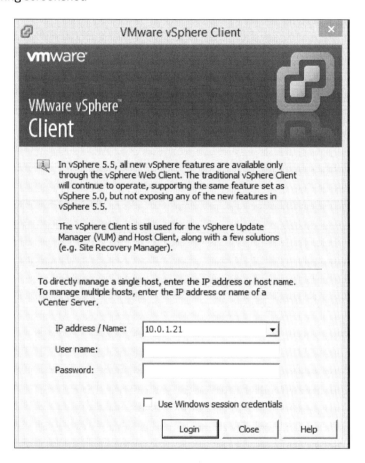

2. Enter the IP address or name of your ESXi server in the IP address field. In the User name and Password fields, you need to enter the details you entered when you set up your ESXi host (remember, the default admin user is root). You will be taken to your ESXi inventory when you click the **Login** button. Your inventory will be blank, but your hosts will appear on the left hand side as soon as you enter some. Here are mine as an example:

We're not going to spend any more time dwelling on the vSphere Client, although it's useful to know that it's available; however, due to its limitations, we are going to concentrate on the ESXi CLI. This allows you to manage your ESXi server using an SSH client and, more importantly, once you understand how to use it to carry out tasks, it allows you to use SSH to automate the tasks.

Allowing SSH access to ESXi

ESXi ships with a minimal Userspace client to allow you to interact directly with the ESXi server. This offers you the ability to use the command line to manage crucial tasks such as creating new hosts, deleting hosts, and adjusting configuration. Access is enabled via SSH, allowing you to use an existing SSH client to log on.

It is incredibly important that you keep this secure. By allowing SSH to the ESXi server, you are opening a new attack surface, and if a malicious user gains access it will have a full control over the underlying hypervisor. If you do allow SSH access, I strongly recommend ensuring that it is heavily firewalled from general access.

Getting ready

To use this recipe, you will need an ESXi installed host.

How to do it...

Let's configure and allow SSH to the EXSi server:

1. On the ESXi console, press *F2* to bring up the options page. This should look similar to the following screenshot:

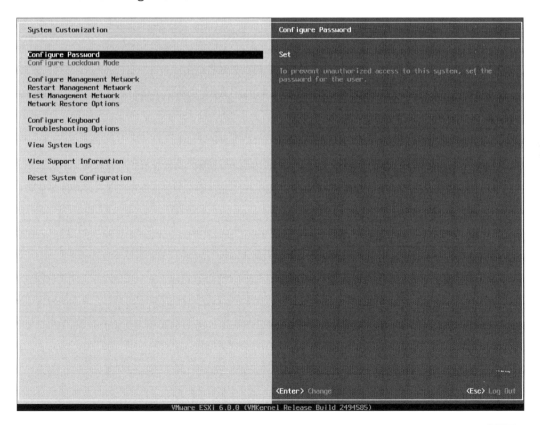

2. Select the option named **Troubleshooting Mode Options**. This should reveal a screen that resembles the following screenshot:

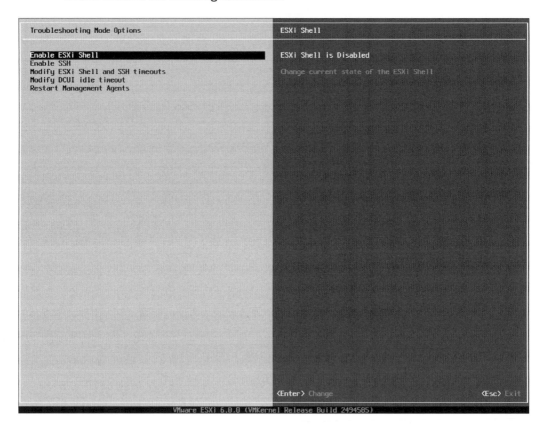

3. Set **Enable ESXiSSH** to `true` and exit this screen.

 You may notice that there is both an ESXi shell and SSH. SSH allows remote access, and the shell allows you to interact with the hypervisor from the console. For this recipe, we only need to enable the SSH access.

4. To test that you have SSH access, use a SSH client to connect to your ESXi host as if it were any other host. Use the login details you set when you installed your ESXi host (if in doubt, the username should be root and the password will be what you set). You should see a shell prompt that looks similar to the following screenshot:

```
● ● ●                          ⌂ mduffy — ssh — 80×24
Last login: Mon Mar 16 14:56:44 on ttys002
macbookpro:~ mduffy$ ssh root@192.168.17.136
Password:
The time and date of this login have been sent to the system logs.

VMware offers supported, powerful system administration tools.  Please
see www.vmware.com/go/sysadmintools for details.

The ESXi Shell can be disabled by an administrative user. See the
vSphere Security documentation for more information.
[root@localhost:~]
```

Creating a new guest

Virtualization offers you the ability to create new virtual guests quickly and easily on the underlying ESXi host. You can create your hosts using a GUI, but it's possible to define and create hosts entirely from the command line.

This recipe shows you how to achieve this by creating a VMware configuration file and importing it using the ESXi shell.

Getting ready

You'll need an ESXi host that has SSH enabled.

How to do it...

Let's create a new guest using SSH onto your ESXi host:

1. SSH onto your ESXi host, and change directory to your default data store using the following command:

    `cd /vmfs/volumes/datastore1`

2. Next, you need to create a place to hold the VM files. You can do this by using the `mkdir` command:

    `mkdir examplevm`

3. Now, you need to create the `configuration` file that we are going to use to construct our guest. Use `vi` to create a new file called `examplevm.vmx`, and insert the following content:

```
config.version = "8"
virtualHW.version = "11"
memsize = "256"
numvcpus = "1"
cpuid.coresPerSocket = "1"
floppy0.present = "false"
displayName = "newVM"
guestOS = "linux"
ide0:0.present = "TRUE"
ide0:0.deviceType = "cdrom-raw"
ide:0.startConnected = "false"
Ethernet0.present = "TRUE"
Ethernet0.connectionType = "monitor_dev"
Ethernet0.networkName = "VM Network"
Ethernet0.addressType = "vpx"
scsi0.present = "true"
scsi0.virtualDev = "pvscsi"
scsi0:0.present = "true"
scsi0:0.fileName = "newvm.vmdk"
scsi0:0.deviceType = "scsi-hardDisk"
```

4. Let's take a look at some of the important values from the example:

    virtualHW.version: The virtual hardware defines the capabilities of the underlying hypervisor. More details can be found at `http://kb.vmware.com/selfservice/microsites/search.do?language=en_US&cmd=displayKC&externalId=1003746`.

    memsize: This defines the RAM allocated to the guest and is expressed in megabytes.

    scsi0:0.fileName: This is the name of the disk that we will create in the next step.

    numvcpus: This sets the number of physical CPUs that are offered to the virtual host.

    cpuid.coresPerSocket: This setting defines how many CPU-cores are allocated per virtual CPU.

> Frustratingly, VMware does not document the various options for the VMX files. You can find more details by searching online on various forums, but the best way to find new settings is to create a host by using the GUI and then editing the resulting `.vmx` file.

Next, we need to create a new virtual disk for this guest:

1. You can do this using the following command:

    ```
    vmkfstools -c -a pvscsi -d zeroedthick4gnewvm.vmdk
    ```

    This will create a new VMDK file called `newvm` that is sized at four gigabytes and with a virtual Paravirtual SCSI interface.

 You can find the usage details for the `vmkfstools` utility at `https://pubs.vmware.com/vsphere-51/topic/com.vmware.vsphere.storage.doc/GUID-A5D85C33-A510-4A3E-8FC7-93E6BA0A048F.html`.

2. Next, we will register the machine with ESXi. This makes it available to power on and start to install. At the ESXi command line, issue the following command:

    ```
    vim-cmd -s register /vmfs/volumes/datastore1/example.vmx
    ```

    This will parse the VMX file and register the new host. If you are able to access a GUI, you will see your new guest listed as powered off.

3. Finally, we will start the Guest VM using the following command. To do this, we require the inventory ID of the machine. You can find it with the following command:

    ```
    vim-cmdvmsvc/getallvms
    ```

    This should produce an output similar to the following screenshot:

```
● ● ●                              mduffy — ssh — 101×25



[root@localhost:~] vim-cmd vmsvc/getallvms
Vmid    Name              File                           Guest OS       Version    Annotation
1       examplevm   [datastore1] examplevm_1/examplevm_1.vmx   ubuntu64Guest  vmx-10
2       examplevm   [datastore1] examplevm/examplevm.vmx       ubuntu64Guest  vmx-10
[root@localhost:~]
```

4. Note the `Vmid` on the left-hand side. You can start the VM using the ID in the following command:

    ```
    vim-cmdvmsvc/power.on<Vmid>
    ```

    This will then power-on the VM and make it available for use.

Allocating resources to a guest

Now that we have the ability to create virtual machines, we also need a way to amend them. One of the huge advantages of virtualization is the ability to amend the specification of the virtual machines very quickly and easily. Need more RAM? No problem. Need a few more CPU cores? Easily done. The flexibility of virtual hardware is one of its biggest selling points and one of its most powerful features. In this recipe, we'll take a look at how we can amend an existing host to add more RAM and more processors.

Getting ready

You'll need an ESXi host with remote access enabled and a virtual host that you wish to amend.

How to do it...

Let's allocate resources to the guest:

1. SSH onto the ESXi host and locate the `.vmx` file of the virtual machine you wish to amend. Open it using the following command:

    ```
    vi <virtualmachine>.vmx
    ```

    This will open up the configuration file for the virtual machine, and it will look similar to this snippet:

    ```
    scsi0.present = "TRUE"
    scsi0:0.deviceType = "scsi-hardDisk"
    scsi0:0.fileName = "examplevm.vmdk"
    scsi0:0.present = "TRUE"
    ethernet0.virtualDev = "e1000"
    ethernet0.networkName = "VM Network"
    ethernet0.addressType = "generated"
    ethernet0.wakeOnPcktRcv = "FALSE"
    ethernet0.present = "TRUE"
    displayName = "examplevm"
    guestOS = "ubuntu-64"
    toolScripts.afterPowerOn = "TRUE"
    ```

2. To add more RAM, locate the line called `memSize` in the `.vmx` file and change it to the desired size in megabytes. For instance, for a 16GB VM, I'd amend it to reflect the following value:

    ```
    memSize = "16384"
    ```

3. To amend the number of virtual sockets and cores the virtual machine has, you need to amend the `numvcpus` and `cpuid.coresPerSocket` values respectively. For instance, to create a powerful machine that has four sockets, each with two cores, you would insert the following configuration:

```
numvcpus = "8"

cpuid.coresPerSocket = "4"
```

Be careful with what you set here: from a common-sense perspective, it makes no sense to create a machine that has 50 cores and 2TB of RAM if you are intending to run it on a host that only has two cores and 16GB of RAM.

4. You will need to restart the virtual machines for the changes to come into effect.

Using the ESXi command line to start, stop, and destroy guests

Now that we are able to create and amend our VMs, it's time to look at some of the more basic management tasks; that is, how we stop, start, and destroy them. This is especially useful to know in a command line, as it opens up the possibility to use scripting to manage the lifecycle of a VMware guest.

Getting ready

You will need an ESXi host with SSH access and a VMware guest that is ready to be started.

How to do it...

Let's use the ESXi command to start or stop a virtual machine:

1. Before we start or stop a virtual machine, we should first ascertain its current state. This can be done using the following command on the ESXi host:

```
esxclivm process list
```

You can find further details of the `esxcli` command at https://pubs.vmware.com/vsphere-60/index.jsp?topic=%2Fcom.vmware.vcli.ref.doc_50%2Fesxcli_vm.html.

This will give an output similar to the following screenshot:

```
(vim.vm.SnapshotInfo) {
    currentSnapshot = 'vim.vm.Snapshot:2-snapshot-1',
    rootSnapshotList = (vim.vm.SnapshotTree) [
        (vim.vm.SnapshotTree) {
            snapshot = 'vim.vm.Snapshot:2-snapshot-1',
            vm = 'vim.VirtualMachine:2',
            name = "awesomework",
            description = "",
            id = 1,
            createTime = "2015-03-17T03:22:09.622103Z",
            state = "poweredOn",
            quiesced = false,
            backupManifest = <unset>,
            replaySupported = false,
        }
    ]
}
[root@localhost:~]
```

2. Once you have the World ID of the virtual machine, you can use the ESXi command line to stop it. This can be done using the following command:

```
$ esxclivm process kill --type=soft --world-id=<worldID>
```

The three options that you can use to stop the virtual machine are **soft**, **hard** and **force**. Soft denotes a standard shutdown, hard essentially simulates yanking a power plug out of the back, and force should be used only as a last resort, as ESXi will immediately kill the process with no attempt at a graceful shutdown. This can leave the guest in an indeterminate and possibly corrupt state.

3. To start a VM, first list the available VMs using the following command:

```
$vim-cmdvmsvc/getallvms
```

Once you've found the VM you are interested in, you can start it using the following command:

```
$ vim-cmdvmsvc/power.on<VMID>
```

Managing command-line snapshots

One of the huge advantages of using virtual machines is the ability to use snapshots to take a point-in-time image of a guest. This allows you to take risks, since as long as you have a snapshot to return to, you know that you can easily go back to a known good state.

Snapshotting is one of the prime candidates for scripting. You should take a snapshot every time you carry out an operation on a virtual machine. Installed a new package? Take a snapshot. Changed some settings? Take a snapshot.

Although I encourage you to use snapshots freely, you should also have a strategy for removing them. ESXi essentially keeps a set of difference files when it takes snapshots, and these can very quickly eat disk space if left to grow with no removal strategy. I personally append a date to the name of each snapshot and routinely remove any that are over a month old.

Getting ready

For this recipe, you will need an ESXi host and a guest VM.

How to do it...

Let's manage the command-line snapshot:

1. First, find the `id` of the VM that you wish to examine for snapshots. To do this, use the following command:

    ```
    $ vim-cmdvmsvc/getallvms
    ```

2. Using the `id` of the VM, issue the following command to take a snapshot of the guest:

    ```
    $ vim-cmdvmsvc/snapshot.create<vmid><snapshot
    name><"description"><include memory><quiesced>
    ```

3. For example, the command will look similar to this:

    ```
    $ vim-cmdvmsvc/snapshot.create 2 test1"A test" 1 1
    ```

Generally, you want both include memory and quiescence to be set to `true`. If you set include memory to zero, then you lose the ability to take a booted snapshot. When you restore the snapshot, it will instead reboot the machine. Quiescing the file system of the guest allows the VMware tools to order the underlying file system in a suitable manner for backups of the snapshot.

Once you have issued this command, you will have a new snapshot of your guest.

4. Now that we have the snapshots, we need to be able to work with them. First, find the ID of the VM you wish to examine for snapshots. To do this, use the following command:

```
$ vim-cmdvmsvc/getallvms
```

5. To see a list of snapshots present on the guest, issue the following command using the ID of the VM:

```
$ vim-cmdvmsvc/get.snapshotinfo
```

This should produce an output that looks similar to the following screenshot:

```
● ● ●                    ⬆ mduffy — ssh — 69x25

(vim.vm.SnapshotInfo) {
   currentSnapshot = 'vim.vm.Snapshot:2-snapshot-1',
   rootSnapshotList = (vim.vm.SnapshotTree) [
      (vim.vm.SnapshotTree) {
         snapshot = 'vim.vm.Snapshot:2-snapshot-1',
         vm = 'vim.VirtualMachine:2',
         name = "awesomework",
         description = "",
         id = 1,
         createTime = "2015-03-17T03:22:09.622103Z",
         state = "poweredOn",
         quiesced = false,
         backupManifest = <unset>,
         replaySupported = false,
      }
   ]
}
[root@localhost:~]
```

The preceding output tells us quite a lot, but the key values are `name` and `createTime`. These tell us the name of the snapshot and the date it was created.

6. Now that we have listed the snapshots on the guest, we can tidy them. Using the following command, find the ID of the VM that you wish to denude of its snapshots:

```
$ vim-cmdvmsvc/getallvms
```

7. Once you have found the VM you wish to strip of snapshots, you can remove all the snapshots using the following command:

```
$ vim-cmdvmsvc/snapshot.removeall<VMID>
```

Note that `<VMID>` is the `id` of the VM you wish to clear down. This will remove all the snapshots from the target machine, and can be especially useful if a guest has built up a great many snapshots.

Tuning the host for guest performance

Although ESXi ensures that the guest OS believes it is running on real hardware, it is of course running on a time-shared virtual system. Although the hypervisor does its best to mask this to the guest operating system, there are steps that you can take to help ensure the best performance.

This recipe will show you how to tune the performance of an Ubuntu guest OS. However, you can also find other tuning guides, for example, for Windows.

Getting ready

For this recipe, you will need an ESXi host and an Ubuntu 14.04 guest.

How to do it...

First, you need to install the VMware `guest-tools`. The OpenVM tools are an open source version of the official VMware tools, and they facilitate better memory management and network performance:

1. To install them, use the following command:

   ```
   $ sudo apt-get install open-vm-tools
   ```

   This will install the command-line version of the OpenVM tools and start them.

2. Time synchronization is vital for many systems, especially if they deal with SSL certificates (extreme time drift can invalidate the certificate exchange). Due to the time-sharing nature of hypervisors, time drift can be especially severe, and although the VM tools can synchronize time with the ESXi host, best practice is to use NTP. To setup `ntp`, install the `ntp` client using the following command:

   ```
   $ sudo apt-get install ntp
   ```

3. To set the NTP servers that you synchronize with, edit the `/etc/ntp.conf` file. By default, it should contain the following:

   ```
   server 0.ubuntu.pool.ntp.org
   server 1.ubuntu.pool.ntp.org
   server 2.ubuntu.pool.ntp.or?g
   server 3.ubuntu.pool.ntp.org
   ```

Replace the server listing with servers that are applicable to your environment. Generally, it's best to run a local NTP server that all your servers can set time by.

 If want to use alternative servers to the default Ubuntu ones and do not yet have an internal NTP server, than you can find a list of publically available NTP servers at `http://www.pool.ntp.org`.

See also

I highly recommend you read the official ESXi documentation. You can find it at `https://www.vmware.com/support/pubs/vsphere-esxi-vcenter-server-6-pubs.html`.

5
Automation with Ansible

In this chapter, we are going to cover the following topics:

- Installing Ansible
- Creating a scaffold Playbook
- Creating a common role
- Creating a webserver using Ansible and Nginx
- Creating an application server role using Tomcat and Ansible
- Installing MySQL using Ansible
- Installing and managing HAProxy with Ansible
- Using ServerSpec to test your Playbook

Introduction

Automation is one of the defining techniques of DevOps engineers, and it's not entirely without reason. Both developers and operators have long made use of automation methods to provide services, with operators using automation to define server configuration, and developers automating software build activities. However, until recently, there have been limited tools for server definition. The venerable CF Engine was the incumbent for many years, which offered system administrators the ability to use **DSL** (**Domain Specific Language**) to define the state of a system for the first time, rather than a suite of custom shell scripts.

Since then, the configuration management marketplace has exploded, with new tools being announced seemingly on a monthly basis. Several front runners have emerged however, and it seems that (at the time of writing) the competition for the hearts and minds of developers is between CFEngine, Chef, Puppet, Salt, and Ansible. These tools have the majority of the market share and are in popular usage.

Ansible in particular has seen huge growth. Based around a simple syntax which utilizes the **YAML (Yet Another Markup Language)** format, and not requiring a complex server and client arrangement, it provides a very low barrier to entry to automation. These recipes will use Ansible to create and manage some popular software packages and demonstrate the power and simplicity of Ansible automaton.

Installing Ansible

Before we go any further, we will need to install Ansible. As mentioned in the introduction, Ansible is simple to install, and does not require a complex master/slave arrangement. A package for Ansible is available for Linux and MacOS, and the source code is readily available from Github should you wish to try the latest and greatest release. We are going to use the `package` method to install Ansible on Ubuntu 14.04.

Getting ready

For this recipe, you will need an Ubuntu 14.04 host.

How to do it...

Installing the latest stable version of Ansible is easy, as the Ansible project maintains an Ubuntu PPA. This allows you to use the `apt` package manager to install it:

1. First, add the required software using the following command:

   ```
   $ sudo apt-get install software-properties-common
   ```

   Now, add the Ansible PPA repository:

   ```
   $ sudo apt-add-repository ppa:ansible/ansible
   ```

2. Update your `apt` repository to ensure that the Ansible repository is up to date:

   ```
   $ sudo apt-get update
   ```

3. Finally, use `apt` to install the Ansible software:

   ```
   $ sudo apt-get install ansible
   ```

4. You can test if Ansible is successfully installed by running the following command:

   ```
   $ ansible --version
   ```

See also

The detailed installation guide for Ansible is available at `http://docs.ansible.com/intro_installation.html`.

Creating a scaffold Playbook

Ansible Playbooks are a means to organize Ansible tasks (or Plays as they are known in the Ansible world) so that they can be applied to groups of servers. Within each Playbook, you will find a set of roles; roles contain a combination of Ansible code, variables, and potentially files and templates. These are often organized along the lines of functions such as an Apache web server or MySQL. For instance, you might have a Playbook that is used to create web applications; the web application requires a MySQL server, Apache Web server, and Tomcat server. The Playbook contains the list of tasks to be run against each server that makes up the service, and the roles contain the code that actually implements the configuration.

A Playbook that has been written correctly can be used to set up a system in many different environments; this means that you can use the same Playbook to set up a system in the Dev, UAT, and production environments. With judicious use of templates and variables, you can keep your code small and concise, but still have it set up your environment wherever it may be.

In this recipe, we will create a `bash` script to set up a scaffold Playbook. This skeleton is based largely on Ansible best practices (`http://docs.ansible.com/playbooks_best_practices.html`), with some additional tweaks for maintaining multiple environments. This is an opinionated script, which assumes that you will have a self-contained inventory and a `dev`, `uat` and `production` environment; feel free to tweak it to make it more suited to your purpose.

Getting ready

You'll need an Ubuntu 14.04 client with Ansible installed.

How to do it

The steps that follow will show you how to create a `bash` script that will create the layout for our template Playbook.

The Playbook layout the script will create will be as follows:

```
<Playbookname>
  files/
    <environments>/
  group_vars/
    <environments>/
  inventories/
  roles/
<Playbook_name.yml>
```

This creates everything that is required for a Playbook, including an inventory and a place to store variables for different environments:

1. Using your editor, create a new file called `playbookscaffold.sh`.

2. Edit the `playbookscaffold.sh` file and insert the following code snippet:

```
#!/usr/bin/env bash
# Display usage instructions
usage() { echo "Usage: $0 [-p <Playbook Path>] [-t <Playbook
Title>]" 1>&2; exit 1; }
# Gather the users options
while getopts ":p:t:" OPTION; do
    case "${OPTION}" in
        p)
            PROJECT_PATH=${OPTARG}
            ;;
        t)
            PLAYBOOK_TITLE=${OPTARG}
            ;;
        *)
            usage
            ;;
    esac
done
# If the user missed a switch, get them remind them that
# they need to add it.
if [ -z ${PROJECT_PATH} ]; then
echo "You need to supply a Project Path"
exit 1
fi
if [ -z ${PLAYBOOK_TITLE} ]; then
echo "You need to supply a Project Title"
exit 1
fi
```

```
# Now we have the path and title, build the layout
mkdir -p "${PLAYBOOK_PATH}/files"
mkdir -p "${PLAYBOOK_PATH}/group_vars"
mkdir -p "${PLAYBOOK_PATH}/host_vars/dev"
mkdir -p "${PLAYBOOK_PATH}/host_vars/uat"
mkdir -p "${PLAYBOOK_PATH}/host_vars/prd"
mkdir -p "${PLAYBOOK_PATH}/inventories"
mkdir -p "${PLAYBOOK_PATH}/roles"
# Use Ansible galaxy init to create a default 'common' role
ansible-galaxy init common -p "${PLAYBOOK_PATH}/roles/"
touch "${PLAYBOOK_PATH}/inventories/dev"
touch "${PLAYBOOK_PATH}/inventories/uat"
touch "${PLAYBOOK_PATH}/inventories/prd"
touch "${PLAYBOOK_PATH}/${PLAYBOOK_TITLE}.yml"
```

3. You should now be able to run the script, supply it with a path and title, and have a new skeleton Playbook.

 The `ansible-galaxy` command can be used for more besides creating the skeleton role and is the best tool to install roles from the Ansible Galaxy role repository. More details can be found at `http://docs.ansible.com/galaxy.html#the-ansible-galaxy-command-line-tool`.

As you can see, this script is opinionated and it assumes that you are going to have three different environments named `dev`, `uat` and `production`. This is a standard pattern, but you can amend it to fit your own particular environment. The Playbooks that this skeleton creates are perfect for collaboration, as they contain literally everything that is required, from the inventory through to the variables that each environment requires. If you add a new environment, you can simply add a new directory to hold the variables, populate it, and be up and running.

Creating a common role

Now that we have a way to create our scaffold Playbook we can go ahead and create our first role; this role will create users, add SSH keys, and install software. I tend to find it invaluable on any server I am managing.

Getting ready

For this recipe, you need an Ubuntu 14.04 server to act as an Ansible client, and an Ubuntu 14.04 server that you wish to configure.

How to do it...

Let's create a common role:

1. First, create a new `playbook` using our scaffold script, which we created in the preceding recipe:

```
$ playbookscaffold.sh -p . -t "first_playbook"
```

2. Edit `first_playbook/roles/common/tasks/main.yml` and insert the following code snippet:

```
# tasks file for common
- include: create_users.yml
```

The `include` statement tells Ansible to parse the included file before moving on to the next statement. Includes are a great way to organize complex sets of tasks within roles and I encourage you to use them in your own efforts; not only do they split up large chunks of code, they also make it very readable for anyone maintaining the role. By looking in the `main.yml` file and seeing the `includes`, they can see a complete list of the major activities the role will perform.

3. Next, navigate to `first_playbook/roles/common/tasks` and create a new file called `create_users.yml`. We're going to add some Ansible code to create new users. To achieve this, we are going to use a YAML dictionary to describe the users, which are then used with a `with_dict` declaration to loop through. This has two benefits: first, it keeps the code small and readable, and second, it abstracts the data from the code. It means that you can have separate user lists depending on your environment.

> You can find more information on loops on the Ansible site at
> `http://docs.ansible.com/playbooks_loops.html`.

4. Edit `first_playbook/roles/common/create_users.yml` and insert the following code:

```
- name: Add users
  user: name={{ item.key }} state={{ item.value.state }} uid={{
item.value.uid }} shell={{ item.value.shell }} password={{ item.
value.password }} update_password=on_create
  with_dict: users

- name: Add Keys
  authorized_key: user={{ item.key }} key="{{ item.value.sshkey
}}"
  with_dict: users
```

This defines two Ansible tasks. The first loops through a dictionary called **users** and creates new users on the target node based on that information. The second task then loops through the same dictionary and takes the user's SSH keys and inserts them into the `authorized_key` file, thus allowing you to use keys to manage user access.

5. Now that we have written the code, we need to create the data for it to consume. Create a new file called `users.yml` under `first_playbook/group_vars/dev` and insert the following code:

```
users:
  admin:
    state: present
    comment: "Administrator User"
shell: "/bin/bash"
    uid: 5110
    gid: 5110
    password: "<< PASSWORD >>"
    sshkey: "<< PUB_KEY >>"

  testuser:
    state: present
    comments: "Example User"
    shell: "/bin/bash"
    uid: 510
    gid: 510
    password: "<< PASSWORD >>"
    sshkey: "<< PUB_KEY >>"
```

Wherever you see `< PUB_KEY >` insert the user's public key as a string and insert the user's encrypted password where you see `< PASSWORD >`. Users can use the `mkpasswd` utility to generate the password using the following command:

`mkpasswd --method=SHA-512`

6. This creates users for the `dev` environment; you can now maintain a different list of keys and users for other environments by creating a `users.yml` file under `first_playbook/group_vars/<<environment>>/`.

7. Now that we have created our users, let's install some packages that we want present on each host. First, let's create a new task within our common role by creating a new file called `install_packages.yml` under `first_playbook/roles/common/tasks/` by inserting the following code:

```
- name: "Install Common packages"
  apt: name={{ item }} state=latest
  with_items:
    - sysstat
    - open-vm-tools
```

8. Again, we will use a loop to perform a repetitive task, and this code will install every package within the `with_items` list.

> `with_items` is an invaluable directive to keep in mind. Often you can shorten very long tasks with adroit use of the `with_items` command.

9. We also need to include this task in our `main.yml` file, so edit the `first_playbook/roles/common/tasks/main.yml` file and ensure that it has the following code:

```
# tasks file for common
- include: create_users.yml
- include: install_packages.yml
```

> Keep in mind that Ansible will parse these in the order presented, so the users will always be created before the packages are installed.

10. Now we will create the `playbook` file itself. The `playbook` file defines which roles to apply against a host or set of hosts, and allows you to configure elements such as which user to run as, and if it should prompt for a `sudo` password when executed. This file should already have been created by the scaffold script, so edit `first_playbook/first_playbook.yml` and insert the following code:

```
- name: Manage Common Items
  hosts: all
  remote_user: "{{ remote_user }}"
  sudo: yes


  roles:
        - { role: common, tags: ['common'] }
```

> Note the `hosts` item; by using `hosts: all`, we ensure that every host within our inventory is configured using the common role. Note the assignment of a tag within the role declaration; this is good practice, and it allows you to selectively run individual elements of a complex playbook.

> This is done using the `--tags` switch in the `ansible-playbook` command. You can find further details at `http://docs.ansible.com/ansible/playbooks_tags.html`.

11. Note that we have used a variable to define the `remote_user`; often, environments have different predefined superusers. By using a variable, we can define the username of the superuser for each individual environment. For example, to define the variable for the `dev` environment, create a file in `first_playbook/group_vars/dev/main.yml` and insert the following configuration:

    remote_user: admin

    Here, `remote_user` is the username of the environment's power user.

12. Now we are missing only one more element: the inventory. As we are aiming to make this `playbook` self-contained, we will create the inventory along with it, rather than relying on the default Ansible location. This means that you will have a `playbook` that you can share with your colleagues, and it will contain every element required to build the targeted environment. We're now going to define our development environment. You should already have a file called named `dev` in `first_playbook/inventories`. Edit it and insert the following code:

    ```
    [<<groupname>>]
    <<targethosts>>

    [dev:children]
    << groupname >>
    ```

13. Where `<<groupname>>` is the group of servers that you wish to collect, and `<<targethosts>>` is the list of the servers you wish to configure within that group. Notice the `[dev:children]` block at the end. This group is the link between your environment variables and your inventory, and it should reflect the environment for which you are creating the inventory. Ensure that any group that you create is also listed within the `dev:children` group of groups to ensure that your variable files are included within the Play.

    > Ansible creates a link to the directories in the `group_vars` folder in the playbook for both hosts and groups in the inventory; thus, in the preceding example, we can use `<<playbook>>/groups_vars/<<hostname>>/main.yml`, `<<playbook>>/group_vars/prerequisites/main.yml`, and `<<playbook>>/group_vars/dev/main.yml` to hold variables. This allows you to set the variables at the most appropriate place in your hierarchy.

14. Once you are happy, you can run your new `playbook`. At the command line, use the following command within the root directory of your `playbook`:

    $ ansible-playbook -i inventories/dev -K first_playbook.yml

The `-i` switch is used to indicate where your inventory is located, and the `-k` to indicate which playbook that is to be executed. This should produce an output that looks similar to the following screenshot:

```
● ● ●                           📁 first_playbook — bash — 100×38
changed: [172.16.84.128] => (item={'key': 'admin', 'value': {'comment': 'Administrator User', 'state
': 'present', 'shell': '/bin/bash', 'uid': 5110, 'gid': 5110, 'password': '$6$5HIi7W8lR.Flg$DWIvV6B/
OGgsiQUtMxfmaP4CkX6fu/t4DplUH3EZL1N5prbSau5soD15P70YPmDsH4Puon8vDnkblfO0745iT/', 'sshkey': 'ssh-rsa
AAAAB3NzaC1yc2EAAAADAQABAAABAQDd/nW7kP+evZOgrc9RklZw6UsiOd/cTs9qLTitk2p3LIGbw4sjlcSLMxd57DPN+J9j+ksv
pZf93lCe0pTW1Fe9H+TNVOjAqX3bXCMFpguEDZY7FjwEQzPdpYw//xxIpCJnQ2MIYtYVaede3zCUifz+cCJaHAuHSxZjhAX5vjVl
srEY5vHvaH+OcNyHzXBQFrOTDh475bFIZv6NMiPs9g3zVi72829lBFluPqWGc0AmfzxMTs6m0AZYaxIPES0RNIy4GvVR0EUaY0TW
JvMV+OI2ISGSrfvthWabL+6hPbqtK8vR70JAy12K21d3DdAWVlkVLUjx7eIfflTfhbuN6pWF'}})
changed: [172.16.84.128] => (item={'key': 'testuser', 'value': {'state': 'present', 'shell': '/bin/b
ash', 'uid': 510, 'gid': 510, 'password': '$6$5HIi7W8lR.Flg$DWIvV6B/OGgsiQUtMxfmaP4CkX6fu/t4DplUH3EZ
L1N5prbSau5soD15P70YPmDsH4Puon8vDnkblfO0745iT/', 'comments': 'Example User', 'sshkey': 'ssh-rsa AAAA
B3NzaC1yc2EAAAADAQABAAABAQDd/nW7kP+evZOgrc9RklZw6UsiOd/cTs9qLTitk2p3LIGbw4sjlcSLMxd57DPN+J9j+ksvpZf9
3lCe0pTW1Fe9H+TNVOjAqX3bXCMFpguEDZY7FjwEQzPdpYw//xxIpCJnQ2MIYtYVaede3zCUifz+cCJaHAuHSxZjhAX5vjVlsrEY
5vHvaH+OcNyHzXBQFrOTDh475bFIZv6NMiPs9g3zVi72829lBFluPqWGc0AmfzxMTs6m0AZYaxIPES0RNIy4GvVR0EUaY0TWJvMV
+OI2ISGSrfvthWabL+6hPbqtK8vR70JAy12K21d3DdAWVlkVLUjx7eIfflTfhbuN6pWF'}})

TASK: [common | Add Keys] ********************************************************
changed: [172.16.84.128] => (item={'key': 'admin', 'value': {'comment': 'Administrator User', 'state
': 'present', 'shell': '/bin/bash', 'uid': 5110, 'gid': 5110, 'password': '$6$5HIi7W8lR.Flg$DWIvV6B/
OGgsiQUtMxfmaP4CkX6fu/t4DplUH3EZL1N5prbSau5soD15P70YPmDsH4Puon8vDnkblfO0745iT/', 'sshkey': 'ssh-rsa
AAAAB3NzaC1yc2EAAAADAQABAAABAQDd/nW7kP+evZOgrc9RklZw6UsiOd/cTs9qLTitk2p3LIGbw4sjlcSLMxd57DPN+J9j+ksv
pZf93lCe0pTW1Fe9H+TNVOjAqX3bXCMFpguEDZY7FjwEQzPdpYw//xxIpCJnQ2MIYtYVaede3zCUifz+cCJaHAuHSxZjhAX5vjVl
srEY5vHvaH+OcNyHzXBQFrOTDh475bFIZv6NMiPs9g3zVi72829lBFluPqWGc0AmfzxMTs6m0AZYaxIPES0RNIy4GvVR0EUaY0TW
JvMV+OI2ISGSrfvthWabL+6hPbqtK8vR70JAy12K21d3DdAWVlkVLUjx7eIfflTfhbuN6pWF'}})
changed: [172.16.84.128] => (item={'key': 'testuser', 'value': {'state': 'present', 'shell': '/bin/b
ash', 'uid': 510, 'gid': 510, 'password': '$6$5HIi7W8lR.Flg$DWIvV6B/OGgsiQUtMxfmaP4CkX6fu/t4DplUH3EZ
L1N5prbSau5soD15P70YPmDsH4Puon8vDnkblfO0745iT/', 'comments': 'Example User', 'sshkey': 'ssh-rsa AAAA
B3NzaC1yc2EAAAADAQABAAABAQDd/nW7kP+evZOgrc9RklZw6UsiOd/cTs9qLTitk2p3LIGbw4sjlcSLMxd57DPN+J9j+ksvpZf9
3lCe0pTW1Fe9H+TNVOjAqX3bXCMFpguEDZY7FjwEQzPdpYw//xxIpCJnQ2MIYtYVaede3zCUifz+cCJaHAuHSxZjhAX5vjVlsrEY
5vHvaH+OcNyHzXBQFrOTDh475bFIZv6NMiPs9g3zVi72829lBFluPqWGc0AmfzxMTs6m0AZYaxIPES0RNIy4GvVR0EUaY0TWJvMV
+OI2ISGSrfvthWabL+6hPbqtK8vR70JAy12K21d3DdAWVlkVLUjx7eIfflTfhbuN6pWF'}})

TASK: [common | Install Common packages] ****************************************
changed: [172.16.84.128] => (item=sysstat,open-vm-tools)

PLAY RECAP **********************************************************************
172.16.84.128                   : ok=4    changed=3    unreachable=0    failed=0

MacBookPro:first_playbook mduffy$ ▯
```

> The preceding screenshot uses the default (and some would say, boring) output. If you want to have a little fun with your configuration management, then install the cowsay package on the host you're running your Ansible scripts from and enjoy a little cow-based joy. You can install cowsay by issuing `apt-get install cowsay`.

See also

- You can find details about the Ansible module user at the following locations:
  - **User**: `http://docs.ansible.com/user_module.html`
  - **Apt**: `http://docs.ansible.com/apt_module.html`
- You can find the documentation for Ansible Playbooks at `http://docs.ansible.com/playbooks.html`
- And you can find the example code for this recipe at `github.com/stunthamster/devops_coobook_first_playbook`

Creating a webserver using Ansible and Nginx

Now we have our common role defined, we can move onto defining specific roles to install and manage applications. One of the more common tasks that underpin many web applications is the installation of an HTTP server. This is a relatively common task that belies a large amount of configuration; installing a package is easy, but applying the configuration and tuning can be non-trivial, especially when you are maintaining multiple servers in a cluster. A simple mistake, such as applying tuning to one host but not the other, can lead to obscure issues, such as a misbalanced cluster, and it can be tricky to track down if each host has been created manually. We are going to create a new role that allows us to install, configure, and tune the powerful Nginx HTTP server across any number of clients.

Getting ready

For this recipe, you will need an Ubuntu 14.04 host to run your Ansible Playbook and at least one Ubuntu 14.04 server to configure as the Nginx server.

How to do it...

1. First, we need to create a new role within our `playbook`. To accomplish this, we are going to use the `ansible-galaxy` command to create a new scaffold role. On the command line, navigate to your `first_playbook/roles` directory and issue the following command:

```
$ ansible-galaxy init nginx --force
```

This will create our new role.

2. Next, we need to start defining our tasks. Let's create a task to install the packages. Within the `first_playbook/roles/nginx/tasks` directory, create a new file called `install_packages.yml` and insert the following code:

```
- name: "Install Nginx packages"
  apt: name=nginx state=present
```

3. To include this within the role, edit `first_playbook/roles/nginx/tasks/main.yml` and ensure that it includes the following:

```
---
# tasks file for nginx
- include: install_packages.yml
```

4. Next, we need to configure Nginx. For this, we are going to use the power of Ansible templates. Create a new file called `nginx.j2` in the `first_playbook/roles/nginx/templates` directory and insert the following code:

```
user www-data;
worker_processes {{ worker_processes }};

pid /run/nginx.pid;

events {
  worker_connections {{ worker_connections }};
  multi_accept {{ multi_accept }};
}

http {
  sendfile {{ send_file }};
  tcp_nopush {{ tcp_nopush }};
  tcp_nodelay {{ tcp_nodelay }};
  keepalive_timeout {{ keepalive_timeout }};
  types_hash_max_size {{ types_hash_max_size }};
  server_tokens {{ server_tokens }};
  include /etc/nginx/mime.types;
  default_type application/octet-stream;
  access_log /var/log/nginx/access.log;
  error_log /var/log/nginx/error.log;
  gzip {{ gzip }};
  gzip_disable "msie6";
  include /etc/nginx/conf.d/*.conf;
  include /etc/nginx/sites-enabled/*;
}
```

This file is a fairly standard Nginx configuration file with Jinja2 template elements applied to it. Whenever you see a set of curly braces, it will be interpolated with data supplied by our Ansible.

Templating is insanely powerful; wherever possible, ensure that you manage your configuration items with a variable, even if it's not a value you are interested in at the moment. Although it's a little bit of upfront work, it pays dividends when you do need to change something further down the line.

5. Now we have created our template, we need to create a place to store the values that we are going to insert into the variables defined within the template. Create a new file called `nginx.yml` within the `first_playbook/group_vars/dev` directory and fill it with the following values:

```
worker_processes: 4
worker_connections: 768
multi_accept: "on"
send_file: "on"
tcp_nopush: "on"
tcp_nodelay: "on"
keepalive_timeout: 65
types_hash_max_size: 2048
server_tokens: "off"
gzip: "on"
```

6. Next, we need a task that will copy the template to an appropriate place on the server. Create a new file called `configure_nginx.yml` under the `first_playbook/roles/nginx/tasks` directory and insert the following code:

```
- name: Deploy Nginx configuration
  template: src=nginx.j2 dest="/etc/nginx/nginx.conf"
  notify: restart nginx
```

Note the `notify:directive`. This makes use of the ability of Ansible to trigger actions if it causes a change of state to a resource. In this case, Ansible will restart Nginx every time there is a change in the `nginx` configuration. This is incredibly useful, as it ensures that whenever you use Ansible to push a change, it gets applied. Let's add the code to manage the restart.

7. Edit the `first_playbook/roles/nginx/handlers/main.yml` file to contain the following code snippet:

```
- name: restart nginx
  service: name=nginx state=restarted
```

As you can see from the directory it resides in, this is known as a handler. A handler is a task that is only called when another task triggers a notify directive. This allows you to trigger events after implementing a change of state within a task. A classic example is the one that we have used, restarting a service after a configuration change.

8. We're going to apply a common tuning technique when running a high-volume web server, and increase the number of open files available to the Nginx user. Within Linux, everything is considered a file, including network sockets; a high-volume web server can chew through the default `1024` extremely quickly, so it's a good practice to allow a high number, especially if the server is dedicated to the Nginx role. Within the `first_playbook/roles/nginx/tasks/configure_nginx.yml` file, add the following code:

```
- name: Add File limits
  lineinfile: dest=/etc/security/limits.conf line='www-data
  -         nofile          65535' owner=root group=root mode=0644
  notify: restart nginx
```

This uses the Ansible `lineinfile` module to insert a value into the `limits.conf` file; note that this value will be inserted at the end of the `limits.conf` file.

 This is a fairly simple use of `lineinfile`, but it is a powerful module and you should be comfortable with it, as it can use a regular expression to insert, amend, and replace values. You can find more details of the `lineinfile` module at `http://docs.ansible.com/ansible/lineinfile_module.html`.

9. One last task remains in configuring Nginx, and that's to remove the default site that's installed when the package is installed. Again, we're going to use our `configure_nginx` task by adding the following code snippet:

```
- name: Remove defaults
  file: path="/etc/nginx/sites-enabled/default" state=absent
```

The `state=absent` declaration ensures that if the file is present then Ansible will remove it.

10. Finally, we add the `configure_nginx` task to our role by adding the following to the `main.yml` file:

```
- include: configure_nginx.yml
```

11. We're now ready to add our own `virtualhost` to `nginx`, and we will use the templates to keep them consistent. First, let's create a template `virtualhost`; create a new file called `virtual_host.j2` in `first_playbook/roles/nginx/templates/virtual_host.j2` and insert the following content:

```
server {

        server_name {{ item.value.server_name }};
        root {{ item.value.vhost_root }};
        index index.html index.htm;
        location / {
            try_files $uri $uri/ =404;
    }
}
```

Again, notice the use of double curly braces to denote an interpolated Ansible variable. The preceding `virtualhost` file is a simple one and we only have two values to configure; the server name, such as `www.example.com`, and the root file system where the HTML files can be found.

12. Now that we have a template, let's create a new variable file to hold the values to insert into it. First, create a new file called `virtualhosts.yml` under the `/first_playbook/group_vars/dev/` directory and insert the following dictionary:

```
virtualhosts:
  test1:
    server_name: test.stunthamster.com
    vhost_root: '/usr/share/nginx/test1'

  test2:
    server_name: test2.stunthamster.com
    vhost_root: '/usr/share/nginx/test2'
```

You can define as many `virtualhosts` as you like within this structure; you'll see in the next part of the recipe that the dictionary is looped over to create them, so you can control anything from `1` to `100` virtual hosts using this method.

> Remember, in the preceding example we have created the `virtualhosts` within the `dev` environment. You can follow the same steps within the `/first_playbook/group_vars/<<environment>>` directory if you wish to configure `virtualhosts` for another environment.

13. Now we have the data that we need to configure our virtual hosts. Create a new file called `configure_vhosts.yml` under the `first_playbook/roles/nginx/tasks` directory and give it the following contents:

```
- name: Create Virtual Host root
  file: path="/usr/share/nginx/{{ item.key }}" state=directory
owner=root
  with_dict: virtualhosts

- name: Add Virtual Hosts
  template: src=virtual_host.j2 dest=/etc/nginx/sites-available/{{
item.key}}.conf
  with_dict: virtualhosts


- name: Add Virtual Host symlink
  file: src="/etc/nginx/sites-available/{{ item.key}}.conf"
dest="/etc/nginx/sites-enabled/{{ item.key}}.}}.conf" state=link
  with_dict: virtualhosts
  notify: restart nginx
```

14. Note the use of `item.key` in the above example; these loops through the dictionary defined in our variable file and retrieves the key of the hash it is currently evaluating. In this case, we have used the hash to name our configuration files, which would be named `test1.conf` and `test2.conf` in this case.

    Don't forget to add this to the `main.yml` so that it runs. By now, your `main.yml` should resemble the following:

```
---
# tasks file for nginx
- include: install_packages.yml
- include: configure_nginx.yml
- include: configure_vhosts.yml
```

15. Now we have a new role, we can add it to the Playbook so that it can be run. We also need to update our inventory to define the servers the Nginx role will be run against. First of all, open the file `first_playbook/first_playbook.yml` and insert the following code:

```
- name: Manage Nginx
  hosts: nginx
  remote_user: "{{ remote_user }}"
  sudo: yes
  roles:
      - { role: nginx, tags: ['nginx'] }
```

16. This will apply the Nginx role against any server that is defined within the inventory as an Nginx node. Next, let's amend our inventory. Edit `first_playbook/inventories/dev` and insert the following configuration:

```
[nginx]
<< NGINX SERVER >>


[dev:children]
nginx
```

Here `<< NGINX SERVER >>` is the IP address or name of the server(s) you wish to configure as `nginx` server(s). This maps against the hosts directive in the Playbook.

17. We're now ready to run our `playbook`. At the terminal, run the following command within the root of the `first_playbook` directory:

```
$ ansible-playbook -i inventories/dev -K first_playbook.yml
```

If all goes well, you should see an Ansible output that looks something like the following screenshot:

```
                          first_playbook — bash — 72×24
': 'present', 'server_name': 'test2.test.com'}})

TASK: [nginx | Add Virtual Hosts] ***************************************
*******
changed: [172.16.84.128] => (item={'key': 'test1', 'value': {'vhost_root
': 'present', 'server_name': 'test.test.com'}})
changed: [172.16.84.128] => (item={'key': 'test2', 'value': {'vhost_root
': 'present', 'server_name': 'test2.test.com'}})

TASK: [nginx | Add Virtual Host symlink] ********************************
*******
changed: [172.16.84.128] => (item={'key': 'test1', 'value': {'vhost_root
': 'present', 'server_name': 'test.test.com'}})
changed: [172.16.84.128] => (item={'key': 'test2', 'value': {'vhost_root
': 'present', 'server_name': 'test2.test.com'}})

NOTIFIED: [nginx | restart nginx] ***************************************
*******
changed: [172.16.84.128]

PLAY RECAP **************************************************************
*******
172.16.84.128              : ok=13    changed=11    unreachable=0    faile
d=0
```

See also

You can find the Nginx documentation at `http://nginx.org/en/docs/`.

Creating an application server role using Tomcat and Ansible

We have explored using Ansible to perform common tasks on a server, and to define selected servers as `nginx` servers. This recipe will demonstrate using Ansible to install and configure a Java application server. For this recipe, we will be installing the venerable Tomcat server. Tomcat is a rock-solid open source container for Java apps, and is used in a huge array of organizations to host applications both small and large.

Currently, Ubuntu ships with a package for Tomcat 7. However, the Tomcat project is already at version 8, so we're going to look at how we can use Ansible to install Tomcat straight from the web.

Getting ready

For this recipe, you need an Ubuntu 14.04 server to act as the Ansible client, and an Ubuntu 14.04 server that you wish to configure.

How to do it...

Let's use Ansible to install and configure Tomcat:

1. First, we are going to create a new role within our `playbook` to hold our tasks. Then, we're going to use the `ansible-galaxy` command to create a new boilerplate role. On the command line, navigate to your `first_playbook/roles` and issue the following command:

    ```
    $ ansible-galaxy init tomcat
    ```

    This will create our new role.

2. Now, we're going to create a new task to install the pre-requisite packages. Generally speaking, we want a JRE at the very least. Create a new file called `install_packages.yml` under the `first_playbook/roles/tomcat/tasks/` directory and insert the following content:

    ```
    - name: "Install Tomcat prerequisites"
      apt: name={{ item }} state=latest
      with_items:
        - default-jre
        - unzip
    ```

3. Next, we amend the main task to execute this code by editing the `first_playbook/roles/tomcat/main.yml` file and inserting the following code:

```
---
# tasks file for tomcat
- include: install_packages.yml
```

4. Generally speaking, we shouldn't run anything as the `root` user, Tomcat included. Let's use Ansible to create a Tomcat user and also a group with which we can run `Tomcat`. Create a new file called `create_users.yml` under the `first_playbook/roles/tomcat/tasks` directory, and insert the following snippet:

```
- name: Create Tomcat Group
  group: name=tomcat gid=5000
- name: Create Athoris User
  user: name=tomcat comment="Tomcat App User" uid=5000  group=5000
```

5. We need to update `main.yml` to include this new task. Edit your `first_playbook/roles/tomcat/main.yml` file and add the following content:

```
- include: create_users.yml
```

6. Now that we have our users and our JRE, it's time to grab the Tomcat 8 zip. We can do this using the `get_url` module. Since this is essentially a package install, we're going to add this code to our existing `install_packages.yml` file. Edit it and add the following code:

```
- stat: path=/usr/local/apache-tomcat-8.0.21
  register: tc

- name: "Fetch Tomcat"
  get_url: url=http://www.mirrorservice.org/sites/ftp.apache.org/
tomcat/tomcat-8/v8.0.21/bin/apache-tomcat-8.0.21.zip dest=/tmp
mode=0440

- name: "Unpack Tomcat"
  unarchive: src=/tmp/apache-tomcat-8.0.21.zip dest=/usr/local/
copy=no
  when: tc.isdir is undefined
```

There are a few things to note in the preceding snippet. The first declaration we need to make is to use the `stat` module to fetch the state of our `Tomcat` directory. This is an important step in making the code idempotent. Next, we fetch the `zip` file containing Tomcat and unpack it. It's here that we make use of the state of the directory that we recorded using the `stat` module. The `unarchive` module will unpack the archive without testing if the Tomcat directory exists This is bad news for two reasons; first, it's not idempotent, so the target node will always take action, and secondly, it will almost certainly overwrite any subsequent changes. Using the `stat` module to test the existence of the directory will cause the `unarchive` task to skip executing if the `Tomcat` directory already exists.

You can find more details about the stat module at `http://docs.ansible.com/ansible/stat_module.html`.

7. Now that we have unpacked Tomcat into our chosen location, we need to perform some tidying up. Tomcat ships with some default apps, which we may not want. Let's create a task to remove these. Add the following snippet to the `install_packages.yml` task:

```
- name: "Remove default apps"
  file: path={{ item }} state=absent
  with_items:
    - /usr/local/apache-tomcat-8.0.21/webapps/docs
    - /usr/local/apache-tomcat-8.0.21/webapps/examples
    - /usr/local/apache-tomcat-8.0.21/webapps/host-manager
    - /usr/local/apache-tomcat-8.0.21/webapps/manager
    - /usr/local/apache-tomcat-8.0.21/webapps/ROOT
```

Again, note the use of `with_items` to remove multiple items with a single task.

8. Now that we've removed the unwanted applications, we can configure `tomcat`. Create a new file called `setenv.j2` under the `first_playbook/roles/templates/tomcat` directory, and insert the following snippet:

```
export CLASSPATH=\
$JAVA_HOME/lib/tools.jar:\
$CATALINA_HOME/bin/commons-daemon.jar:\
$CATALINA_HOME/bin/bootstrap.jar
export CATALINA_OPT="{{ tomcat.catalina.opts }}"
export JAVA_OPTS="{{ tomcat.java.opts }}"
```

9. Next, let's create a place to hold the variables we're interpolating. Create a new file called `tomcat.yml` under the `first_playbook/group_vars/dev` directory, and insert the following code:

```
tomcat:
  appgroup: tomcat
  appuser: tomcat
  gid: 5000
  uid: 5000
java:
    home: '/etc/alternatives/java'
    opts: '
      -Duser.timezone=UTC
    -Dfile.encoding=UTF8
    -Xmx6g
    -Xms6g
```

```
    '
  catalina:
    home: '/usr/local/apache-tomcat-8.0.21/'
    pid:  '/usr/local/apache-tomcat-8.0.21/temp/tomcat.pid'
    opts: '-Dcom.sun.management.jmxremote
           -Dcom.sun.management.jmxremote.port=8082
 -Dcom.sun.management.jmxremote.authenticate=false
 -Dcom.sun.management.jmxremote.ssl=false'
```

10. We've inserted two new data structures here, one to hold our Java options and the other to hold the Tomcat specific Catalina data. Let's create the code to add this configuration to our target node. In the `first_playbook/roles/tomcat/tasks` folder, create a new file called `configure_tomcat.yml` and insert the following code snippet:

```
- name: "deploy setenv.sh"
  template: src=setenv.j2 dest=/usr/local/apache-tomcat-8.0.21/
bin/setenv.sh owner=tomcat group=tomcat
```

This will place the `setenv.sh` file in place and fill it with the options we've configured.

11. The final element is the startup script. As we have downloaded Tomcat from the packaged distribution, it's up to us to supply our own. Create a new file in the templates directory called `tomcat.j2` and insert the following code:

```
#!/bin/sh

SHUTDOWN_WAIT=30

export APP_USER="{{ tomcat.appuser }}"
export JAVA_HOME="{{ tomcat.java.home }}"
export CATALINA_HOME="{{ tomcat.catalina.home }}"
export CATALINA_PID="{{ tomcat.catalina.pid }}"

SU="su"

start() {
  isrunning

  if [ "$?" = 0 ]; then
    echo "Tomcat is already running"
    return 0
  fi

  # Change directory to prevent path problems
```

```
  cd $CATALINA_HOME

  # Remove pidfile if still around
  test -f $CATALINA_PID && rm -f $CATALINA_PID

  $SU $APP_USER -c "umask 0002; $CATALINA_HOME/bin/catalina.sh
start" > /dev/null
}

stop() {
  isrunning

  if [ "$?" = 1 ]; then
    echo "Tomcat is already stopped"
    rm -f $CATALINA_PID # remove pidfile if still around
    return 0
  fi

  echo -n "Waiting for Tomcat to exit (${SHUTDOWN_WAIT} sec.): "

  count=0
  until [ "$pid" = "" ] || [ $count -gt $SHUTDOWN_WAIT ]; do
    $SU $APP_USER -c "$CATALINA_HOME/bin/catalina.sh stop -force"
> /dev/null
    findpid

    echo -n "."
    sleep 3
    count=$((count+3))
  done

  echo ""

  if [ "$count" -gt "$SHUTDOWN_WAIT" ]; then
    echo "Forcing Tomcat to stop"
    /bin/kill -9 $pid && sleep 5
  fi

  # check if tomcat is still around, this will be our exit status
  ! isrunning
}

findpid() {
  pid=""
```

```
   #pid=$(pgrep -U $APP_USER -f "^$JAVA_HOME/bin/java.*cpatalina.
base=$CATALINA_HOME")
   pid=$(ps -fu $APP_USER | grep "Dcatalina.home=$CATALINA_HOME" |
awk {'print $2'})

   # validate output of pgrep
   if ! [ "$pid" = "" ] && ! [ "$pid" -gt 0 ]; then
     echo "Unable to determine if Tomcat is running"
     exit 1
   fi
}

isrunning() {

   findpid

   if [ "$pid" = "" ]; then
     return 1
   elif [ "$pid" -gt 0 ]; then
     return 0
   fi
}

case "$1" in
  start)
    start
    RETVAL=$?

    if [ "$RETVAL" = 0 ]; then
      echo "Started Tomcat"
    else
      echo "Not able to start Tomcat"
    fi
    ;;

  stop)
    stop
    RETVAL=$?

    if [ "$RETVAL" = 0 ]; then
      echo "Stopped Tomcat"
    else
      echo "Not able to stop Tomcat"
    fi
```

```
    ;;

    restart)
      stop
      sleep 5
      start
      RETVAL=$?

      if [ "$RETVAL" = 0 ]; then
        echo "Restarted Tomcat"
      else
        echo "Not able to restart Tomcat"
      fi
    ;;

    status)
      isrunning
      RETVAL=$?

      if [ "$RETVAL" = 0 ]; then
        echo "Tomcat (pid $pid) is running..."
      else
        echo "Tomcat is stopped"
        RETVAL=3
      fi
    ;;

    *)
      echo "Usage: $0 {start|stop|restart|status}."
    ;;

esac

exit $RETVAL
```

12. Next we need to add the Ansible code to place the template onto the server. Add the following snippet at the bottom of the `configure_tomcat.yml` file,:

```
- name: "Deploy startup script"
  template: src=tomcat.j2 dest=/etc/init.d/tomcat owner=root
mode=700
```

13. Now, let's add this set of tasks into the main `playbook`. You can do this by adding the highlighted code to the `main.yml` file:

```
---
# tasks file for tomcat
- include: create_users.yml
- include: install_packages.yml
- include: configure_tomcat.yml
```

14. Next, we should amend our inventory to add our Tomcat servers to it. Edit the inventory located in `first_playbook/inventories/dev` and insert the following code:

```
[tomcat]
<<Node>>
```

Now, replace `<<Node>>` with the *nodes* you wish to configure as a Tomcat node.

15. Finally, we add the role to our playbook file. Edit `first_playbook/first_playbook.yml` and insert the following code:

```
- name: Manage Tomcat
    hosts: tomcat
    remote_user: "{{ remote_user }}"
    sudo: yes
    roles:
            - { role: tomcat, tags: ['tomcat'] }
```

16. You can now run this role and you will have a Tomcat 8 container ready to run your code.

See also

You can find the documentation for Tomcat at `http://tomcat.apache.org/tomcat-8.0-doc`.

Installing MySQL using Ansible

We now have an Ansible Playbook that can manage common items. It can install and configure Nginx, and also finally, install and configure Tomcat. The next logical step is to install some form of data storage, and for this, we are going to look at MySQL.

MySQL is arguably one of the most popular databases deployed due both to its relative ease of use, and its open source heritage. MySQL is powerful enough for sites both large and small, and powers many of the most popular sites on the Internet. Although it may lack some of the enterprise features that it's more expensive cousins, such as Oracle and Microsoft SQL, have, it more than makes up for that by being relatively simple to install and able to scale without license costs.

Getting ready

For this recipe, you need an Ubuntu 14.04 server to act as your Ansible client, and an Ubuntu 14.04 server that you wish to configure for MySQL.

How to do it...

Let's install MySQl using Ansible:

1. As with the previous recipes, we're going to create a new `role` within our `playbook`. Navigate to the `tasks` folder and issue the following command:

   ```
   $ ansible-galaxy init mysql --force
   ```

   This will create our new role and the underlying folder structure.

2. We're going to start by installing the packages for MySQL. Create a new file called `install_packages.yml` under the MySQL role's `tasks` folder, and insert the following code:

   ```
   - name: 'Install MySQL packages'
     apt: name={{ item }} state=latest
     with_items:
        - python-dev
        - libmysqlclient-dev
        - python-pip
        - mysql-server

   - pip: name=MySQL-python
   ```

   There are a couple of things going on here. First, we are installing a few more packages aside from MySQL itself. This is to support the Ansible `MySQL` module, and to allow us to use the `pip` package manager to install another prerequisite package.

3. Now that we have installed MySQL, we can configure it. First, start by changing the password of the `root` `MySQL` user; by default, it is set to nothing. Create a file called `configure_mysql.yml` in the `tasks` directory, and insert the following code snippet:

```
- name: Set root password
mysql_user: name=root host={{ item }} password={{
mysql_root_password }}
  with_items:
    - "{{ ansible_hostname }}"
    - 127.0.0.1
    - ::1
    - localhost
```

4. Remember to add this task to the `main.yml` file by adding the following to the bottom of the file:

```
- configure_mysql.yml
```

There are two things to notice here. First, we're iterating over the list of hosts. This ensures that the `root` user has their password changed in all the various permutations that it might exist in. Second, we're using a variable to contain the `root` password. Note the use of `{{ansible_hostname}}` in the `with_items` list. This uses details gathered from the target host to populate certain reserved variables; this is incredibly useful for situations such as these.

 You can find more details of Ansible facts at `http://docs.ansible.com/ansible/playbooks_variables.html#information-discovered-from-systems-facts`.

5. Next, we're going to create a `.my.cnf` file. This is a convenience file that allows you to insert certain options that the MySQL client can use, and saves you the effort of typing at the command line. Normally, this is used to save key strokes but in this case it is used to ensure that when Ansible runs for the second time, it can access the database using the password we have set. Create the `.my.cnf` file using this code snippet:

```
- name: Create .my.cnf file
    template: src=my.cnf.j2 dest=/root/.my.cnf owner=root
mode=0644
```

6. As you've noticed, this makes use of a template to create the file. Create the template by creating a new file called `my.cnf.j2` under the templates directory in the MySQL role and insert the following code:

```
[client]
user=root
password={{ mysql_root_password }}
```

7. Normally, we would create a file under the `group_vars/dev` directory to hold the MySQL root password variable, and this will work. However, since this is sensitive information, we want to make sure that casual prying eyes don't stumble across the `root` password of our shiny new MySQL server. Instead, we are going to use the Ansible `vault` feature. This will create an encrypted file that will hold our password, and Ansible will be able to read it at runtime. Run the following command from the root of the playbook:

```
$ ansible-vault create group_vars/dev/mysql.yml
```

8. You'll be prompted to enter a vault password. Make sure it's something you can remember, as you'll need it every time you run your Ansible Playbook. Once you enter and confirm the password, you will be handed over to an editor to enter your data. Insert the following data:

```
mysql_root_password: <<ROOTPASSWORD>>
```

Here, `<<ROOTPASSWORD>>` is your chosen MySQL password. Save the file and exit, and Ansible will encrypt it for you. If you open the file in your editor now, you will find it has content similar to this:

```
$ANSIBLE_VAULT;1.1;AES256
63353039653738663232383465343235353166363034306361436373239616638
65386137316263
31333832376166626538376139663966666653732376136620a3561396339373838
30613732336533
37393465396431613737383961316265336331373637373316661643039323383265
35366333303632
36616432373032663670a3461616635336434366433316161653661643261636362
34633932336364
34376437323737653566323261666613364383435393832303130386536539623662
38
```

> Using the Ansible `crypt` feature is a fantastic way to keep sensitive data a secret, and can be used on a variable file. You can find more details on the crcypt feature at `https://docs.ansible.com/playbooks_vault.html`.

9. Now that we have our `.my.cnf` file, we can tidy up. Within the default install on Ubuntu 14.04, an anonymous user is created along with a test database; we're going to use the Ansible MySQL module to remove both of these. Insert the following code snippet into the `configure_mysql.ym` file:

```
name: delete default user
  action: mysql_user user="" state="absent"
- name: remove the test database
  action: mysql_db db=test state=absent
```

10. Now that we have installed and configured our MySQL server, it's time to use the Ansible MySQL module to create a new database and database user. In this case, we're going to create a database for a blog. Create a new task within the MySQL role called `create_blog_db.yml` and insert the following content:

```
- name: Create MyBlog DB
mysql_db: name=myblog state=present

- name: Create MyBlog User
mysql_user: name=myblog_user password=agreatpassword
priv=myblog.*:ALL state=presentpresent
```

This code snippet uses the Ansible MySQL module to create a new database and a matching user with the correct privileges to use it.

11. Finally, we just need to update our `main.yml` file to include our various tasks. Edit it to include the following content:

```
---
# tasks file for mysql
- include: install_packages.yml
- include: configure_mysql.yml
- include: create_blog_db.yml
```

12. Our new role is complete and ready to use. Now, we just need to update our playbook and inventory to include it. First, open up the `first_playbook.yml` file in your editor and add the following content:

```
- name: Manage MySQL
    hosts: mysql
    remote_user: "{{ remote_user }}"
    sudo: yes

    roles:
          - { role: mysql, tags: ['mysql'] }
```

13. Now, we need to update our inventory. Open the `inventories/dev` file and insert the following snippet:

```
[mysql]
<< mysql_server >>

[dev:children]
nginx
tomcat
mysql
```

Where `mysql_server` is the server (or servers) that you wish to configure MySQL on.

14. Now, if you run the `playbook` you will find your selected host will have MySQL installed, with the new database ready for use. As we now have an encrypted file, you will need to add the `--ask-vault-pass` switch; your command should now look something similar to the following:

```
$ ansible-playbook --ask-vault-pass -i inventories/dev -k first_
playbook.yml
```

This will prompt you for your vault password and it will then decyrpt and use the values contained within.

See also

▶ You can find out more about the Ansible MySQL module at:

http://docs.ansible.com/mysql_db_module.html

▶ You can find details of the Ansible MySQL User Module at:

http://docs.ansible.com/mysql_user_module.html

▶ You can find details of the Ansible Playbook vaults at:

https://docs.ansible.com/playbooks_vault.html

Installing and managing HAProxy with Ansible

One key element of high-performance web applications is the ability to scale, and the easiest way to achieve this is to use a load balancer to direct traffic to multiple nodes. This can provide both horizontal scale and, just as importantly, the ability to survive individual node failures.

There are many load balancers available, both open source and commercial, but HAProxy is certainly one of the more popular. Open Source, high performance, and highly configurable, HAProxy is a good choice for any site that requires load balancing.

This recipe will demonstrate how to install HAProxy, configure it, and add both a frontend and backend service to it.

Getting ready

For this recipe, you need an Ubuntu 14.04 server to act as our Ansible client and an Ubuntu 14.04 server that you wish to configure for HAProxy.

How to do it...

Let's install and manage HAProxy and Ansible:

1. We are going to use the `ansible-galaxy` command to create our role scaffold. Do this by issuing the following command:

```
$ ansible-galaxy init haproxy -p "${PLAYBOOK_PATH}/roles/"
```

2. Now we have the role, let's start with the tasks that will deal with installing the packages. By default, Ubuntu 14.04 ships with HaProxy 1.4, whereas 1.5 is the latest version and brings important features such as SSL termination. Fortunately, there is a PPA available which allows us to install the more recent version. Start by creating a new file called `install_packages.yml` under the `roles/tasks` directory, and insert the following snippet:

```
name: "Add HAProxy repo"
  apt_repository: repo="deb http://ppa.launchpad.net/vbernat/
haproxy-1.5/ubuntu trusty main" state=present

- name: Install HAProxy
  apt: name=haproxy state=installed force=yes
```

3. This will add the PPA to the package list and install HAproxy; however, we're also going to install the `hatop` package. Hatop is a fantastic tool for monitoring HAProxy and allows you to see detailed traffic statistics quickly and easily. Add the following code in the `install_packages.yml` file:

```
- name: Install HATop
  apt: name=hatop state=installed
```

This will install `hatop` to allow you to monitor your load balancer. Next, we're going to configure HaProxy. Create a new file called `configure_haproxy.yml`, and insert the following code:

```
- name: Deploy HAProxy configuration
  template: src=haproxy.cfg dest=/etc/haproxy/haproxy.cfg
  notify: Restart HAProxy
```

4. Remember to add this task to the `main.yml` file by appending the following code at the bottom:

```
- configure_haproxy.yml
```

5. As you can see, this writes a template into the `/etc/haproxy` directory; you need to create the template by creating a new file under the `haproxy` role, in the templates directory, and add the following content:

```
global
        log 127.0.0.1    local0 notice
        stats socket /var/run/haproxy.sock mode 600 level admin
        stats timeout 2m
        maxconn {{ haproxy.maxconns }}
        user haproxy
        group haproxy


defaults
        option http-server-close
        log     global
        option dontlognull
        timeout http-request {{ haproxy.http_timeout }}
        backlog {{ haproxy.backlog }}
        timeout queue {{ haproxy.timeout_q }}
        timeout connect {{ haproxy.timoutconnect }}
        timeout client {{ haproxy.timeoutclient }}
        timeout server {{ haproxy.timoutserver }}


frontend default_site
        bind {{ haproxy.frontend_ip }}:{{ haproxy.frontend_port }}
        mode http
        option httplog
        default_backend app_server



backend app_server
        balance {{ haproxy.balance }}
        mode    http

        {% for node in groups['tomcat'] %}
        server {{node}} {{node}}:8080 check
        {% endfor %}
```

6. As you can see, we're using a lot of variable interpolation in this template; this is good practice. If you think you might be changing a value, it's best to template it. Also, take a look at this snippet:

```
        {% for node in groups[nginx] %}
        server {{node}} {{node}}:8080 check
        {% endfor %}
```

This code is interesting as it uses the data included in the Ansible inventory to build the template values. This essentially means that whenever we add a new host to the Nginx role, not only will it be configured for Nginx, it will be added to the load balancer automatically.

7. Now that our template is ready, we can create a file to hold the values that it's going to interpolate. Create a new file called `haproxy.yml` inside the `group_vars/dev` directory and insert the following:

```
haproxy:
    frontend_ip: 192.168.1.1
    maxconns: 4096
    backlog: 2
    timeout_q: 400ms
    timoutconnect: 5000ms
    timeoutclient: 5000ms
    timoutserver: 5000ms
    http_timeout: 15s
    balance: leastconn
    frontend_port: 83
```

8. Next, we need to add the role and host into the playbook and inventory respectively. First, let's amend the playbook to add our new role. Open the `first_playbook.yml` file, and insert the following:

```
- name: Manage HAProxy
  hosts: haproxy
  remote_user: "{{ remote_user }}"
  sudo: yes
  roles:
        - { role: haproxy, tags: ['haproxy'] }
```

9. Now, we amend the inventory. Open the `inventories/dev` file in your editor and insert the following snippet:

```
[haproxy]
<<SERVER NAME>>
```

10. Also, remember to add the `haproxy` role to the children as the highlighted code in this snippet:

```
[dev:children]
nginx
tomcat
mysql
haproxy
```

Now when you run your playbook, you will find that the servers you have configured as HAproxy hosts will be configured with HAproxy; they will also add the servers you have configured as Nginx nodes to the load balancer.

See also

▸ The HAproxy documentation can be found here:

```
http://www.haproxy.org/#docs
```

▸ There is a module within Ansible that can be used to control the HAproxy; this can be used to integrate a load balancer with a deployment script:

```
http://docs.ansible.com/haproxy_module.html
```

Using ServerSpec to test your Playbook

As mentioned in the introduction of this book, the DevOps methodology is built on some of the best practices already in use within software development. One of the more important ideas is the concept of unit testing; in essence, a test that ensures that the code performs the correct operations under certain scenarios. It has a two-fold advantage; first of course, you can test for code correctness before it even arrives in a test environment and you can also ensure that when you refactor code, you don't inadvertently break it. It is the second of these advantage that truly shines for Ansible Playbooks. Due to the way Ansible works, you can guarantee that a certain state will appear when you declare it; Ansible is almost running unit tests itself to ensure that an operation has been carried out correctly. However, you might need to ensure that certain elements are there on a server, and it's incredibly easy to drop these accidently, especially if you are carrying out a large-scale refactoring exercise having ServerSpec on hand can help stop this from happening.

Getting ready

You will need an Ubuntu 14.04 client to run the `serverspec` code.

How to do it...

Let's test our Playbook:

1. First, we are going to install the packages we need. ServerSpec is written in Ruby, so we can use the Gem package manager to install it; however, first we need to install Ruby. You can do this using the following command:

    ```
    $ sudo apt-get install ruby
    ```

2. Once Ruby is installed at the command line, enter the following command:

   $ geminstall serverspec highline

   This will install both ServerSpec and its dependency highline.

3. Next, we are going to use serverspec to create a new skeleton project. Since this is going to test our playbook, ensure that you are in the root of the playbook directory when you issue the next command:

   $ serverspec-init

   This command is going to prompt you for a few details; see the following screenshot for some example entries:

```
● ● ●                                            devops_cookbook — bash
Alita:devops_cookbook mduffy$ serverspec-init
Select OS type:

  1) UN*X
  2) Windows

Select number: 1

Select a backend type:

  1) SSH
  2) Exec (local)

Select number: 1

Vagrant instance y/n: n
Input target host name: test.example.com
 + spec/
 + spec/test.example.com/
 + spec/test.example.com/sample_spec.rb
 + spec/spec_helper.rb
 + Rakefile
 + .rspec
```

Remember, this will be run against a test server; ideally this is something like a Virtual Machine that runs on your desktop. ServerSpec can also integrate with Vagrant, and this is also an excellent method to test your code without needing a dedicated server.

4. Now, we need to do a little clean up. When you use the `serverspec-init` command, it creates a file called `sample_spec.rb` under a folder named after your test server; we don't need this, so remove it.

5. Now, we are going to create our test file for our Nginx Role. Create a new file under `spec/{testserver}` called `nginx_role_spec.rb` and insert the following:

```
require 'spec_helper'

require 'yaml'
```

These require statements will bring in the libraries that we will need to run our tests.

6. We're going to start by testing the basics; check if the Nginx package installed, and if the service is running and listening on the correct port; insert the following code into the test:

```
describe package('nginx'), :if => os[:family] == 'ubuntu'
do
   it { should be_installed }
end


describe service('nginx'), :if => os[:family] == 'ubuntu' do
   it { should be_enabled }
end

describe port(80) do
   it { should be_listening }
end
```

These three blocks of code use the additional functions provided by the spec_helper library to allow us to describe a test; much like Ansible, it abstracts you away from needing explicit commands to test something and instead provides preset resources that you can easily access

 You can find the complete list of ServerSpec resources at:`http://serverspec.org/resource_types.html`

7. Now that we have the basics covered, let's use some data from our Playbook to power the next test. As mentioned above, ServerSpec tests are written in pure Ruby, so we can use the features of that language to help write more tests that are complex. In this case, we're going to load the contents of our variables in Ansible to iterate over our virtual hosts and check if the configuration files are present and linked properly; insert the following code into your test file:

```
vh_list = YAML.load_file('group_vars/dev/virtualhosts.yml')
vh_list['virtualhosts'].each do |key|
  describe file ("/etc/nginx/sites-enabled/#{key[0]}.conf")do
    it { should be_linked_to "/etc/nginx/sites-
available/#{key[0]}.conf"}
  end
```

8. We are using a basic Ruby loop to open our `virtualhosts.yml` file, extract the values of each hash, and use it to build a test against the file. This is a great technique to keep in mind, as it means that your test can use the data in your playbook automatically.

9. We can now run our test suite using the following command:

```
$ rake spec
```

If we now run the tests against a test server that hasn't had Ansible run against it, you should see output similar to the following:

```
Finished in 0.10308 seconds (files took 2.98 seconds to load)
5 examples, 5 failures

Failed examples:

rspec ./spec/test.stunthamster.com/nginx_role_spec.rb:5 # Package "nginx" should be installe
d
rspec ./spec/test.stunthamster.com/nginx_role_spec.rb:9 # Service "nginx" should be enabled
rspec ./spec/test.stunthamster.com/nginx_role_spec.rb:13 # Port "80" should be listening
rspec ./spec/test.stunthamster.com/nginx_role_spec.rb:20 # File "/etc/nginx/sites-enabled/te
st1.conf" should be linked to "/etc/nginx/sites-available/test1.conf"
rspec ./spec/test.stunthamster.com/nginx_role_spec.rb:20 # File "/etc/nginx/sites-enabled/te
st2.conf" should be linked to "/etc/nginx/sites-available/test2.conf"
```

This is exactly what we want to see; since we haven't configured anything yet, all the tests should fail. If we run Ansible to configure Nginx on the server and run the tests now, you should see an output similar to the following:

```
Package "nginx"
  should be installed

Service "nginx"
  should be enabled

Port "80"
  should be listening

File "/etc/nginx/sites-enabled/test1.conf"
  should be linked to "/etc/nginx/sites-available/test1.conf"

File "/etc/nginx/sites-enabled/test2.conf"
  should be linked to "/etc/nginx/sites-available/test2.conf"

Finished in 0.10165 seconds (files took 5.71 seconds to load)
5 examples, 0 failures
```

By writing unit tests for your Ansible code, you are ensuring that changes can be applied with far more confidence, and can reduce incidences of broken code.

See also

You can find more details at the ServerSpec home page at `http://serverspec.org`.

6
Containerization with Docker

In this chapter, we are going to cover the following topics:

- ▶ Installing Docker
- ▶ Pulling an image from the public Docker registry
- ▶ Performing basic Docker operations
- ▶ Running a container interactively
- ▶ Creating a Dockerfile
- ▶ Running a container in detached mode
- ▶ Saving and restoring a container
- ▶ Using the host only network
- ▶ Running a private Docker registry
- ▶ Managing images with a private registry

Introduction

Containerization is not a new technology, but it has enjoyed a recent renaissance; this has been due to the emergence of Docker, which has made using containerization reasonably straightforward, and it has enjoyed a rapid uptake of both developers and system administrators. However, despite all of the enthusiasm, Docker is based on existing and well-understood technology.

Containers have been around in some form or other for a very long time, but until Docker debuted they lacked an especially compelling tool chain. This has caused them to languish, with most users electing to spin up full fat virtual machines rather than containers. This is a shame, as there are many compelling benefits to using containers over full virtualization in many use cases. To understand these benefits, we need to consider how a container works versus virtual machines. Unlike a virtual machine which runs a full kernel user space and application within an isolated system, a container uses the underlying kernel of the container host and runs the user space and Applications in its own sandbox. This sharply reduces overhead on contended hosts, as you are only running a single kernel, rather than many. Docker also makes use of a layered file system; it builds images by layering many immutable layers together and creates an isolated writable space for the container. This means that if you have a hundred containers based on Ubuntu 14.04, you are only consuming the disk space for a single Ubuntu image; you use the disk space only to store the changes made to the running container.

It's important to understand the difference between a container and an image. An image is an immutable template, which is generally built from a set of instructions called a Dockerfile. The image cannot be changed once it is built, and is used as the basis for a container. When you run a container, the image is used to *boot* it, and from there the container writes any changes to a new mutable layer.

Docker debuted in March 2013 as an Open Source project, and has grown explosively; it is now used by startups and large enterprises alike. It has also attracted a great deal of interest from investors, and at the time of writing, the Docker project has grown into one of the most funded startups in the world, and is partnering with companies as diverse as Microsoft and Red Hat to bring containers to a vast array of differing platforms. It's not just the operating system vendors who have embraced Docker, and many of the **Platform-as-a-Service** (**PAAS**) vendors either rolled out Docker support or are planning to in the near future.

There are many reasons why Docker appeals to developers. Primarily, it helps solve the problem of packaging. For many years, there has been an enduring question over what should constitute a deployable package, and how much of the underlying operating system should be encompassed within it. Docker offers the ability to create a *complete* deployable with every dependency, from operating system up, managed in an easily deployable artifact. Secondly, Docker makes it easy to scale elastic applications, as containers are generally small and fast to start. The most time consuming part of standing up a new container is the time it takes to download the initial image; this can be ameliorated by creating a local Docker registry, and we will be looking at how to achieve that later in this chapter.

Although it is easy to create and destroy containers at will, it does bring new challenges; such a free flowing infrastructure creates confusion over which apps are hosted where. Fortunately, now there is a growing ecosystem of applications that offer orchestration of Docker containers, and this is set to be an area of growth within the Docker ecosystem.

Installing Docker

Before we go any further, we will learn how to install the software that allows us to host Docker containers.

Getting ready

For this recipe, you will need an Ubuntu 14.04 server.

How to do it...

The Docker developers have gone to great lengths to make the installation of Docker as simple as possible, and this recipe should have you up and running within minutes:

1. First, ensure that you have the `wget` tool installed by issuing the following command:

    ```
    $ sudo apt-get install wget
    ```

2. Once you have `wget` installed, issue the following command to run the Docker installer:

    ```
    $ wget -qO- https://get.docker.com/ | sh
    ```

3. The installer will prompt you for the `sudo` password, which once entered will install Docker and any dependencies. Once the install is complete, you can verify that Docker is correctly installed by running the following command:

    ```
    $ docker -v
    ```

    You should receive output similar to the following screenshot:

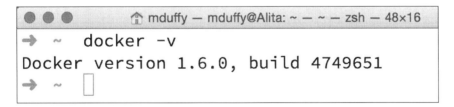

See also

You can find the Docker installation instructions for various operating systems at: `https://docs.docker.com/installation/`.

Pulling an image from the public Docker registry

Now that we have installed Docker, we can use it to run a container from the public Docker registry. The public Docker registry contains thousands of ready to use images that cover hundreds of different packages, from databases, through to app servers. The public registry also includes official images from certain software providers, offering you a quick method to start developing with those packages, and the surety that the image is correct and secure.

For this recipe, we're going to use a combination of two different images to run a basic WordPress blog.

Getting ready

To use this recipe, you will need an Ubuntu 14.04 server with Docker installed.

How to do it...

This recipe will use some simple Docker commands, and will use the public Docker images for MySQL and WordPress to install a blog:

1. The first task that we need to accomplish is to create a MySQL container to hold our data. We can do this using the following command:

   ```
   $ sudo docker run --name test-mysql -e MYSQL_ROOT_
   PASSWORD=password -d mysql:latest
   ```

2. This command will connect to the Docker public registry and pull the container image tagged as `mysql:latest` down to the server. Once it's downloaded, a new Docker container called `test-mysql` will be started with a MySQL root password of `password`. You can confirm it's running by issuing the following command:

   ```
   $ docker ps
   ```

   This should produce output similar to this:

```
● ● ●                    ⬆ mduffy — mduffy@Alita: ~ — — — zsh — 82×22
➜  ~   docker ps
CONTAINER ID       IMAGE              COMMAND                 CREATED
 STATUS             PORTS              NAMES
296c18cc81ca       mysql:latest       "/entrypoint.sh mysq    10 days ago
 Up 2 seconds        3306/tcp           test-mysql
```

3. Now that we have a MySQL container, we can turn our attention to WordPress. As with MySQL, the WordPress developers have created an official container image, and we can use this to run WordPress using the following command:

```
$ docker run --name test-wordpress -p 80:80 --link test-mysql:mysql -d wordpress
```

4. This command will retrieve and run the official WordPress image, and will name it `test-Wordpress`. Note the `--link` option; this links the MySQL container to the WordPress container without creating an explicit network between the two.

 Keep in mind that you can only link two containers on the same host; if the containers are on different hosts, you will need to map ports for them to be able to communicate.

5. Note the `-p` option, this exports TCP port `80` from the container to port 80 on the host, making the WordPress installation accessible. It will not be available to the outside world without the port mapping, even though the container has port `80` open. The mapping essentially creates a firewall rule on the Docker host that bridges between the host network and the virtual network created for the Docker containers to run on.

6. Open a browser, point it to the address of your Docker host, and you should see the following page:

See also

- ▶ You can find the official MySQL image at `https://registry.hub.docker.com/_/wordpress/`

- ▶ In addition, you can find the official WordPress image and documentation at `https://registry.hub.docker.com/_/wordpress/`

Performing basic Docker operations

Now that we have the ability to create Docker containers, let's have a look at how to control them. Docker has a comprehensive set of tools that allows you to start, stop, and delete containers.

Getting ready

For this recipe, you will need an Ubuntu 14.04 server with Docker installed.

How to do it...

This recipe demonstrates the basic commands used to manage Docker containers. By using these commands, you can manage the full lifecycle of the container:

1. Use the following command to list the running containers on your system:

   ```
   $ sudo docker ps
   ```

    This only shows the running containers. To see the containers that have been stopped, use the following command:

   ```
   $ sudo docker ps -a
   ```

2. To stop a running container, use the following command:

   ```
   $ docker stop <dockerID>
   ```

   Here the `ID` is derived from running `docker ps` and selecting the ID of the image you wish to stop.

3. To remove a `docker` container, use the following command:

   ```
   $ sudo docker rm <CONTAINER ID>
   ```

Remember, this only removes the CONTAINER and not the underlying image.

4. Use the following command to list the Docker images that have been downloaded to the host:

```
$ sudo docker images
```

This should produce output that looks something similar to this:

```
→  ~  docker images
REPOSITORY          TAG          IMAGE ID           CREATED          VIRTUAL SIZE
wordpress           latest       7dc926dab9fb       2 weeks ago      460.3 MB
mysql               latest       56f320bd6adc       3 weeks ago      282.9 MB
→  ~
```

5. Use the following command to remove an image:

```
$ sudo docker rmi < IMAGE ID >
```

 Removing images is a safe operation; Docker uses reference counting to keep track of containers that have image dependencies. If you attempt to remove an image that is in use by a container (started or stopped) on your host, you will receive a warning, and it will not be removed.

See also

You can find instructions on how to work with images and containers at https://docs.docker.com/userguide/.

Running a container interactively

You will want to run containers in a detached mode; however, there are times when it is very useful to be able to run the container interactively to diagnose issues.

Running a container interactively essentially gives you a shell on the container, and from within the container you can work in the same way, as you would with any other Linux system.

Getting ready

For this recipe, you will need an Ubuntu 14.04 server with Docker installed.

How to do it...

You can start any Docker container in an interactive mode using the following command:

```
$ sudo docker run -i -t ubuntu /bin/bash
```

See also

Refer the documentation on Docker at: `https://docs.docker.com/articles/basics/`.

Creating a Dockerfile

Although there are many premade images available on the Docker registry, it is inevitable that you will want to create your own images as the basis for your containers. One of the standout features of Docker is its straightforward build tools, and you can easily create new images with a simple text file.

In this recipe, you will learn how to use Docker to package the Gollum Wiki software and push it to the Docker public repository.

Getting ready

For this recipe, you will need a server with Docker installed.

How to do it...

The following steps outline how to create a new Dockerfile, build it, and finally push it to the Docker Registry:

1. First, we are going to create a new Docker registry account. Start by visiting `https://registry.hub.docker.com` and follow the signup instructions that you will find on this page to create a new account. By creating your account, you create a namespace within the Docker registry, which allows you to upload your own images.

2. We have created a Docker registry account, so we can now turn our attention to creating our first Dockerfile. A Dockerfile is the list of steps used to create a complete Docker image. These steps can include copying files into the image, or running commands, but every Dockerfile needs to start with a FROM command. The FROM command allows you to choose the Docker image that will form the basis for this container; generally speaking, this will be an OS image, and many Linux distributions now ship an official image that can be used.

It might strike you as slightly recursive that you need to use an image to create an image. If you wish to create your own OS image to serve as your base, you can follow the instructions given at: `https://docs.docker.com/articles/baseimages/`.

3. Let's use the Ubuntu image for our Gollum container. Do this by creating a new file called Dockerfile and inserting the following code:

    ```
    FROM ubuntu:14.04
    ```

    This will use Ubuntu 14:04 as our base image.

4. Next, we can insert a little metadata that allows people to see who is currently maintaining the image. This allows people to see who authored the image, and who to contact if they have questions or issues. This takes the form of a text field, and it's generally accepted to put your name and e-mail address in it. You can do this by adding the following command in the Docker file:

    ```
    MAINTAINER Example User example@adomain.com
    ```

5. Now that we have taken care of the metadata for our container, we can turn our attention to installing software. As we are using the Ubuntu base image, we use the `apt` package manager to install our software; however, the base image may have an out-of-date package list cached, so it's best to update it. To update the package list, add the `RUN` directive. In your Dockerfile, insert the following code:

    ```
    RUN apt-get update && \
    ```

 The `RUN` directive is one you are going to see a lot, as it allows you to run commands within the container. Be careful, though, as you need to ensure that the commands you run are non-interactive; interactive commands will cause your image build to fail as you have no way to interact with it at build time.

6. Notice the `&& \`; this is a shell function that runs a subsequent command if the previous command was successful, allowing us to chain commands in one line. This is useful for keeping the number of Docker layers small. The `\` is a line break, allowing you to keep your Dockerfile readable.

When you run a Docker build, each command creates a new layer, and each
layer is placed on top of the next, building your eventual Docker image.
However, each layer carries a small amount of internal metadata, which
although small, can add up. Perhaps more importantly, there is a limit to the
amount of layers an image can contain, a constraint of the underlying AUFS
filesystem; at the time of writing, the limit is 127 layers. Although you can
use alternative file systems with Docker that might remove this limitation, it's
worth designing with it in mind.

7. Now, we can start to install our prerequisite software. Since Gollum is a Ruby
   application, it requires Ruby, plus some additional build tools. Again, we are going
   to use the RUN command and have apt install these packages for us. Insert the
   following code inside your Dockerfile:

```
RUN apt-get update && apt-get install -y ruby1.9.1 ruby1.9.1-dev
make zlib1g-dev libicu-dev build-essential git
```

This will install the software that we need to install Gollum.

8. Next we want to install Gollum itself. Gollum is distributed as a Ruby gem, so we can
   use the Gem package manager to install it for us. To do this, add the following code:

```
RUN apt-get update && \
apt-get install -y ruby1.9.1 ruby1.9.1-dev make zlib1g-dev libicu-
dev build-essential git && \
gem install gollum
```

As you can see, we are performing the installation as a chained set of commands
rather than using an individual RUN directive for each new line.

9. We now need a directory to store our wiki content. Unlike many wikis that rely on a
   database to store content, Gollum uses a Git repository as its persistent store. All
   that is required is a file system to store the Git repository on, and it takes care of the
   versioning. Let's create it now; insert the following code into your Dockerfile:

```
RUN mkdir -p /usr/local/gollum
```

10. Now, we are going to set the work directory. By default, Docker runs all directives within the root directory of the container; by setting the work directory, we can run the commands in the directory of our choice. To set the work directory, add the following directive to your Dockerfile:

```
WORKDIR /usr/local/gollum
```

11. With the work directory set, we can now create the initial repository to hold our wiki content; this is achieved using the Git command. Add this code to your Dockerfile:

```
RUN git init .
```

This command will be run in the work directory we set in the previous command, and it will create an empty Git repository ready for our content.

12. Now, we need to expose a network port. By exposing the port, we will be able to connect to the service from the network; it also allows other containers to connect to the service via linking. Gollum runs by default on TCP port 4567; add the following code to expose it:

```
EXPOSE 4567
```

13. Finally, we add a default command that will be run when the container is started. In this case, the Gollum package installs a binary that can be used to start the wiki. Add the following command to execute it when the container starts:

```
CMD ["gollum"]
```

14. We are now ready to build our Docker container. At the command line, navigate to the directory containing your Dockerfile and issue the following command:

```
$ sudo docker build -t <username>/gollum:4.0.0 .
```

Where <username> is the Docker registry username that you setup earlier. Notice the -t: this is the tag. The tag is used both to name your image and to version it. In this case, I have used the version of the software.

> Versioning is as always a contentious issue, and it is best to use your existing standards if in doubt. I tend to create a container version that matches the version of the application I am packaging, as it allows me to see at a glance which host is running which version of a given piece of software.

15. Once you trigger this command, you should see output similar to the following screenshot:

```
● ● ●           gollum — docker build --no-cache -t stunthamster/gollum:4.0.0 . — docker — docker — 96×34
→ gollum   docker build --no-cache -t stunthamster/gollum:4.0.0 .
Sending build context to Docker daemon 43.52 kB
Sending build context to Docker daemon
Step 0 : FROM ubuntu:14.04
14.04: Pulling from ubuntu
e9e06b06e14c: Pull complete
a82efea989f9: Pull complete
37bea4ee0c81: Pull complete
07f8e8c5e660: Already exists
ubuntu:14.04: The image you are pulling has been verified. Important: image verification is a te
ch preview feature and should not be relied on to provide security.
Digest: sha256:125f9479befe1f71562b6ff20fb301523a2633902ded6d50ade4ebcd7637a035
Status: Downloaded newer image for ubuntu:14.04
 ---> 07f8e8c5e660
Step 1 : MAINTAINER Michael Duffy <michael@stunthamster.com>
 ---> Running in 0126728037c6
 ---> 336fb4837b48
Removing intermediate container 0126728037c6
Step 2 : RUN apt-get update
 ---> Running in a8d91d6643a3
Ign http://archive.ubuntu.com trusty InRelease
Ign http://archive.ubuntu.com trusty-updates InRelease
Ign http://archive.ubuntu.com trusty-security InRelease
Hit http://archive.ubuntu.com trusty Release.gpg
Get:1 http://archive.ubuntu.com trusty-updates Release.gpg [933 B]
Get:2 http://archive.ubuntu.com trusty-security Release.gpg [933 B]
Hit http://archive.ubuntu.com trusty Release
Get:3 http://archive.ubuntu.com trusty-updates Release [63.5 kB]
Get:4 http://archive.ubuntu.com trusty-security Release [63.5 kB]
Get:5 http://archive.ubuntu.com trusty/main Sources [1335 kB]
Get:6 http://archive.ubuntu.com trusty/restricted Sources [5335 B]
Get:7 http://archive.ubuntu.com trusty/universe Sources [7926 kB]
Get:8 http://archive.ubuntu.com trusty/main amd64 Packages [1743 kB]
```

16. Once your build is complete, you can push it to the Docker repository. By pushing your image to the repository, you make it straightforward to deploy it to other machines. To push the container, issue the following command:

```
$ sudo docker push <username>/gollum:4.0.0
```

This will push the image to the Docker repository and make it ready to be distributed. If you wish to make it private, then you can sign up for a premium account and make use of the private repository feature; alternatively, you can host your own Docker registry.

See also

The Docker build documents can be found at: `https://docs.docker.com/reference/builder/`.

Running a container in detached mode

You should run your container in a detached mode. This ensures that the applications that are running within your container are able to run unattended, much in the same way as a daemonized service. In this example, we are going to take the container we created in the previous recipe, and run it as a detached process.

Getting ready

For this recipe, you will need an Ubuntu 14.04 server with Docker installed. You should also have completed the previous recipe, *Creating a Dockerfile*, or have a suitable image to use.

How to do it...

The following steps show you how to use the `docker` command to run a container in a detached fashion:

1. Running a container in detached mode is relatively straight forward. On your Docker host, run the following command:

    ```
    $ sudo docker run -d -t <username>/gollum:4.0.0 --name gollum -p
    4567:4567
    ```

2. Let's take a look at these options. The `-d` tells Docker to run the container in a detached mode; this means that it will run in the background, non interactively. Next we use the `-t` option and supply the tag of our image, telling it which image we wish to start our container from. Then, we use the `--name` option to allocate a name to the container; without this option, a random name will be allocated.

3. The final option (`-p`) bridges the network between the container and the host, allowing you to connect to your Gollum Wiki. This is presented as `<container port>:<host port>` and allows you to connect to the host on a different port to the one that is presented by the container; this can be very useful if you want to run multiple versions of the same app, as it allows you to export the service onto several different ports, and use technology such as `haproxy` to load balance between them.

4. Once you have issued the command, you should be able to connect to your new Wiki. In your browser enter the `url ::4567`. You should be presented with a page that looks similar to this:

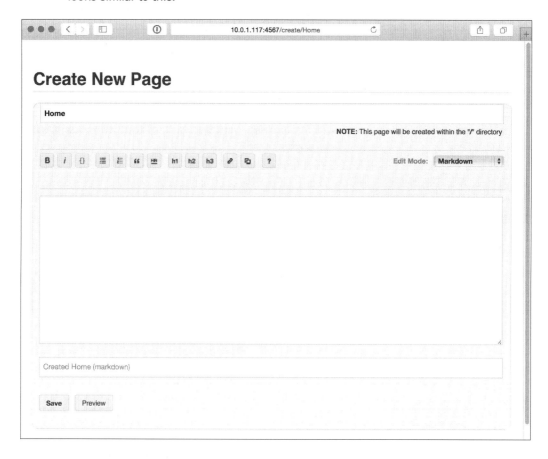

See also

▸ You can find the Docker run command reference at `https://docs.docker.com/reference/run/`

▸ You can find the Gollum documentation at `https://github.com/gollum/gollum/wiki`

Saving and restoring a container

One of the powers of containers is the flexibility that they provide, and part of this is the ease with which you can take snapshots of running containers and restore them onto other Docker hosts. This can be used both to back up containers and to diagnose issues. If you have a production issue with a particular container, you can use a snapshot to restore the problematic container to a test host and test the exact same container in a controlled environment.

Getting ready

For this recipe, you will need an Ubuntu 14.04 Docker host and a running Docker container.

How to do it...

The following steps will show you how to save a Docker container and then restore it on another machine:

1. First we need to locate the container we are interested in. Using the `docker ps` command, locate the container you wish to snapshot and make a note of its `ID`.

2. Once you have located the container you wish to commit, issue the following command:

   ```
   $ sudo docker commit <containerid> <imagename>:<imageversion>
   --pause=false --author=<yourname>
   ```

   Let's go through some of these options in more detail. The `containerid` should be the `id` of the container you wish to commit, and the `imagename` and `imageversion` are the name and version you wish to give to the image you're creating. The `pause` flag is important for production instances, as this controls the behavior of the running container when committing. By default, Docker will pause the image whilst the commit takes place; this is to ensure that the data is consistently captured. However, it also renders the container unable to serve requests during this time. If you need the container to continue to run, you can use the `--pause=false` flag to ensure this. Be aware, though, the image you create may contain corrupted data if a write takes place during the commit. Finally, we also add an author name, as this helps the people who examine the image to know who took it.

3. Once you have issued the command, you can use the following command to check if it has been created:

   ```
   $ docker images | grep "<imagename:imageversion>"
   ```

   This should show your newly created image.

4. Now that we have our image, we can push it to the Docker repository using the following command:

```
$ docker push -t <imagename:imageversion>
```

5. We can now make the image available for diagnosis on a test machine using the following command:

```
$ Docker pull -t   <imagename:imageversion>
```

6. Alternatively, you can skip pushing the image to the Docker repository by using the Docker `save` command. The `save` command creates a `tar` file of the image, which is suitable to be passed around with tools such as SCP, or shared file systems such as NFS. To use the `save` command, issue the following at the command line:

```
$ docker save <imagename:imageversion> > /tmp/savedimage.tar
```

7. This will create a `tar` file of the image. Copy it to your test host using the tool of your choice, and issue the following command on the test host:

```
$ docker load < savedimage.tar
```

Now, if you check the Docker images on your test host, you will find that your saved image is available to run.

See also

You can find details of Docker save, load, and commit commands at: `https://docs.docker.com/reference/run/`.

Using the host only network

Docker uses a bridge to connect to the underlying virtual network and present services within a container, and by and large, this is perfectly satisfactory. However, there are some edge cases where this can cause issues; a perfect example is an application that makes use of multicast. To get around this, you can present the host networking stack to the container, allowing it to make full use of the host network. This allows items such as multicast to work at the expense of some flexibility and convenience.

Wherever possible, you should avoid using this technique. Although it can help avoid certain issues, it also breaks one of the underlying ideas of containerization by making a container rely on features of the host. It also stops you from being able to run multiple containers that rely on the same port. For instance, under normal circumstances you can run multiple Nginx servers using Docker, and also map the host ports of 80, 81, and 82 to three containers listening on port 80. You cannot do this by tying the host network to the container, as the port is tied to a single process.

Getting ready

For this recipe, you will need an Ubuntu 14.04 host and a container with which it can network.

How to do it...

The following recipe shows you how to run a container in a detached fashion and give it access to the host network:

1. First, we're going to start a new container; in this example, we're going to use the Gollum container from earlier in the chapter. Start it using the following command:

   ```
   docker run -d --name gollum --net=host -t <username>/gollum:4.0.0
   ```

   Note the additional option of `--net=host`; this directs Docker to start the container with the host network rather than bridging. Also note the lack of the `-p` option to map ports; this option becomes superfluous as the container communicates directly with the host network, so no bridge is required.

2. As we are no longer mapping a port, Docker cannot take care of configuring the IP Tables for use. Due to that, you will need to insert a new rule to allow traffic to reach the service running in the container. You can do this by using the following command:

   ```
   iptables -I INPUT 5 -p tcp -m tcp --dport <serviceport> -j ACCEPT
   ```

   Substitute `<<serviceport>>` with the TCP port number of the service that you're running on.

See also

You can find more information on advanced Docker networking techniques at:
`https://docs.docker.com/articles/networking/`.

Running a private Docker registry

Although the Docker registry offers a robust and cost effective place to store Docker images, for some companies this can be limiting, either due to the cost involved, or possibly due to security policies. Luckily, it is possible to run your own private Docker repository, allowing you to keep your images completely within the boundaries of your own network.

In this recipe, we are going to set up a minimal Docker registry. We are not going to delve into items such as authentication mechanisms or alternative storage mechanisms. This is left as an exercise for the reader, and you can find excellent guidance within the Docker documentation at: `https://docs.docker.com/registry/`.

The registry we create will contain some minimal security in the form of SSL, and we are going to export the filesystem to the underlying host. Docker registries can consume massive amounts of disk space and ideally, you should hold the data on a robust storage device, such as an NFS server with both a large capacity, and solid redundancy.

Getting ready

For this recipe, you will need an Ubuntu 14.04 host with Docker installed.

How to do it

The following steps will show you how to create a new Docker repository and secure it using SSL:

1. By default, the Docker registry does not ship with SSL enabled. To enable it, we need to download the source code. Create a folder to contain it and download it using the following command:

   ```
   $ wget -q https://github.com/docker/distribution/archive/
   v2.0.0.tar.gz
   ```

2. Next, unpack the source code using the `tar` command:

   ```
   $ tar -xvf v2.0.0.tar.gz
   ```

3. Move to the `distribution` directory and create a new `certs` directory using the following command:

   ```
   $ cd distribution-2.0.0 && mkdir certs
   ```

4. Now we create the SSL certificates for our Docker host using the following command:

   ```
   $ openssl req -newkey rsa:2048 -nodes -keyout certs/registery.key
   -x509 -days 730 -out certs/registery.crt
   ```

5. This command will trigger some prompts asking for further details about the new certificate you are creating:

```
● ● ●          distribution-2.0.0 — openssl req -newkey rsa:2048 -nodes -keyout certs/registery.key -x509 -days  — openssl — openssl — 96×34
→ distribution-2.0.0  openssl req -newkey rsa:2048 -nodes -keyout certs/registery.key -x509 -da
ys 730 -out certs/registery.crt
Generating a 2048 bit RSA private key
...........................+++
...............................+++
writing new private key to 'certs/registery.key'
-----
You are about to be asked to enter information that will be incorporated
into your certificate request.
What you are about to enter is what is called a Distinguished Name or a DN.
There are quite a few fields but you can leave some blank
For some fields there will be a default value,
If you enter '.', the field will be left blank.
-----
Country Name (2 letter code) [AU]:
```

Pay special attention to the hostname when you fill these in, as this should match the hostname of registry you are creating.

6. Next, we need to amend the registry configuration to recognize the new certificates. Edit the `/cmd/registry/config.yml` file within the registry source code and find the block marked http, then amend the code to look similar to this:

```
http:
    addr: :5000
    secret: asecretforlocaldevelopment
    debug:
        addr: localhost:5001
    tls:
        certificate: /go/src/github.com/docker/distribution/certs/
registry.crt
        key: /go/src/github.com/docker/distribution/certs/
registry.key
```

7. Next, locate the key named `filesystem:` and amend it so that it resembles the following snippet:

```
filesystem:
    rootdirectory: /var/spool/registry
```

8. Now we have finished our changes, we can build our custom registry image using the following `docker build` command:

```
$ docker build -t docker_registry .
```

9. Once the build is complete, you can run the registry using the following command:

```
$ docker run -p 5000:5000 -v /var/spool/registry:<host_dir>
docker_registry:latest
```

Where `host_dir` is a directory on the host machine.

10. Since we are using a self-signed certificate, we need to configure any Docker client that wishes to use this repository to recognize the new certificate. On each Docker client, copy the `registry.crt` into `/etc/docker/certs.d/<<registrydomain>>:<<registryport>>/ca.crt`. Ensure that you replace `registrydomain` with the DNS name of your Docker registry, and the `registryport` with the port it will be running on. This will then suppress any warnings you may encounter due to untrusted certificates.

11. We can check if our registry has started correctly by querying the API. Point your browser at the address of your new registry (remember to ensure it's `https` rather than `http`). You should see a response similar to this:

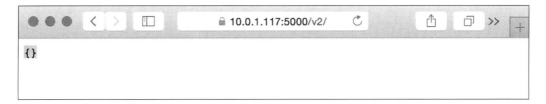

This is exactly what we expect; by returning a `200` response and an empty JSON array, you can see that the API is ready to go.

See also

You can find details on how to deploy and use the Docker Registry at: `https://docs.docker.com/registry/`.

Managing images with a private registry

Once you have created your own Docker registry, you can start to push your Docker images to it. By pushing your images to a self-hosted Docker registry, you are not only gaining security, you are also making the build and deployment of further images much faster. Pushing to a self-hosted registry is straightforward, and there is nothing to stop you from pushing an image to multiple registries; this can be useful if you maintain registries for certain environments.

Getting ready

For this recipe, you will need an Ubuntu 14.04 Docker host and a self-hosted Docker registry.

How to do it...

I have split this recipe into two sections, the first dealing with pushing images to your registry, and the second for how to pull images.

Pushing images

The following steps deal with taking an image and pushing it to a private Docker registry:

1. For this recipe, we are going to use the Gollum Dockerfile, which we created previously. Change the directory to the Dockerfile directory and trigger a build using this command:

   ```
   $ sudo docker build -t <username>/gollum:4.0.0 <<docker_registry_
   name_and_port>>
   ```

   Note that, instead of your usual Docker registry username, you are inserting the name and port number of your own Docker registry into the image tag. This is going to act as a pointer to Docker, for both where to push the image to and where to pull it from.

2. Next, we can push the image using the following command:

   ```
   $ docker push <docker_registry_name_and_port>/gollum:4.0.0
   ```

3. If all goes well, you should see output similar to this:

```
distribution-2.0.0 — mduffy@alita: ~/Downloads/distribution-2.0.0 — ..ibution-2.0.0 — zsh — 83×26
➜  distribution-2.0.0  docker push registry.stunthamster.com:5000/gollum:4.0.0
The push refers to a repository [registry.stunthamster.com:5000/gollum] (len: 1)
bffb8c4a03ea: Image already exists
99d63ab110f9: Image successfully pushed
7b9ee66207cb: Image successfully pushed
2e971bf03a20: Image successfully pushed
57a21dbeb512: Image successfully pushed
393b01244176: Image successfully pushed
71dae6be4417: Image successfully pushed
bd1eaf07f014: Image successfully pushed
ca0f230b927e: Image successfully pushed
f1bec3d7a3c2: Image successfully pushed
4a386c8c854d: Image successfully pushed
2c006467b059: Image successfully pushed
cf87a463dca8: Image successfully pushed
33e1becc4d89: Image successfully pushed
86c1ba2f46fd: Image successfully pushed
f3d5a2ae5530: Image successfully pushed
e3dfcb7c6e5a: Image successfully pushed
c032a945ed19: Image successfully pushed
05bacbdfa6eb: Image successfully pushed
e66a33f451f4: Image successfully pushed
41b730702607: Image successfully pushed
3cb35ae859e7: Image successfully pushed
Digest: sha256:433e2671bc64abc9561f916b166e37076fa851a8eb42670ad7f29591f6e21222
➜  distribution-2.0.0
```

4. Now, we can also use the Registry API to check if our image has been correctly pushed. At the command line, enter the following command:

```
curl -v -X GET  address>:5000/v2/gollum/tags/list
```

5. You should see a response along the lines of the following screenshot:

```
distribution-2.0.0 — mduffy@alita: ~/Downloads/distribution-2.0.0 — ..ibution-2.0.0 — zsh — 103×30
→ distribution-2.0.0   curl -v -X GET http://registry.stunthamster.com:5000/v2/gollum/tags/list
* Hostname was NOT found in DNS cache
*    Trying 172.16.84.135...
* Connected to registry.stunthamster.com (172.16.84.135) port 5000 (#0)
> GET /v2/gollum/tags/list HTTP/1.1
> User-Agent: curl/7.37.1
> Host: registry.stunthamster.com:5000
> Accept: */*
>
< HTTP/1.1 200 OK
< Content-Type: application/json; charset=utf-8
< Docker-Distribution-Api-Version: registry/2.0
< Date: Fri, 15 May 2015 04:54:59 GMT
< Content-Length: 35
<
{"name":"gollum","tags":["4.0.0"]}
* Connection #0 to host registry.stunthamster.com left intact
→ distribution-2.0.0 []
```

If you see this, then you have successfully pushed the image to your own Registry.

Pulling images

Now that we have pushed images to our Docker registry, we can look at how we can subsequently pull them. Again, we can use the Gollum example, which we uploaded in the previous examples.

At your command line, enter the following command:

```
$ docker run -d -t <<docker_registry_name_and_port>>/gollum:4.0.0
```

This will pull the image from your registry and run it.

See also

You can find more details of working with a self-hosted Docker registry at: `https://docs.docker.com/registry/spec/api/#overview`.

7
Using Jenkins for Continuous Deployment

In this chapter, we are going to cover the following topics:

- ▶ Installing Jenkins
- ▶ Installing the Git plugin
- ▶ Installing a Jenkins slave
- ▶ Creating your first Jenkins job
- ▶ Building Docker containers using Jenkins
- ▶ Deploying a Java application to Tomcat with zero downtime using Ansible

Introduction

Continuous integration is one of the most powerful techniques you can use when developing software and it underpins a great deal of what many consider a DevOps tool-chain. **Continuous integration** (**CI**) essentially entails taking your code and building it on a frequent schedule and deploying it into a representative environment for the purpose of testing. This automated job should both build and test, if the tests are passed, you can deploy your software into a nominated environment. Without the ability to automate code deployment, you are left with an enormous piece of manual labor in your deployment pipeline. It's one thing to be able to build servers and deploy configuration automatically, but if you are unable to build your code in a reliable manner and then push it to a test environment, then you are going to be wasting a lot of time and energy.

Continuous integration is an incredibly valuable tool and something that most development teams should be working towards if they don't already have it. Once you have a CI tool in place you will be deploying and testing code very frequently and increasing the visibility of bugs before they can be deployed any further than an integration environment.

How often you run the integration job is something for the team to agree on. I've worked with systems that deploy every time a developer checks in and I've also worked in teams where it happens once every hour. I will suggest that you run the integration at least once a day. If your integration tests are long, the best time will be when the last developer goes home; so that, when you return the next day, you can see the state of your last build and fix any issues that may have occurred overnight.

Taken to extreme, continuous integration can be used to take code from the repository and take it right through to production deployments and indeed, there are companies that utilize continuous integration in this fashion. Even if you don't take your system to such a degree, you will still find that the judicious use of continuous integration can help you identify bugs in the code quicker.

The key to continuous integration is to leverage the existing tools. You almost have the existing testing suites in place, so re-purpose those to be used in the continuous integration environment. We can also re-use the automation tools and techniques we use to build the environments. This not only re-uses existing tools but also ensures that any deployment tool you use is tested regularly, ensuring that these are as bug free as possible.

In this chapter, we are going to focus on using Jenkins as the basis of our continuous integration recipes. Jenkins is a fork of the Hudson CI system and has a thriving and active development community with many plugins to enhance its functionality.

Although Jenkins is a fork of Hudson, I recommend that you stick with Jenkins rather than its progenitor. It has a much more active developer community and more plugins.

Jenkins allows the use of a master and slave arrangement and this allows you to scale it out for truly massive builds. The Jenkins master controls the slaves and with a few select plugins, you can use technologies such as Docker to keep your build environment elastic; alternately, you can use plugins to drive build slaves using AWS, Digital Ocean, and many other PAAS providers.

We will also be making use of both Ansible and Docker to build and configure our integration environment. If you are not up to speed with either of these, I suggest that you have a look at *Chapter 5*, *Automation with Ansible*, and *Chapter 6*, *Containerization with Docker*. Both of these chapters contain everything you need to get up and running with these technologies.

Installing Jenkins

This recipe will show you how to install a basic Jenkins server. The Jenkins server will form the basis of the continuous integration environment, and this is where you define your build jobs and also manage build users, plugins, and environment details. We are also going to cover some basic setup tasks, ensuring that your new Jenkins servers is secured from anonymous usage is a very important step if your hosting your build platform on a publicly accessible host.

We are going to use Ansible to install our Jenkins master; this allows us to easily re-create the basic server if we have a problem or allows us to create a new one if we need a second master, perhaps for a new project.

 This recipe will setup the Jenkins master but you will quickly realize that the Jenkins master is not the important part; the crucial parts are the jobs you create. Make sure that once you start to use Jenkins, you back up your system regularly. If disaster strikes and you haven't backed up your Jenkins master, you will have a very tedious time re-creating jobs from scratch.

Getting ready

For this recipe, you will need an Ubuntu 14.04 server and an Ubuntu 14.04 host with Ansible installed. If you need more information on how to use Ansible, please consult *Chapter 5, Automation with Ansible*.

How to do it...

The following steps will show you how to write a basic Ansible role to install the Jenkins server and how then to setup some basic security:

1. We're going to create a new Ansible role to manage the installation of our Jenkins Master; use the following command to create the new role:

```
ansible-galaxy init jenkins
```

2. Now, we have our new template role ready and we can start adding code. Edit `jenkins/tasks/main.yml` and add the following snippet:

```
- name: Add Apt key
  apt_key: url=http://pkg.jenkins-ci.org/debian/jenkins-ci.org.key
state=present
- name: Add Jenkins Repository
  apt_repository: repo='deb http://pkg.jenkins-ci.org/debian
binary/' state=present update_cache=yes
```

```
- name: Install Jenkins
  apt: name=jenkins state=present

- name: Start Jenkins
  service: name=jenkins state=started
```

This code is straightforward and performs the following tasks:

- Adds the Jenkins repository key
- Adds the Jenkins repository to the apt sources
- Installs the Jenkins package
- Starts the Jenkins service.

If you now use your browser to point at the DNS/IP address of your build server on port 8080 you should be presented with the following page:

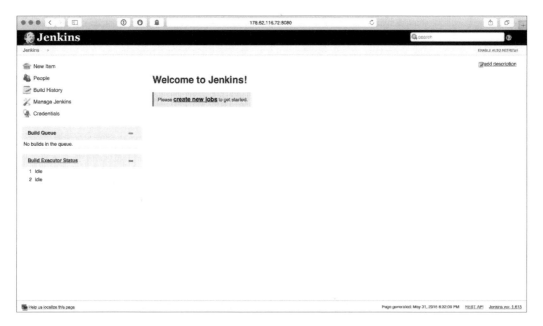

3. Now that you have installed Jenkins, we should at least add a minimum amount of security; this is especially important if you are hosting your Jenkins server on a public facing server. Click on the **Manage Jenkins** on the left-hand side of the home page marked as:

4. The next page allows you to manage some of the features of Jenkins. If you have not already setup your security, you should find a banner that looks similar to the following screenshot at the top of the screen:

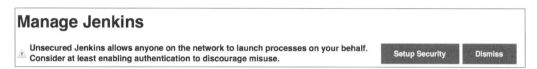

5. Click on the button marked as **Setup Security**. This should take you to the next screen, which looks like the following screenshot:

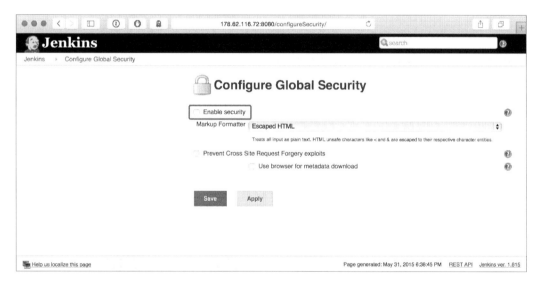

6. Check the highlighted checkbox and then click on the **Save** button; it will take you to the next screen of the setup, which should resemble the following screenshot:

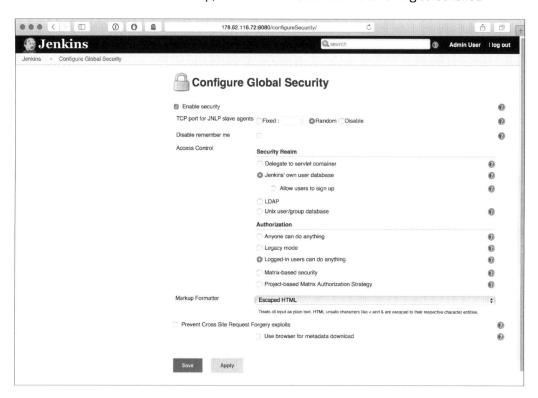

Note the selected settings. This will configure Jenkins to use it's own in built user directory and ensure that only logged in users are able to perform any actions.

This only stops users from being able to perform actions within Jenkins, but it does not stop unauthenticated users from seeing information on your build server. If you are hosting this on an externally available site, I strongly urge you to get additional security; at the very least a reverse proxy, such as an Apache or Nginx server in front of your Jenkins with basic authentication. Alternatively, you can also add a user called **Anonymous**, and remove all the rights; this will effectively stop unauthenticated users from being able to take any actions or see any data.

Once you are happy with the settings, hit **Save** and you will be taken back to the configuration page.

7. Finally, we need to create a user to log in with. From the management page, find and click on the link that looks like this:

Manage Users
Create/delete/modify users that can log in to this Jenkins

8. This will take us to the user management page. On the left-hand side, you will find a link called **Create User**, click on it and you will be taken to a page that looks similar to the following screenshot:

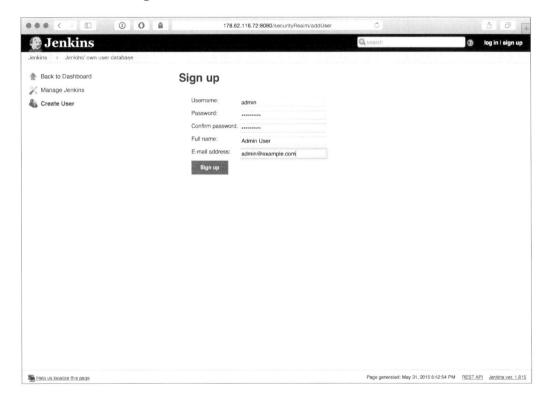

Add the details of your user as shown in the preceding instance and hit the **Sign up** button. You should now be able to login to Jenkins as that user and start to create jobs. If you don't supply user details, you can still see some of the less secure elements of Jenkins; however, you will be unable to alter anything.

See also...

▶ You can find further details of how to install Jenkins at `https://wiki.jenkins-ci.org/display/JENKINS/Installing+Jenkins`

▶ You can find details of Jenkins authentication methods at `https://wiki.jenkins-ci.org/display/JENKINS/Authentication`

▶ You can find details of how to administer Jenkins at `https://wiki.jenkins-ci.org/display/JENKINS/Administering+Jenkins`

Installing the Git plugin

By default, Jenkins is shipped with the ability to connect to CVS and Subversion; despite the growing popularity of Git, it's still not available by default. Fortunately, Jenkins has a plugin that allows you to use Git as your repository of choice. This recipe will show you how to install the plugin and configure the credentials to connect to your repo.

Getting ready

For this recipe, you will need a Jenkins server and a Git repo to connect to.

How to do it...

The following steps use a combination of Ansible and a Jenkins plugin to add Git client functionality to the Jenkins Server.

1. First, we need to install the Git client on to our Jenkins server. Rather than doing this manually, we are going to adjust the Ansible role from the installation recipe. Within the Jenkins role, edit the following file: `Jenkins/tasks/main.yml`, and insert the following code:

```
- name: Install Jenkins
  apt: name=jenkins state=present
- name: Install Git
  apt: name=git state=present
```

2. Re-run the Ansible role against your server; this should install the Git client. You can test this by issuing the following command on your Jenkins server:

```
git --version
```

This should return the version of the Git client that you installed.

3. Now, since we have the Git client installed, we can install the Jenkins Git plugin. From the front page of the Jenkins console, click on the **Manage Jenkins** button found on the left-hand side of the page.

 Although not covered in this recipe, it's possible to use Ansible to manage the plugins, a great example can be found at: `https://github.com/ICTO/ansible-jenkins`.

4. On the manage Jenkins page, find and click on the **Manage Plugins** button, found around halfway down the page and then click on the **Available** tab.

5. In the filter box, type **Git Plugin**; it should return a list of plugins similar to the following screenshot:

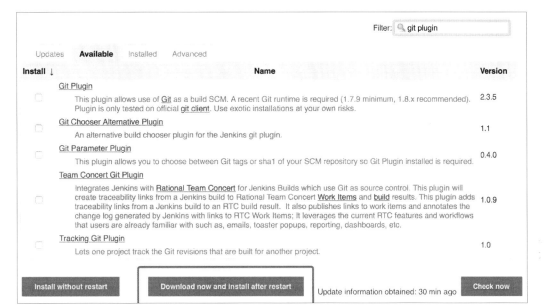

 As you have probably noticed, each of the plugins has a link in the title; this takes you through to the documentation and is worth looking at before installing them.

Tick the checkbox next to the **Git Plugin**, click on the **Download now, and install after restart** button. This will prompt Jenkins to download the plugin, install it, and restart Jenkins to make it available for use.

6. Next, we need to configure our credentials to connect to Git.

When setting up Git credentials, I recommend that at the very least, your build system should have its own credentials. Although it's tempting to re-use existing credentials, it makes it both hard to audit and more susceptible to intrusion. It's also creating a problem for the future, when the builds stop working and you revoke the key of the person who setup the build server when they leave.

7. Log on to your Jenkins server and issue the following command:

    ```
    $ sudo su Jenkins
    ```

8. Now, we can create a new SSH key with the following command:

    ```
    $ ssh-keygen -t rsa -b 4096 -C "jenkins@example.com"
    ```

9. You will be greeted with a response similar to the following screenshot:

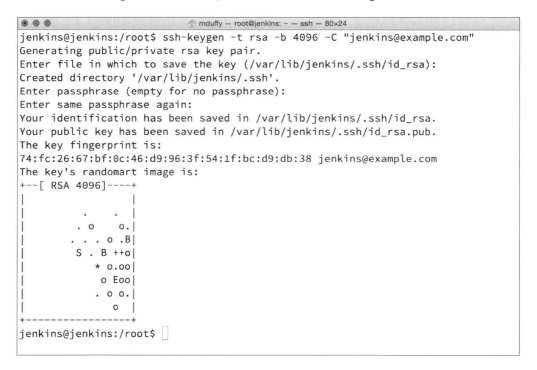

As you can see, I've left the responses at their default values.

 This will create the key without a password. If you wish, you can create a key with a password and the password can be passed via Jenkins.

10. Log on to your Jenkins server and click on the link on the left-hand side marked as **Credentials**. This will take you into credentials management page, which should look something similar to the following screenshot:

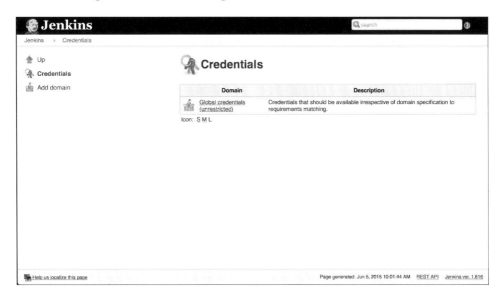

11. Click on the global credentials link and select the link on the left-hand side marked as **Add Credentials**; this will bring up a screen that will allow you to add your Git credentials; look at the following screenshot to get an idea of how it should look when you enter your credentials:

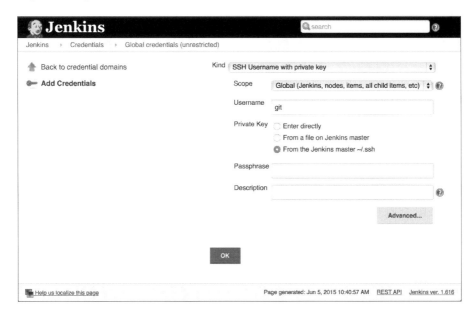

As you can see, we're asking the Jenkins server to simply look-up the key that we generated earlier. Alternatively, you can add it directly to Jenkins or keep it in a different place than the SSH default on the server itself. Tweak these details to fit your build infrastructure.

See also

▶ You can find the details of the Git plugin at `https://wiki.jenkins-ci.org/display/JENKINS/Git+Plugin`

▶ You can find more details about the credentials plugin at `https://wiki.jenkins-ci.org/display/JENKINS/Credentials+Plugin`

Installing a Jenkins slave

As we've already covered, Jenkins can be scaled by adding additional build slaves. These slaves can be used to distribute builds amongst many different servers. This allows you to have a single low-powered server, which acts as the Jenkins master and then as many slaves as you need to perform the build jobs.

Getting ready

For this recipe, you will need a Jenkins master and a server running Ubuntu 14.04 with a JDK installed to act as the slave.

How to do it...

The following steps will show you how to add a Jenkins slave to the Jenkins master:

1. On your slave node, add a new Jenkins-user with the following command:

```
$ adduser jenkins
```

Login to your Jenkins Master and add new credentials. These are going to be the credentials used to connect to your new Slave; it should look similar to the following screenshot:

As you can see, I'm using a `username` and `password` to connect to my slave; however, you can also use an SSH key if you prefer.

2. Once you have created your credentials, you now need to add the new slave. On the main screen, click on **Manage Jenkins** and then select the option marked as **Manage Nodes**. Inside the management panel, you should find that the master is already listed and should look something like this:

3. Click on the button on the left-hand side of the management panel marked as **New Node**; this will open the following dialog box:

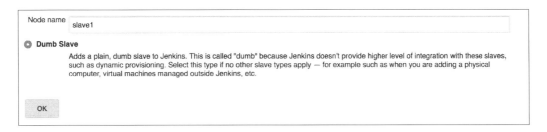

As you can see, you need to name your node. This is descriptive and doesn't necessarily need to the be same name as the actual node. As you can see, there is only one option available for slave nodes but you can add more via an appropriate plugin. Click on **OK** to move to the next step.

4. The next step allows you to enter the details of your slave node; have a look at the following screenshot:

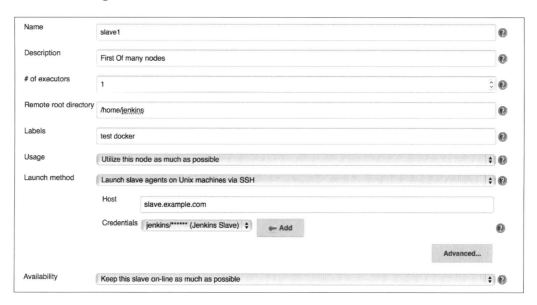

These options allow you to configure some fairly important settings for your node. First of all, it allows you to set the name and description of this node; It's best to be as descriptive as possible. Next, you can set the number of executors and this sets the number of parallel jobs the node can perform at one time. Generally speaking, the more powerful the server, the more jobs it should be able to perform. Mine is a tiny server, so I'll leave it at the default of one.

Next up, we have the remote root directory; this is where the Jenkins workspaces will be kept. So it's best to make sure that this is a location that has the majority of the disk space. Next, we have labels. Labels are a mechanism to allow you to use certain nodes for certain jobs; for instance, in my case, I've set two tags on my `slave`, `test` and `Docker`. This means that any Jenkins job that has that tag will have this node available to them. If no node with that tag exists, it will fail.

This is a great way to separate out nodes by capability; so for instance, you could label some nodes as being Redhat, Ubuntu, Beta, and so on.

Finally, we have our launch options. In the case of my slave, I'm using SSH to connect to it using the credentials we created in step 2. Once you have entered your details, click on **Save**.

5. If you now navigate to the node management page, you should find that it now looks something similar to this:

S	Name ↓	Architecture	Clock Difference	Free Disk Space	Free Swap Space	Free Temp Space	Response Time	
	slave1	Linux (amd64)	In sync	25.86 GB	0 B	25.86 GB	2535ms	
	master	Linux (amd64)	In sync	51.87 GB	0 B	51.87 GB	0ms	
	Data obtained	3 min 11 sec	3 min 11 sec	3 min 11 sec	3 min 11 sec	3 min 11 sec	3 min 11 sec	

Refresh status

Your new node is now available for building with.

Remember, your slave node will need the appropriate tools installed for your build; for instance, Git, maven and so on. It's a good practice to automate this using a tool such as Ansible. This makes it quick and easy to spin up new slaves.

See also

For further details on the SSH plugin, you can see the documentation at `https://wiki.jenkins-ci.org/display/JENKINS/SSH+Slaves+plugin`.

Creating your first Jenkins job

The basic building blocks of Jenkins are jobs. A Jenkins job is a series of steps that normally check software out of a repository, run unit tests, and builds the artifact ready for deployment; however, they are versatile and can be used to perform almost any task you can think of.

When we talk of an artifact in this context, we are referring to the deployable object your build job produces. This is commonly an object, such as an executable binary, library, or software package. An artifact is the object you wish to take from your build server, deploy, and execute on your environments to test.

At its core, you add steps to a Job and it can trigger another when it succeeds; generally speaking, these are command-line jobs but as with many Jenkins items, this capability can be extended with the use of Jenkins plugins.

For this example job, I am going to build my blog. This is based on the excellent Hugo static blog engine (`http://gohugo.io`). Hugo allows us to create a relatively straightforward job that will download the code from a Git repository and run a task that will build our end product; we're then going to use Jenkins to archive this ready for distribution.

Getting ready

For this recipe, you will need a Jenkins server. You should also have a blog ready to process within Hugo. You can find an example blog at `https://github.com/spf13/hugo/tree/master/examples/blog`.

How to do it...

The following steps will show you how to install the Hugo blog engine and create a Jenkins job that will fetch an example site and build it:

1. Our first task it to install the Hugo blog engine; you can do this by issuing the following command on either the Jenkins server or Jenkins slave that will run this job:

```
$ wget https://github.com/spf13/hugo/releases/download/v0.14/
hugo_0.14_amd64.deb && dpkg -i hugo_0.14_amd64.deb
```

2. Next, we are going to create a new job. Login to your Jenkins server and click on **New Item** button:

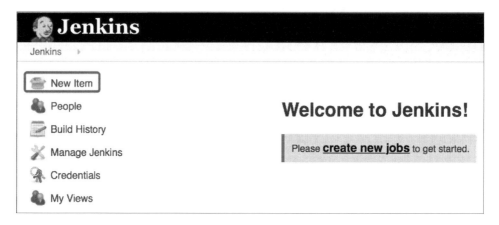

3. In the next window, give your project a descriptive name and select **Freestyle project**.

You can find the differences between the different project types at `https://wiki.jenkins-ci.org/display/JENKINS/Building+a+softwar e+project#Buildingasoftwareproject-Settinguptheproject`.

4. In the next screen, you start to fill in the details that comprise your job. Take a look at the following screenshot:

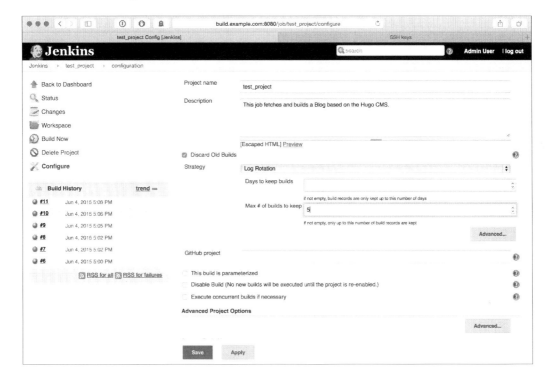

As you can see, I've added a description for the project and also selected the **Discard old builds** option. This is important; if left unconstrained, Jenkins can eat a stupendous amount of disk space. I've left it at five builds but you can also use the number of days instead. As with many Jenkins elements, there are plugins that allow you to tune this in more detail.

5. Next, we define our code repository options. As you can see in the succeeding screenshot, I've used Git to store the code for this particular project:

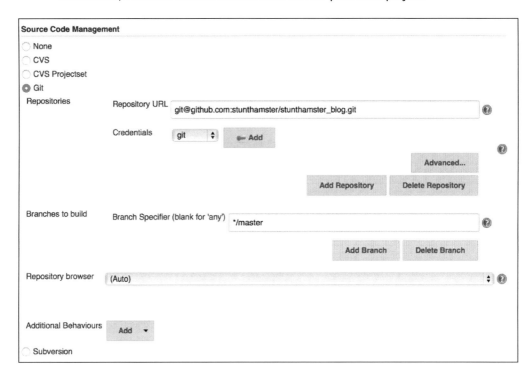

This makes use of the Git credentials that we set up in the earlier recipe. If you choose to use a different type of repository, then amend your configuration to fit it.

6. Now we can configure how Jenkins will schedule the builds. You could leave this as a manual job but that rather flies in the face of a CI server; instead, I have set mine to periodically poll Git; have a look at the following screenshot:

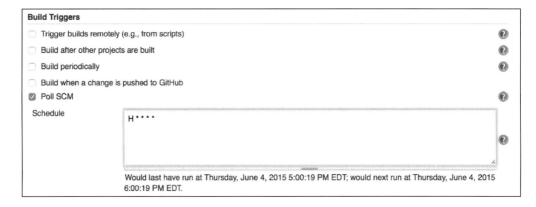

The Poller uses a similar syntax to cron to set out the schedule, with a few notable differences. You can see one of these above; the H denotes a hash, which ensures that the job will run at a randomized time within that period; in this case, my schedule is to run at a random minute, every hour, day, month and year. This helps to keep the load light on the upstream server; perhaps not as important on a scalable public platform such as Github, but very important when you run your own server.

7. Finally, we setup both our build and post-build steps. The build steps are what command you to run once you have cloned your source code; have a look at the following screenshot:

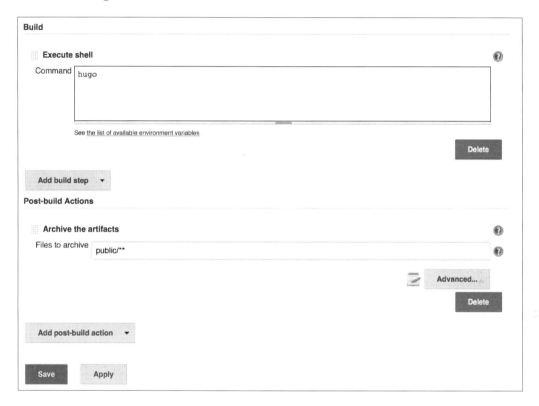

For my job, I am calling the `hugo` command. Hugo is a statically generated CMS. It takes the content, processes it, and creates the HTML, CSS and also the images that make up the site. This has a huge performance boost over CMS systems such as WordPress, as content is not generated on the fly; it also makes it very easy to use with a **Content Distribution Network** (**CDN**).

After we execute our build, we add a post-build action to archive the artifacts. This will produce a zip file containing the selected items from our build. In this case, I'm zipping up the public files that comprise the deployable part of the blog. Each time a build is successful, you will be able to open it in Jenkins and find the artifact available for download from within it.

 Don't forget, you're not limited to one-step for either the build or post-build; you can have as many as you like and they can be ordered using drag and drop.

At this point, hit the save button and we're ready to run our job.

8. Back at the job screen, hit the **Build now button**. This will trigger an immediate build. To the left of the screen, you should see the **Build History**; it looks similar to the following screenshot:

As long as the icon is blue, the build is a success. Clicking on the icon will take you to results of that particular build and its here that you can see the console output from the job, and most importantly, the build artifact. If the icon is red, it means that something didn't quite go right in your build and you need to examine the console output to derive what might have occurred.

See also

You can find detailed documentation around Jenkins jobs at `https://wiki.jenkins-ci.org/display/JENKINS/Building+a+software+project`.

Building Docker containers using Jenkins

One of the important elements of creating an automated build is to ensure that the environment is consistent; unless you ensure consistency, you may find that integration tests pass when they should fail. Docker is perfect for this. By building your environment within a Docker container, you can ensure that your environment is the same from the initial build, right through to the production deployment and you can dispose of this environment after the build.

By utilizing Docker, you are also preparing for continuous deployment. A successful build within a container can be promoted to the next environment without needing to be amended. If it passes that environment, it can be passed onto the next and so on. If you trust your automated testing sufficiently, you can even push your container into service in production.

 You can find more about continuous deployment patterns in the seminal book on the subject, *Continuous Delivery* by *Jez Humble*.

Getting ready

For this recipe, you will need a Jenkins server with Docker installed.

How to do it...

The following steps will show you how to install Docker and use it to create a deployable artifact using Jenkins:

1. Follow the instructions in *Chapter 6, Containerization with Docker* of recipe *Installing Docker*, to install Docker on your Jenkins server.

2. For Jenkins to be able to use the `docker` commands during a build, we need to give the Jenkins user the correct permission. We need to create a `docker` group and add the Jenkins user to it. You can do that by issuing the following command on the Jenkins server:

   ```
   $ usermod -aG docker Jenkins
   ```

   If your Jenkins server is running it will not pick up these changes; restart it with the following command:

   ```
   $ service Jenkins restart
   ```

3. If you want your automated build to be able to be able to publish to the Docker registry, then you need to sign in. Use the following commands to enable your Jenkins user to access your registry:

```
$ sudo su sudo Jenkins
$ docker login
```

Enter your details when prompted; they will then be stored for use within Jenkins.

4. Now that we have finished our setup steps, we are ready to build our container. We are going to take the Hugo blog from the previous recipe and use a Docker container to host the built artifact. We will also add an Nginx HTTP server to serve the blog.

First, we are going to move the contents of our blog into a new folder structure. Open a terminal session in the root of your blog project and issue the following command:

```
$ mkdir -p files/hugo
```

Issue the following command to move your blog content into your new directory structure:

$ mv * files/hugo

5. Next, we are going to create our `Dockerfile`. This `Dockerfile` will install Nginx and add the contents of our Hugo blog into the default location to be served by Nginx. Create a new file called `Dockerfile` in the root of your project and insert the following code:

```
FROM ubuntu:14.04
MAINTAINER <MAINTAINER DETAILS>
RUN apt-get update && apt-get upgrade -y
RUN apt-get install -y nginx
ADD files/hugo/public /usr/share/nginx/html
# Expose ports.
EXPOSE 80
CMD ["nginx", "-g", "daemon off;"]
```

Once you are done editing, save the file and check your project into your Git repository and push to your remote.

6. Now, we can edit our build to create a Docker image. Login to your Jenkins server and locate the job used to build your Hugo blog; click on the configure button.

7. The first item we need to edit is the first build step. Previously, we simply triggered the `hugo` command in the root of the work directory; since we have moved the files into a sub-directory, this will no longer work. Instead, edit it to resemble the following:

The -s switch enables you to give `hugo` a path to its input file and we can then supply the new directory structure.

8. Now, we need to add a new build step. Underneath the first step, click the button marked **Add build step**, and select **Execute Shell** Script as the action. This will add a new textbox underneath the original build step; add the following content:

As you can see, this is using the Docker command to perform the build for us and add the tag of **Latest** to it.

9. Now, we shall add a step to push the built image to the Docker registry. Again, click on the **Add build step** button and select **Execute Shell Script**. This time, add the following command:

10. This final step is optional, but recommended. As with all Docker hosts, repeated builds create containers and these can add up over time. You can alleviate this by deleting old containers and images using the following command:

This will remove all Docker images and containers after each build and will stop your disk space from disappearing into the ether.

This can cause your build to go slower as Docker will be unable to use a build cache; depending on the size of your image, locality of Docker registry, and speed of Internet connection, this may not matter. However, if you want the quickest possible build, omit this step and police your Docker storage using other means.

11. We're now ready to build. Save your job and hit the build button. Once it's complete, examine the build-log by locating and clicking on the last build on the build history panel on the left-hand side. Once you have opened the build, click on the button on the left-hand marked **Console Output**; it should look something like this:

If all goes well when you scroll down, it should look something like this:

```
da7142e65a7c: Buffering to Disk
da7142e65a7c: Image successfully pushed
407d8dcbfcaf: Buffering to Disk
407d8dcbfcaf: Image successfully pushed
d1078fde300d: Buffering to Disk
d1078fde300d: Image successfully pushed
9dab3f34d9be: Buffering to Disk
9dab3f34d9be: Image successfully pushed
cd033ab9d10d: Buffering to Disk
cd033ab9d10d: Image successfully pushed
fa81ed084842: Buffering to Disk
fa81ed084842: Image successfully pushed
e04c66a223c4: Buffering to Disk
e04c66a223c4: Image successfully pushed
7e2c5c55ef2c: Buffering to Disk
7e2c5c55ef2c: Image successfully pushed
e118faab2e16: Buffering to Disk
e118faab2e16: Image successfully pushed
Digest: sha256:2ce464bb252802ebd063ee0ee27fbce6e364f3a8876afef6f4867dc949cd6a20
Finished: SUCCESS
```

Notice the message is telling you **Finshed: SUCCESS**; if it says something differently, then you have a problem; otherwise, you should now have a new Docker image ready to use. You can double check by examining your Docker registry; you should find a new build within it.

Of course, it is understood that this is the tip of the iceberg. Using this recipe as a base, you can easily extend this job to build your software, package it into a Docker image once it has passed its unit tests and then automatically promote the image to an integration environment for testing. Be creative and with a small amount of work, you can save yourself a vast amount of manual testing.

Deploying a Java application to Tomcat with zero downtime using Ansible

Docker is not the only way to perform deployments using Jenkins, and indeed, for many organizations their container efforts are still in the nascent stages. For many, Java and Tomcat are still the mainstay of most platforms and will continue to be so for some considerable time.

Tomcat is now in its eighth version and is still one of the most common Java containers in use, both due to it's Open Source heritage and battle tested stability. Over time, it has also learned some interesting new tricks, with a particularly innovative one being a function called parallel deployment. Parallel deployment allows you to deploy a new version of an application alongside an existing one and Tomcat will then ensure that any existing connections to the application will be satisfied, while new connections will be passed to the new version. From a user perspective, there is no downtime and they simply flip from one version to another the next time they connect to the application.

Using a combination of Ansible, Tomcat, and Parallel deployment, you can promote builds seamlessly, and even better, if you deploy a bad build, you can roll it back relatively easily; all without causing downtime to your platform.

It goes without saying that this is great for your app but you need to design your architecture around this capability. It is no good using parallel deployments, if your app is dependent on a manual database migration or if you have a heavy dependency on state. A state in particular will not be passed from one application to another.

Getting ready

For this recipe, you are going to need a Jenkins server to host the build and a tomcat server to act as the app server plus a repository to hold the example code. Ensure that your Jenkins server also has the Ansible installed; you can see instructions on how to do this in *Chapter 5, Automation with Ansible*, in recipe, *Installing Ansible*.

How to do it...

The following steps will demonstrate how to use Jenkins, Ansible and Tomcat to deploy a very simple test application:

1. To demonstrate how parallel deployment works, we are going to create a very simple web app and package it in a `war` file. Use the following command to create a new directory structure:

    ```
    $ mkdir -p testapp/WEB-INF
    ```

2. Next, edit a new file under `testapp/WEB-INF` called `web.xml` and insert the following content:

    ```
    <web-app></web-app>
    ```

    This is a very simple `web app` configuration file.

    Save this file and create another file called `index.jsp` and insert the following code:

    ```
    <html>
        <head>
          <meta http-equiv="refresh" content="1">
        </head>
        <body>
            <H1>Test App</H1>
            <%= date = new java.util.Date() %>
            <p>Greetings, this is the first version of our test app. The
    time is currently: <%= date %></p>
        </body>
    </html>
    ```

This is a remarkably simple application, whose only role in life is to print out a pithy greeting, the date and time, use the HTML META tag to force the browser to refresh the page; however, it's perfectly suited to demonstrate the power of parallel deployment.

3. Next, we are going to create a new Ansible playbook to perform our deployment. Create a new directory to hold our playbook using the following commands:

```
$ mkdir -p appdeploy/inventory
$ mkdir -p appdeploy/group_vars/appdeploy
```

This creates a basic structure to house our Ansible code, including a place to hold our inventory and variables.

 If you have an existing Ansible setup, you would like to use this code. In this recipe, we are going to add a new playbook and inventory item, both of which can happily live inside an existing project.

4. Next, we're going to create our Ansible inventory and create a new file called `appdeploy/inventory/appinventory` file and insert the following code:

```
[appdeploy]
<< tomcatserver >>
```

Where `<< tomcatserver >>` is the name/ip address of your tomcat server.

5. Now that we have our inventory, we are ready to create our playbook. Create a new file called `appdeploy.yml` under the `appdeploy` folder and insert the following content:

```
- hosts: appdeploy
  gather_facts: false
  sudo: true
  tasks:
    - name: Deploy App
      copy: src=/var/lib/jenkins/jobs/workspace/tomcat_test /
testapp.war dest="/usr/local/apache-tomcat-8.0.23/webapps/
testapp##{{ buildnum }}.war" owner=tomcat group=tomcat
```

This is a simple playbook. First, we declare that this will only run against the servers that are tagged as `appdeploy` hosts. We are also declaring that this playbook does not need to gather facts. Not gathering facts can be a good way to speed up a playbook and is an excellent practice when you know that your Ansible code does not make use of them, as it skips a relatively expensive fact of gathering task. As usual, this is a trivial time saver against one host but when you scale out to hundreds of hosts, it can make a difference.

> You may need to amend the paths in the preceding example, especially if you are using a slightly different version of Tomcat

Next, we declare the tasks that we are going to carry out. In our case, we are only performing a single task, copying a war file to the remote host. Notice the `{{ buildnum }}` variable; this is going to be our link between Ansible and Jenkins and it will be explained later in the recipe.

6. In the `appdeploy/group_vars/appdeploy` directory, create a new file called `main.yml` and insert the following code:

    ```
    # Intentionally left blank
    ```

    This is a simple kludge to ensure that the directory is added if you are using a Git repository. We are going to fill the content of this file by dynamically using Jenkins but Git has a nasty habit of not adding empty directory structures. This ensures that it will be included when we check it in and push it to our remote.

> A `.gitignore` file also suffices well for this purpose.

Once you have finished editing your files, create, check in, and push your code to your repository.

7. Now, we can create our new Jenkins job. Log on to your Jenkins server and create a new item called `tomcat_test` and ensure that it's set as a freestyle project. Once created, we can set the basic job options. We want to ensure that our job doesn't fill the disk of our Jenkins server, which is a real and immediate issue with builds that can generate large artifacts; ensure that your build matches the options listed in the following screenshot:

As you can see, I'm limiting the job to only keeping 10 builds at a time; you should edit this to suit your particular needs.

8. Next, we're going to configure our source code repository options. These will be different depending on your Git hosting options and repository name; you can use the following screenshot as a guide to configure your repository options:

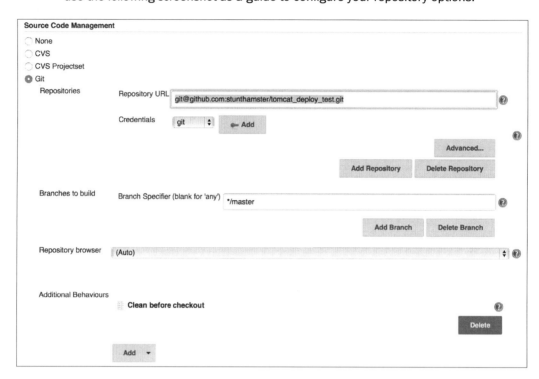

Now we can set our build triggers. Since we are creating a CI process, we should poll our code repository regularly to look for changes, the idea being, that when a developer checks in code, it is immediately picked up and a build is attempted. Have a look at the following screenshot:

As you can see, I'm polling the SCM (Source Control Manager) every minute. You can amend this to fit the capabilities/spec of your repository, especially if you have many builds. Having a periodic polling can completely crush an SCM with a lowly spec, so be cautious with this option and be ready to scale when your job list gets relatively big.

> As with all things Jenkins, there are many plugins that allow you to control the polling behavior; it is worth browsing the plugin directory to see if it can help on this front. Alternatively, you may find that your SCM supports hooks that allow you to push build events rather than polling for them. This is ideal as the SCM is only being called when there is actually something to do, rather than being battered with needless traffic.

9. Now we have our schedule in place, it's time to get on and construct our build steps. First, we're going to use the jar command to create our Java archive. Add a new execute shell build step and ensure that it has the following command:

    ```
    mv chapter7/testapp/* . && jar cf testapp.war WEB-INF/index.jsp
    ```

    This is a simple command that takes the checked out code and moves it into the working directory and uses the jar command to create the archive.

10. Next, we need to create the variable that will inform Ansible, which builds the application we are pushing. Create a new execute shell build step and add the following content:

    ```
    echo "buildnum: $BUILD_NUMBER" > chapter7/appdeploy/group_vars/
    appdeploy/main.yml
    ```

11. This command makes use of one of the environment variables that Jenkins sets as part of its build. These environment variables are astonishingly powerful, as they allow you to act on the output of your build.

> You can find the list of available variables at your Jenkins server at the `/env-vars.html/` URL; you can also act on other environment variables that you set yourself.

12. Finally, we can trigger our Ansible build. Add another execute shell build step and add the following command:

    ```
    ansible-playbook -i chapter7/appdeploy/inventory/appinventory
    chapter7/appdeploy/appdeploy.yml
    ```

    This invokes Ansible to use your inventory and playbook.

If all goes well, your build steps should resemble the following screenshot:

Once you are happy that your job looks correct, save it and return to the main Jenkins screen.

13. Before we can run our project, we need to make some changes to our servers. As our Ansible code is being run as the Jenkins user we need to ensure that it has access to the target server and it has a `sudo` access on each server. If you are using Ansible to control the tomcat servers, then you can add a Jenkins user and key via Ansible; see *Chapter 5, Automation with Ansible*, for an example. You will also need to add `sudo` access; this can be done by adding the following task into the Role that manages your user:

```
- name: Add Jenkins Sudo access

  lineinfile: dest=/etc/sudoers state=present line='jenkins
ALL=(ALL) NOPASSWD:ALL' validate='visudo -cf %s'
```

This code uses the Ansible `lineinfile` module to insert a new rule into the `sudoers` file; it will also use the `visudo` command to double check that the new rule is valid.

Regardless of how you achieve it, ensure that your Jenkins user has both access to your target servers and a `sudo` access.

It is understood, that when using Jenkins in this manner it's vitally important to ensure that the Jenkins server is secure, especially if you use this technique in production deployments. I tend to air gap the development and production servers in this scenario and ensure that the production Jenkins is heavily monitored and locked down.

14. We're now ready to run our Jenkins build. Hit the Build now button and wait a few seconds. If all goes well, you should have a successful build and console output that resembles the following:

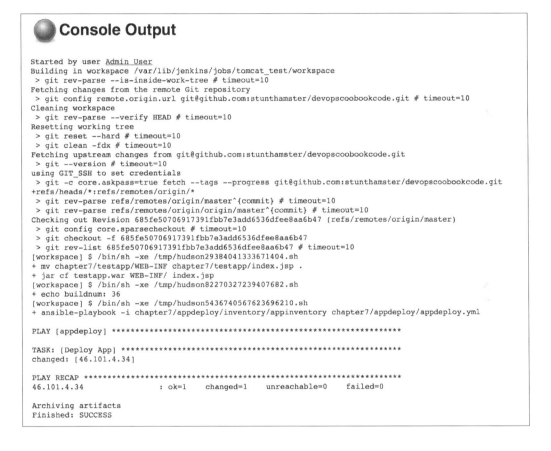

Console Output

```
Started by user Admin User
Building in workspace /var/lib/jenkins/jobs/tomcat_test/workspace
 > git rev-parse --is-inside-work-tree # timeout=10
Fetching changes from the remote Git repository
 > git config remote.origin.url git@github.com:stunthamster/devopscoobookcode.git # timeout=10
Cleaning workspace
 > git rev-parse --verify HEAD # timeout=10
Resetting working tree
 > git reset --hard # timeout=10
 > git clean -fdx # timeout=10
Fetching upstream changes from git@github.com:stunthamster/devopscoobookcode.git
 > git --version # timeout=10
using GIT_SSH to set credentials
 > git -c core.askpass=true fetch --tags --progress git@github.com:stunthamster/devopscoobookcode.git
+refs/heads/*:refs/remotes/origin/*
 > git rev-parse refs/remotes/origin/master^{commit} # timeout=10
 > git rev-parse refs/remotes/origin/origin/master^{commit} # timeout=10
Checking out Revision 685fe50706917391fbb7e3add6536dfee8aa6b47 (refs/remotes/origin/master)
 > git config core.sparsecheckout # timeout=10
 > git checkout -f 685fe50706917391fbb7e3add6536dfee8aa6b47
 > git rev-list 685fe50706917391fbb7e3add6536dfee8aa6b47 # timeout=10
[workspace] $ /bin/sh -xe /tmp/hudson29384041333671404.sh
+ mv chapter7/testapp/WEB-INF chapter7/testapp/index.jsp .
+ jar cf testapp.war WEB-INF/ index.jsp
[workspace] $ /bin/sh -xe /tmp/hudson82270327239407682.sh
+ echo buildnum: 36
[workspace] $ /bin/sh -xe /tmp/hudson5436740567623696210.sh
+ ansible-playbook -i chapter7/appdeploy/inventory/appinventory chapter7/appdeploy/appdeploy.yml


PLAY [appdeploy] ***************************************************

TASK: [Deploy App] ***********************************************
changed: [46.101.4.34]

PLAY RECAP ********************************************************
46.101.4.34                 : ok=1    changed=1    unreachable=0    failed=0

Archiving artifacts
Finished: SUCCESS
```

Open your browser, and point it at your test application. You should see something similar to the following screenshot:

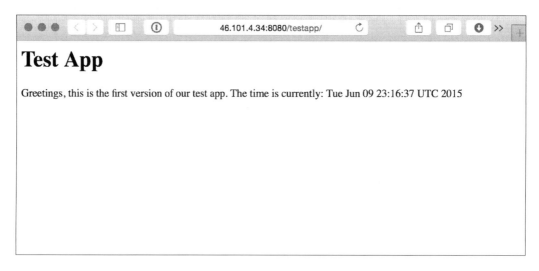

If you see this, then excellent; your automated build has succeeded in taking a code from a developer and deploying it to a target machine without any manual interactions.

15. Now that we have deployed the first version of our code, it's time to make an amendment and deploy the second version. Keep your browser window open in the background and open up the code in `testapp/index.jsp` and edit it to resemble the following code example:

```
<html>
    <head>
      <meta http-equiv="refresh" content="1">
    </head>
    <body>
        <H2>Test App</H2>
        <%= date = new java.util.Date() %>
        <strong>Greetings, this is the second version of our test
app.</strong>
<p>The time is currently: <%= date %></p>
    </body>
</html>
```

As you can see, this a slight tweak to our original code. Adding the maximum amount of style that a DevOps engineer generally decorates their apps with. Once you have made the tweak, save the code and check-in to your repository and push to your remote.

16. In addition to your existing browser window, open a new session and point it at `server>:8080/testapp`. You should see the new content showing, with the original content in your original browser window. Here's a general idea of what you should see:

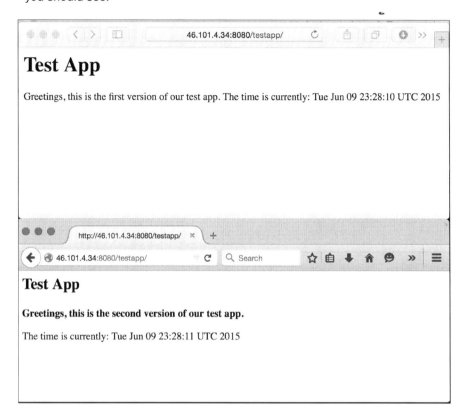

As you can see, two versions of the same app are running at the same time and will continue to do so as long as we have our browser window open with the old application. As soon as we close the window with the old application, it will be unloaded and will not be used again.

It's worth going over the details of what this recipe is doing. At its most basic form, this recipe is using Jenkins to construct an artifact and packaging it into a WAR file. Once this file is created, we use Ansible to transfer the built file to our targeted tomcat server, into the webapps directory. The important detail is that it appends the build number onto the WAR file, prepended with ## before the file extension.

When Tomcat sees a WAR file with ## in front of its file extension, it works on the assumption that this is a versioned application and as with any app, it will attempt to explode and automatically deploy the code. When a newer version of the app is placed into the web apps directory, it explodes and deploys this as well, but it ensures that the existing app is also ran alongside it until all user sessions are expired. This is incredibly powerful and allows for true zero-downtime deployment using Tomcat; however, there are several issues:

- ► Old applications are not removed and will stay on the server until you house keep them
- ► When running two apps side by side, you need to ensure that you have enough memory to service both, even if it's only for a short time.
- ► This only works with numeric build numbers; any other characters are not supported.
- ► As noted in the stat of this recipe, your app needs to be able to cope with an in service upgrade.

See also

You can find more details around parallel deployment at `https://tomcat.apache.org/tomcat-7.0-doc/config/context.html#Parallel_deployment`.

8
Metric Collection with InfluxDB

In this chapter, we are going to cover the following topics:

- ► Installing InfluxDB
- ► Creating a new InfluxDB database
- ► Logging events with the InfluxDB REST API
- ► Gathering host statistics with Telegraf
- ► Exploring data with the InfluxDB data explorer
- ► Installing Grafana
- ► Creating dashboards with Grafana

Introduction

The importance of monitoring cannot be overstated and it is seen as one of the core elements of a DevOps approach to a system. Monitoring takes many shapes; however, it's common to stop once you've added state monitoring, such as *Is the database up?* or *Is the site responding?*. These are indeed critical things to monitor, but they don't cover important questions such as *How fast am I responding to requests?* And *How many things have I done?*. This is where a time series database can be a valuable addition to the monitoring and information stack that you have to hand not handle.

A time series database is a storage technique that is designed to be fast at both storing and retrieving points of data. For instance, you can measure CPU usage in percentiles from one second to the next or alternatively measure the number of times a particular service call has been made. Once you have a different series, you can start to use this data for correlation. In the above example, we can overlay the CPU statistics across the service call information and start noting where the CPU spikes correlate with the service calls. This starts to form the basis for an **Application Performance Monitoring** (**APM**) solution; thus, allowing you to drill into the detail of where your platform is spending time and where improvements can be made.

A time series databases are becoming increasingly popular as people are realizing the value of the data their platform produces, and there are several dedicated open source TSD providers (such as InfluxDB and Whisper), and the industry heavy-weights, such as Microsoft and Oracle, are also enhancing their time series offerings.

For this chapter, we are going to use InfluxDB. InfluxDB is relatively a newcomer but it has many interesting features. That being said, it has yet to hit a 1.0 release and is a rapidly evolving, product especially with items such as clustering. However, InfluxDB is fast, easy to use, and extremely easy to deploy, and is being used by an increasing set of companies as their preferred time series database.

Installing InfluxDB

Installing InfluxDB is straightforward and it has no external dependencies; it also has packages for many operating systems. This recipe will show you how to install InfluxDB on an Ubuntu 14.04 server. The following steps are manual; however, you should consider automation using a tool such as Ansible (if you decide to use InfluxDB in production). You can find details of Ansible in *Chapter 5*, *Automation with Ansible*.

Getting ready

For this recipe, you need an Ubuntu 14.04 server.

How to do it...

The following steps will show you how to download, install, and configure InfluxDB:

1. On your server, issue the following commands:

    ```
    $ wget http://influxdb.s3.amazonaws.com/influxdb_0.9.3_amd64.deb
    $ sudo dpkg -i influxdb_0.9.3_amd64.deb
    ```

    This will fetch the InfluxDB package and install it.

2. Next, we can configure our InfluxDB server. You can find a ready-made configuration file in `/etc/opt/influxdb/influxdb.conf`, which is already populated with default `InfluxDB` values.

   There are a few configuration options that you should set specifically; first, locate the following entry in the configuration file:

   ```
   [data]
       dir = "/root/.influxdb/data"
   ```

   This should be amended to reflect your preferred storage location.

> It goes without saying, that you should aim to make your storage location both large and high-performance. Wherever possible, aim to use SSD storage. Time series data can lead to a staggering amount of IO, so always plan for your future requirements where possible.

3. You should also find the following configuration item:

   ```
   [meta]
       dir = "/root/.influxdb/meta"
       hostname = "localhost"
   ```

4. Change the value for the host name to reflect the host name of this particular node. Once you have made your changes, save the file and start InfluxDB using the following command:

   ```
   $ sudo /etc/init.d/influxdb start
   ```

5. You can test your new installation by issuing the following command:

   ```
   $ /opt/influxdb/influx -version
   ```

6. This should return a response similar to this:

   ```
   InfluxDB shell 0.9.4
   ```

7. You should be able to access the built-in graphical user-interface by opening the following URL in your browser:

   ```
   http://localhost:8083
   ```

This will give you a page similar to the following screenshot:

You will be ready to start with your InfluxDB instance one you see this screenshot.

See also

You can find the InfluxDB installation document at `https://influxdb.com/docs/v0.9/introduction/installation.html`.

Creating a new InfluxDB database

This recipe outlines how to create a new database in InfluxDB using the in-built GUI that is shipped as a part of the installation. This will create a new and empty database ready for data.

Getting ready

For this recipe, you need an Ubuntu 14.04 server with InfluxDB installed.

How to do it...

Let's create a new database in InfluxDB using the GUI:

1. Open the GUI in your browser by opening the following URL: `http://localhost:8083`.

2. You should be presented with a blank query field. At this point, you can either enter the query manually or select the **Query Templates** button on the bottom right-hand side. If you do so, you can select the option entitled **Create Database**. This will fill out the query for you as follows:

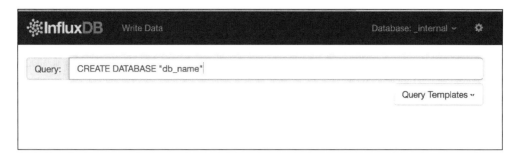

3. To create your new database, simply give it a name (one word and no special characters) and hit `return`. If all goes well, you should see a message telling you that the database was successfully created. You can then use the query **SHOW DATABASES** in the query field to list your current database. It should look something like this:

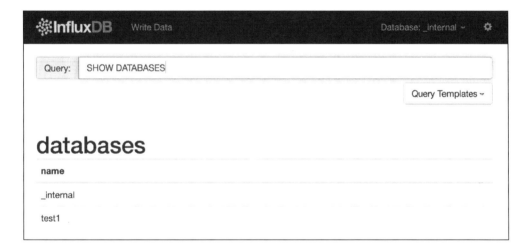

4. We can test that our database is ready for use by entering some data. To manually enter a new piece of data, click on the **Write data** link. This will create a new pop-up window that allows you to write a new piece of data in InfluxDB line protocol. Insert the following code to create an example data:

```
numOrders,site="www.testsite.com",currency="GBP" value=15.50
```

> You can find more details of the InfluxDB line protocol at `https://influxdb.com/docs/v0.9/write_protocols/line.html`.

If all goes well, you will see a success message; your new database is now ready for data.

See also

You can see the official InfluxDB instructions at `https://influxdb.com/docs/v0.9/introduction/getting_started.html`.

Logging events with the InfluxDB REST API

InfluxDB can be used to log events and other statistics. An event can be anything from a user clicking on a button on your website to performing deployments. The latter is especially useful, as it means that you can have a single place to log any event that might occur on the platform.

This recipe will show you how to enter data using the REST API provided with InfluxDB. It allows you to create your own applications to enter extremely useful data. By leveraging the REST API, you will be able to use a wide spectrum of existing tools to enter data from Jenkins jobs to Ansible and beyond.

Getting ready

For this recipe, you need an InfluxDB instance.

How to do it...

The following steps will show you how to create a new InfluxDB database and populate it using the REST API:

1. First, we need to create a database in which we can log our events. We can use the REST API rather than using the GUI and you an use the following command to do this:

   ```
   $ curl -G http://localhost:8086/query --data-urlencode "q=CREATE
   DATABASE events"
   ```

   You should receive a JSON response that is similar to the following:

   ```
   {"results":[{}]}
   ```

   Although it's slightly abstract, this empty response indicates that the command was successful.

2. Now, we can add data to our new database. Let's start with a deployment and use the following `curl` command to input the data:

   ```
   $ curl -i -XPOST 'http://localhost:8086/write?db=events' --data-
   binary 'deployment, deployer=mduffy,app=test_app,version="1.1",env
   ironment="test" value="sucess"'
   ```

3. Let's take a look at this command. First, we have the details of the InfluxDB server we want to connect to; in this case, I've chosen to connect to my local instance on port `8086`. Next, let's decide on the action we wish to take and the database we wish to take it on; in this case, we wish to write a value and target the events db.

4. We move to the contents once we have set the target. First, we need to give the measurement a name; in this case, deployment. We then give this measurement a set of fields and values; in this case, the `deployer`, app, version, and environment. Finally, we give the measurement a value; in this case, success. This will create a new data point that we can query.

5. Now, since we have inserted a value, we can query it. Use the following command to do the same:

```
$ curl -G 'http://localhost:8086/query?pretty=true' --data-urlencode "db=events" --data-urlencode "q=SELECT * FROM deployment WHERE deployer='mduffy'"
```

6. This should produce a JSON response that looks something like this:

```
{
    "results": [
        {
            "series": [
                {
                    "name": "deployment",
                    "columns": [
                        "time",
                        "app",
                        "deployer",
                        "environment",
                        "value",
                        "version"
                    ],
                    "values": [
                        [
                            "2015-09-
                             16T21:17:54.799294876Z",
                            "test_app",
                            "mduffy",
                            "\"test\"",
                            "success",
                            "\"1.1\""
                        ]
                    ]
                }
            ]
        }
    ]
}
```

As you can see, we can use InfluxDB to track more than just measurements, and its simple API makes it very easy to integrate into other tools. By extending this into your tool set, you can quickly build up an easy-to-query and simple-to-graph time line of events; ranging from alerts to deployments and errors. Use your imagination and you will be able to build a wealth of data very simply.

See also

You can find more details of the InfluxDB REST API at `https://influxdb.com/docs/v0.9/guides/index.html`.

Gathering host statistics with Telegraf

One of the most useful examples of a time series database is to contain statistical information, and this is especially relevant and useful when it comes to tracking host performance. Due to the type of data, server resource monitoring can collect a great deal of measurements very quickly across a wide range of data points. Using the InfluxDB Telegraf tool, this can be done in a relatively straightforward manner and the data can be easily queried using InfluxDB's powerful set of query tools.

Getting ready

For this recipe, you need a server with InfluxDB installed and configured, and an Ubuntu 14.04 server to install `telegraf` onto.

How to do it...

The following steps will show you how to both install the tools and configure the Telegraf agent onto an Ubuntu host. Once this is done, we will look at how to configure it to log to an InfluxDB server:

1. Use the following command to fetch the `telegraf` package:

   ```
   $ wget http://get.influxdb.org/telegraf/telegraf_0.1.8_amd64.deb
   ```

2. Now, install the package using the following command:

   ```
   $ sudo dpkg -i telegraf_0.1.8_amd64.deb
   ```

3. Before we can start to send data to InfluxDB, we need to create a database for it to log information to. Use the following command to create a new database:

   ```
   $ curl -G http://localhost:8086/query --data-urlencode "q=CREATE DATABASE telegraf"
   ```

4. Next, we need to configure `telegraf` to log data on to the selected InfluxDB instance. On the host you have installed `telegraf`, to edit `/etc/opt/telegraf/telegraf.conf` and look for the following configuration item:

```
[outputs.influxdb]
    url = "http://localhost:8086"
database = "telegraf"
```

5. Edit the values to match your setup and ensure that the database matches the one that you created in step three.

6. Start the `telegraf` service using the following command:

```
$ sudo service telegraf start
```

At this point, Telegraf should start logging data into your InfluxDB.

7. You can select some sample data using the following command:

```
$ curl -G 'http://localhost:8086/query?pretty=true' --data-urlencode "db=telegraf" --data-urlencode "q=SELECT * FROM io_write_bytes WHERE host='<<INFLUXHOST>>'"
```

8. Where `<<INFLUXHOST>>` is the same as your InfluxDB host. This will select the number of bytes written to the disks on the host and should produce an output similar to the following:

```
{
    "results": [
        {
            "series": [
                {
                    "name": "io_write_bytes",
                    "columns": [
                        "time",
                        "host",
                        "name",
                        "value"
                    ],
                    "values": [
                        [
                            "2015-09-16T21:25:54Z",
                            "influxdb1",
                            "vda1",
                            1259130880
                        ],
                    ]
                }
            ]
        }
    ]
}
```

You can easily use this data to create real time charts of important metrics with the help of a tool such as Grafana. You can also use a tool such as Sensu to alert you about certain thresholds.

See also

You can find more information about Telegraf at `https://github.com/influxdb/telegraf`.

Exploring data with the InfluxDB data explorer

InfluxDB comes with a ready-to-use GUI to query your data; this makes exploring your data quick and easy. Although it's not a comprehensive tool and lacks niceties such as exporting, reporting, and so on, the built-in data explorer is great to get a feel for your time series data. Using this, you can easily pull certain data out of your InfluxDB database and use it to test queries for use in other tools.

Getting ready

For this recipe, you will need an InfluxDB server installed and configured and a data set to query.

How to do it...

Let's explore the data using the InfluxDB data explorer:

1. Log on to the **InfluxDB** server using a browser to visit the following URL:

    `http://<INFLUXDBSERVER>:8083`

    You should see a screen similar to the following:

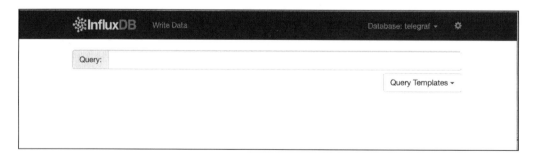

This panel allows you to run ad-hoc queries against your data sources. Select your database by clicking on the **Database telegraf** list on the top right menu and pick a database that has data to query.

> For those of you who already have SQL experience, the following recipe will seem familiar; this is because the InfluxDB query language has been designed to be as SQL like as possible; however, it's worth checking the manual to understand the nuances of the query language. You can find a useful comparison at `https://influxdb.com/docs/v0.9/concepts/crosswalk.html`.

2. The first query we can execute is the one that allows us to see the measurements that are available to use. In the query panel, enter the following code:

```
SHOW MEASUREMENTS
```

This should return a list of all the measures in the selected database and should look something like this:

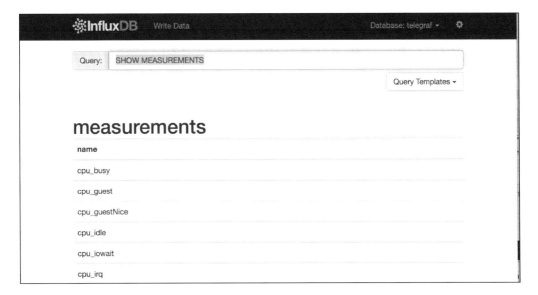

Using this query, we can list the measurements currently available in the database.

> This and several other simple queries are available from the query template drop-down menu located underneath the query panel. The query template menu is a fantastic way of exploring some common InfluxDB queries.

3. Next, we can start querying to our data. From the data I have, I'm interested in the contents of the `cpu_busy` data set. The `cpu_busy` data is made up of several measures and I'm particularly interested in the statistics of the first CPU (cpu0). Now, we can use the following queries:

```
SELECT * FROM cpu_busy WHERE cpu = 'cpu0'
```

This command will return the following output:

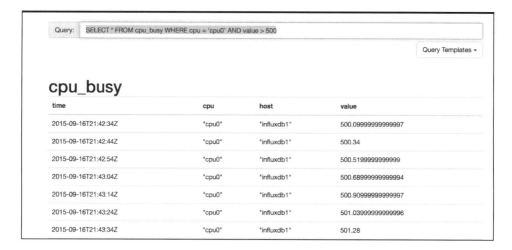

4. Next, we can start to whittle down the data by adding conditions. In this case, we'll be looking into the CPU values higher that 500 (in this case, 500mhz). We can do this using the following query:

```
SELECT * FROM cpu_busy WHERE cpu = 'cpu0' AND value > 500
```

This command will return the following output:

Query:	SELECT * FROM cpu_busy WHERE cpu = 'cpu0' AND value > 500		

Query Templates ▾

cpu_busy

time	cpu	host	value
2015-09-16T21:42:34Z	"cpu0"	"influxdb1"	500.09999999999997
2015-09-16T21:42:44Z	"cpu0"	"influxdb1"	500.34
2015-09-16T21:42:54Z	"cpu0"	"influxdb1"	500.5199999999999
2015-09-16T21:43:04Z	"cpu0"	"influxdb1"	500.68999999999994
2015-09-16T21:43:14Z	"cpu0"	"influxdb1"	500.90999999999997
2015-09-16T21:43:24Z	"cpu0"	"influxdb1"	501.03999999999996
2015-09-16T21:43:34Z	"cpu0"	"influxdb1"	501.28

5. Now I want to look at this data on a host-by-host basis; we can do this using the GROUP BY statement by extending our query to look like this:

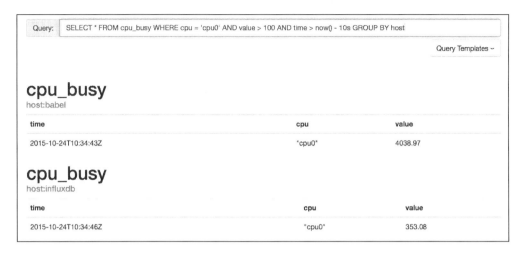

As you can see, the results are now returned grouped by the host. Note that I'm also adding an additional parameter limiting the query by time. I'm asking for any data less than ten seconds from the system timestamp.

 You can find more details about using the query language, including **Time Ranges**, at https://influxdb.com/docs/v0.9/query_ language/query_syntax.html.

See also

You can find more details of the data explorer at https://influxdb.com/docs/v0.9/ query_language/data_exploration.html.

Installing Grafana

Gathering data is a relatively useless task without an accessible method for both accessing and displaying it. This is especially true of time series data, which can produce a huge mass of information made of many small points of data. Without a tool that allows you to easily spot trends, the noise can easily become overwhelming; thus rendering your carefully gathered data useless.

InfluxDB can make use of an open source visualization tool called **Grafana**. Grafana is a sleek and stylish tool that allows you to take time series data and display it in many different fashions, including good-looking graphs. These can be combined into dashboards, which are perfect to display on TV's.

This recipe will show you how to install Grafana.

Getting ready...

For this recipe, you will need an InfluxDB data source with some data to query, and a server to host Grafana.

How to do it...

1. We start by fetching the latest `grafana` release using the following command:

    ```
    $ wget https://grafanarel.s3.amazonaws.com/builds/grafana_2.1.3_
    amd64.deb
    ```

2. Next, use the following command to install the Grafana pre-requisites:

    ```
    $ sudo apt-get install -y adduser libfontconfig
    ```

3. Now, we can install the `grafana` package using the following command:

    ```
    $ sudo dpkg -i grafana_2.1.3_amd64.deb
    ```

4. Now that `grafana` is installed, you can start it using the following command:

    ```
    $ sudo service grafana-server start
    ```

5. You should now be able to connect to Grafana by going to the following URL:

    ```
    http://<GRAFANA SERVER>:3000
    ```

    Here, `<GRAFANA SERVER>` is the name or IP address of your Grafana instance. You should be able to see a page similar to the following:

6. You can log in to the panel with the following user details:

   ❑ **User**: admin

   ❑ **Password**: admin

   When logged in, you should be greeted with a page similar to the following:

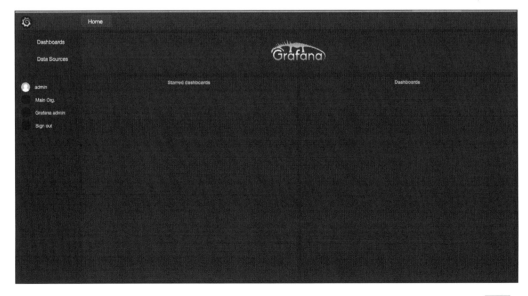

This is the default view of Grafana. When you create dashboards, you can see them listed on the pane on the far right, and you can add your favorites to the pane on the left for easy access.

7. Next, click on the **Data source** button, as shown in the following screenshot:

This will take you to a page that lists your configured data sources; this will currently be blank. On the top menu there is a button entitled **Add New**. Click on this and it will take you through to a panel that allows you to add a new source. This requires the details of your InfluxDB and when filled in, it should resemble the following screenshot:

There are a few points to note. First, you can make this your default data source, to make the creation of new views on the data easier. Secondly, you can choose between several different types of data sources; this includes different versions of InfluxDB, so ensure that you choose correctly.

Once you are happy with your details, click on the **Save** button; you can also use the **Test Connection** button to test if Grafana can connect. Click on **OK** before saving.

See also

You can find further details about Grafana at `http://docs.grafana.org`.

Creating dashboards with Grafana

Once you have installed Grafana, you will have the ability to create attractive and informative dashboards that are ideal for display on devices such as projectors or TVs. The dashboards can display information from several different data sources, allowing you, for example, to display combined CPU statistics from a cluster of servers, alongside the number of orders taken in the same time period and the HTTP return codes. Grafana can hold any number of dashboards and makes it easy to embed links within dashboards to other dashboards. So, feel free to make specific dashboards for your data and they should remain easy to access.

Getting ready

For this recipe, you need to have a server with InfluxDB and Grafana installed.

How to do it...

Let's create a dashboard with Grafana:

1. Log into the `grafana` panel. In the top menu, click on the menu item titled **Home**. Click on the option marked as **New dashboard** that you see at the bottom of the drop-down menu.

2. Next, you will see a screen that looks similar to the following screenshot:

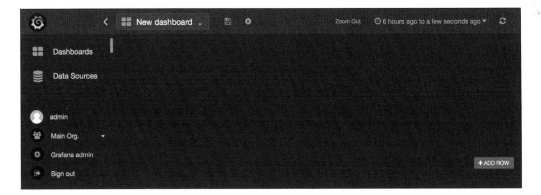

3. This is a blank dashboard that is ready for new content to be added. Observe the green strip to the right of the **Dashboards** menu items; this is a menu. When you click on it you will be presented with the following options:

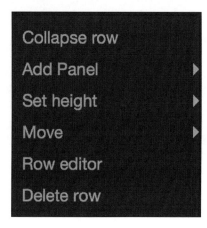

This menu allows you to edit your panel options. Let's start by clicking on the **Add Panel** link. This will open another menu listing the available options, which are as follows:

- **Graph:** This is a line graph of a selected data series
- **Single Stat**: This is a singular number derived from a selected series
- **Text**: This is a free text field that allows you to enter your own text
- **Dashboard list**: This allows you to construct links to further dashboards

4. Let's start by adding a new **Graph**. Click on the **Add panel** option and select **Graph**. This should add a new graph that looks like this screen shot:

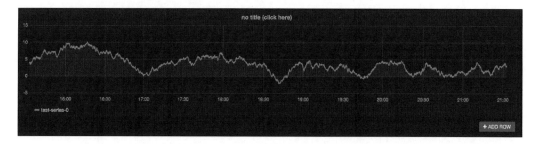

This is a default graph based on example data; let's change that to real data. Click on the graph title and click on the edit option. This will create a new window underneath the graph that looks like the following screenshot:

5. This panel allows you to edit your new graph. Note the option at the bottom:

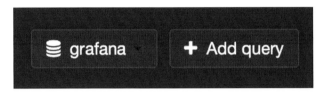

6. This allows you to set your data source. Click on the button titled **grafana** and select your data source. For these examples, I'm using the information derived from Telegraf. When you select your data source you are offered the option to select a query, as shown:

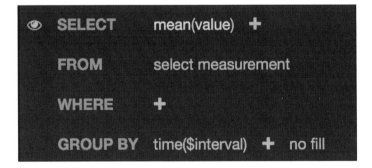

    The FROM entry will allow you to select any measurement from your data source. Go ahead and select both your measurements and, if needed, a query to whittle the data down into the selection you want.

     By clicking on the + icon next to the WHERE clause, you will be taken into the interactive query builder; this will help you define queries to narrow down the data.

7. Once you are happy with your graph, click on **Back to Dashboard**.

8. Now that we have our first graph, we can add another item. Click on the button entitled **ADD ROW** in the pop-up menu and select **Text**. This will add a new blank text box to the dashboard. Click on the title of the text box and you will be offered a menu; click on the **Edit text** button. This will open a new panel that allows you to add a text suh as the following example:

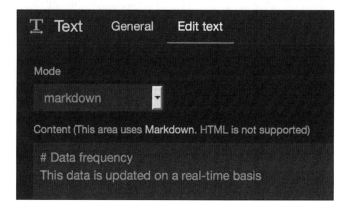

Once you've added your text, click on **Back to Dashboard**.

9. Click on the green bar next to your new text panel and select **Add panel**. This will create a new panel next to your text panel. In this case, select **Single stat**. Once again, this will be a panel with example text. Click on the title and it should present a new panel; this is the same as the graphing panel and allows you to create a new query to select your data. Once you've selected your data, go back to the dashboard. Your dashboard should look similar to this:

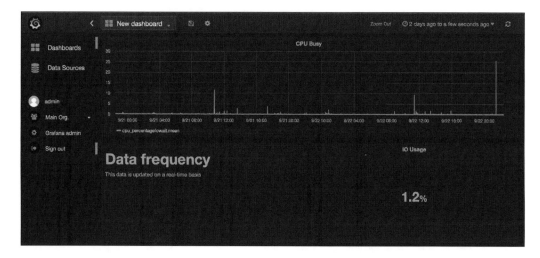

Although basic, this dashboard is a great start. You can continue to add panels, but keep in mind that it needs to fit whichever device you are using to display it (TV, monitor, and so on). If you need to add a lot of data, the best approach is to create links that allow you to drill down into more detailed dashboards.

See also

You can find further information about dash boarding at `http://docs.grafana.org/reference/graph/`.

9
Log Management

In this chapter, we are going to cover the following subjects:

- ▶ Centralizing logs with syslog
- ▶ Using syslog templates
- ▶ Managing log rotation with the Logrotate utility
- ▶ Installing Elasticsearch, Logstash, and Kibana
- ▶ Importing logs into Elasticsearch with Logstash
- ▶ Using Kibana queries to explore data
- ▶ Using Kibana queries to examine data

Introduction

Log management is one of the most essential roles that systems administrators have been performing since the term came into being, and it's a crucial part of running any system. Without log management the logs will overflow, disks will fill up, and eventually data will be lost.

Until recently, the true value of logs has been understated by many systems administrators. Generally looked upon as a troubleshooting mechanism, logs had been consigned to being looked at only as a last resort and had been left to gather digital dust on a shelf somewhere. However, recently, there has been a renaissance in how logs are perceived, with developers and operators alike considering the humble log file more in the perspective of an event stream; that is, a continuous stream of information that not only indicates if you have issues, but can also be used to check for underlying patterns that can highlight significant state changes.

A good example of this can be found in the HTTP server access logs. These tend to contain not only issues (404, 500, and so on) but also successful transactions. This data is generally enriched to contain additional data, such as a client IP, pages access, response time, and so on. This additional metadata can then be further added to; for instance, using the originating IP to derive geographical location, which can give you a real-time view on business processes.

Event stream analysis is becoming a very large element of successful and scalable infrastructure, and many of the pioneers in the industry are embracing it to underpin items such as automated security scanning, platform scaling, and so on.

The recipes in this chapter will introduce you to several valuable tools for the management of logs, running the whole gamut of log management tasks, from centralization to rotation and finally into analysis. Armed with these recipes you should be ready to capture and explore many facets of data that your platform gathers in the course of the day and use them to scale, secure, and improve your platform.

Centralizing logs with Syslog

Generally speaking, most applications will have a logging facility that will produce text logs that can be written into an arbitrary location on a storage device (normally, defaulting to a local disk partition). Although this is an essential first step, it also produces problems; you need to provide adequate storage for logs and you need to put in place rotation to stop them from growing too large. If they contain vital information, you need to ensure that they are rotated to a safe location, but you may also need to ensure that they remain secure if they contain sensitive information, such as credit card numbers. On top of all of this, you will lose the current logs if you have a disaster on that node.

A good solution to manage these issues is to use a central location to store logs. This allows you to provide appropriate storage and gives you a central place to back up, secure, and examine logs. As long as the logging mechanism that your application uses supports syslog, it is straightforward. Syslog was originally used as the logging mechanism for the venerable Send mail MTA and was developed in the early 80s. Since then, it has been standardized and is now in use as the standard logging mechanism for most *nix based operating systems, with many implementations of the standard available.

Getting ready

For this recipe, you will need two Ubuntu 14.04 hosts; one to act as the Syslog server and another to act as a sending host.

How to do it...

This recipe will show you how to set up a server to act as a central Syslog server and how to configure a client log to utilize it. This will use the default syslog implementation on Ubuntu 14.04, Rsyslog:

1. Rsyslog is the default `syslog` package for Ubuntu 14.04 and should be pre-installed; you can double check this by issuing the following command:

   ```
   $ sudo apt-get install rsyslog
   ```

   This should return a message that states that `rsyslog` is already installed.

2. Next, we need to change the configuration of the Rsyslog package so that it listens for network connections. By default, Rsyslog is set only to listen to local socket connections. Edit the file `/etc/rsyslog.conf` and locate the following lines:

   ```
   # provides UDP syslog reception
   #$ModLoad imudp
   #$UDPServerRun 514

   # provides TCP syslog reception
   #$ModLoad imtcp
   #$InputTCPServerRun 514
   ```

3. Uncomment them so that they resemble the following:

   ```
   # provides UDP syslog reception
   $ModLoad imudp
   $UDPServerRun 514

   # provides TCP syslog reception
   $ModLoad imtcp
   $InputTCPServerRun 514
   ```

> In the preceding configuration, we have enabled both UDP and TCP log reception. Generally speaking, I recommend using UDP to forward logs; it has a much lesser impact on performance than TCP as it is fire and forget. The downside is that some log messages might be lost if the server is too busy to receive the UDP packets. Use TCP where your logs are critical; otherwise, stick with UDP.

4. Restart the `rsyslog` service by issuing the following command:

```
$ sudo service rsyslog restart
```

Your Rsyslog server is now ready to use. Next, we can turn our attention to the Rsyslog client.

5. On the Rsyslog client, ensure that Rsyslog is installed.

6. We are going to start by ensuring that all logs dealing with the user login activity are forwarded to the Syslog server. This is an excellent place to start, as monitoring who logged into which server and when is a crucial part of securing your systems, and sending it off-host makes it harder to tamper with. Edit the `/etc/rsyslog.d/50-default.conf` file and find the following line:

```
auth,authpriv.*                    /var/log/auth.log
```

Change it to the following:

```
auth,authpriv.*                    @<Syslog server>:514
```

 When you prepend your remote host with a single @ symbol, you are using UDP. To use TCP, use @@ instead.

7. Restart the Rsylsog service on the client using the following command:

```
$ sudo service rsyslog restart
```

8. Log on to the host server while monitoring the `/var/log/auth.log` log on your Syslog server; you should be able to see entries similar to the following snippet:

```
Jun 29 07:47:05 syslognost sshd[19563]: Accepted publickey for
root from 178.251.183.111 port 33241 ssh2: RSA f0:0c:25:c1:9a:94:f
f:20:6e:f7:57:70:9f:3c:9c:5c
Jun 29 07:47:05 syslognost sshd[19563]: pam_unix(sshd:session):
session opened for user root by (uid=0)
```

Notice the highlighted text; this is the hostname of the server that has sent the log entry and it can be used to search for specific entries.

 The field after the date in the syslog entry is always the hostname of the host sending that particular log entry.

This can be very useful when you have more than a handful of servers reporting to your Syslog server and it enables you to use tools such as `grep` to quickly search for information across many servers at once.

You can find the Rsyslog documentation at `http://www.rsyslog.com/doc/master/index.html#manual`.

Using syslog templates

Although it's advantageous to be able to send all the logs to a single location, there are times when you will want to be able to split logs out into separate log files based on certain criteria; for instance, a per-host log for certain elements.

Rsyslog supports this using a system of templates and the property replacer feature; this allows you to distribute logs of your choice into the location you need.

Getting ready

For this recipe, you will need an Ubuntu 14.04 server acting as a Syslog server and a host to send logs to it.

How to do it...

Let's use the syslog templates for the:

1. As with the previous recipe, we're going to take the `auth` logs from our Ubuntu host and send them to our Syslog server. On the shipping host, ensure that you have a line that resembles the following in your copy of `/etc/rsyslog.d/50-default.conf`:

   ```
   auth,authpriv.*                    @<Syslog server>:514
   ```

2. Restart the `syslog` Daemon using the following command:

   ```
   $ sudo service rsyslog restart
   ```

3. On your Syslog server, open `/etc/rsyslog.d/50-default.conf` and edit it to include the following snippet:

   ```
   $template Remote, "/var/log/%HOSTNAME%/%syslogfacility-text%.log"
   auth,authpriv.*                    -?Remote
   ```

4. Locate the following line and comment it out with a #:

   ```
   auth,authpriv.*                    /var/log/auth.log
   ```

5. In the preceding code, we are disabling the default log settings for the `auth` log and using variables to replace the filename and path.

6. Restart the Syslog server using the following command:

```
$ sudo service rsyslog restart
```

7. You should now find that when you log in to the host server, its `auth` messages will be sent to a file that will be located at `/var/log/<hostname>/auth.log`.

 As you may have considered, this technique can be used to organize any log that you want to be forwarded onto the remove Syslog server; indeed, for ephemeral hosts, it can be very useful, as you can create and destroy them at will and still retain all logs created over their life cycles.

See also

You can find details on the Rsyslog property replacer at `http://www.rsyslog.com/doc/property_replacer.html`.

Managing log rotation with the Logrotate utility

It's often surprising how much space can be consumed by something as simple as a plain text file, and without constant care and attention logs can grow to fill the available free space on a host. Fortunately, given their nature as plain text, they are compressible. Indeed, you can expect compression ratios of 80% or more on most log files.

The Logrotate utility is shipped with most Linux distributions and offers a simple yet powerful method to manage logs, allowing you to rotate, compress, and remove on the schedules you set. It also has the ability to run scripts both pre- and post-rotation, thus allowing you to send signals to applications to gracefully restart or to send logs to a remote location after compression. Most applications that are packaged with the operating system should come with a Logrotate configuration, but you should also ensure that any applications you develop or deploy are catered for.

Getting ready

For this recipe, you will need an Ubuntu 14.04 host.

How to do it...

This recipe will show you how to create a new `logrotate` configuration, for example, app and also point out important configuration options:

1. In this example, we're going to rotate the logs on notional app located in `/usr/local/exampleapp/logs`.

2. To start, create a new file in `/etc/logrotate.d` called `exampleapp` (no extension) and insert the following content:

```
/usr/local/exampleapp/logs/*.log {
        daily
        rotate 31
        copytruncate
        compress
        notifempty
}
```

3. This is a relatively straight forward Logrotate entry, which will do the following:

    □ Rotate any files with a `.log` extension in the directory `/usr/local/exampleapp/logs`

    □ Rotate the log files daily

    □ Keep 31 days' worth of logs

    □ Will truncate files without removing them

    □ The logs will be compressed using `gzip`

    □ The logs will not be rotated if they are already empty, saving on empty archived logs

Be careful with the `copytruncate` option. It's useful when you have an application that can't accept a signal to reload and use a new `logfile`. Using `copytruncate` avoids the need for this by copying the contents of the current log and zeroing out the existing one; however, in the time between copying the log and zeroing it, there may be new entries that will be subsequently lost.

This example should serve as a good starting point for most applications. Use the Logrotate documentation to explore some further options that your application might require.

See also

You can find the documentation for Logrotate by issuing the following command:

```
$ man logrotate
```

Installing ElasticSearch, Logstash, and Kibana

Once you have established a policy to control retention, archiving, and centralization of your logs, you can consider how best to extract the data from them. Log analysis software has seen some serious growth in recent years, as an increasing number of systems administrators, developers, and managers realize the value of the data they can provide. Currently, Splunk has gained a great number of traction, offering both an easy-to-install and easy-to-use product with a great deal of integrations; however, it can be costly with a pricing model that ratchets up along with the quantities of data you wish to analyze. This has led to open source projects springing up and aiming to rival Splunk, in particular, it has been popularized by the trifecta of ElasticSearch, Logstash, and Kibana. Together these form what is popularly known as an ELK stack. These three products combine to offer a compelling alternative to Splunk; thus, allowing you to ship, analyze, and present data derived from your log streams.

This recipe will deal with the ElasticSearch and Kibana elements of the stack, allowing you to create a server that is ready to have logs shipped to it via Logstash.

Getting ready

For this recipe, you will need an Ubuntu 14.04 server.

How to do it...

1. To start, we need to install a Java virtual machine to run ElasticSearch; either the Sun or the OpenJDK implementation is supported; we're going to use the OpenJDK distribution as it is packed into the Ubuntu repositories. Install the OpenJRE by issuing the following command:

    ```
    $ sudo apt-get install default-jre
    ```

2. Next, install the public signing key for the ElasticSearch repository with the following command:

```
$ wget -O - http://packages.elasticsearch.org/GPG-KEY-
elasticsearch | sudo apt-key add -
```

3. Next, create a new file within `/etc/apt/sources.list.d/` called `elasticsearch.list` and insert the following:

```
deb http://packages.elastic.co/elasticsearch/1.7/debian stable
main
```

4. Now, install ElasticSearch using the following command:

```
$ sudo apt-get update && sudo apt-get install elasticsearch
```

5. Next, start your ElasticSearch instance by issuing the following command:

```
$ sudo service elasticsearch start
```

6. Now, since we have ElasticSearch, we can install Kibana. Start by downloading the most recent release using the following command:

```
$ wget https://download.elastic.co/kibana/kibana/kibana-4.1.0-
linux-x64.tar.gz
```

7. Next, issue the following command to create a new user to run the Kibana process:

```
$ adduser kibana --home /opt/kibana-4.1.0-linux-x64
```

8. Now, decompress the installation using the following command:

```
$ cd /opt && tar -xvf <<fullpathtokibana.tar.gz>> && chown -R
kibana:kibana .
```

Make sure you replace the `<<fullpathtokibana>>` text with the path to where you downloaded the `Kibana gzip`.

9. Run the following command to start the Kibana instance as a background process using the user we created in step six:

```
$ sudo su kibana -c '/opt/kibana-4.1.0-linux-x64/bin/kibana > /
opt/kibana-4.1.0-linux-x64/kibana.log &'
```

 This isn't as robust as a true startup script and you may want to consider writing a more complete `init` script for production use.

10. You can now test your Kibana instance by going to the URL
    `http://<kibanaserver>:5601`. You should see a screen that looks similar to this:

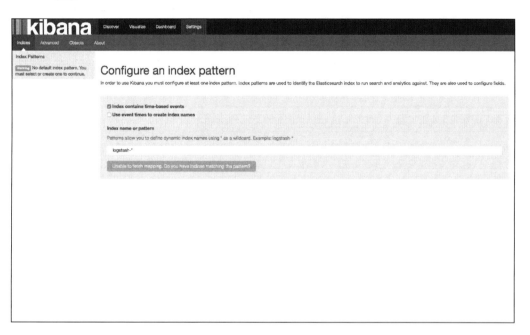

This indicates that Kibana is ready for use. Next, we'll turn our attention to the Logstash server.

11. First, create a new file in `/etc/apt/sources.list.d/` called `logstash.list` and insert the following:

    ```
    deb http://packages.elasticsearch.org/logstash/1.5/debian stable
    main
    ```

12. Install the signing key using the following command:

    ```
    wget -qO - https://packages.elasticsearch.org/GPG-KEY-
    elasticsearch | sudo apt-key add -
    ```

13. Next, install the package using `apt-get`:

    ```
    $ sudo apt-get update && sudo apt-get install logstash
    ```

14. Now, we need to configure the Logstash server. The bulk of Logstash configuration comprises inputs and outputs; inputs take log streams in and outputs forward them onto a given system. In our case, we are going to create a new output for ElasticSearch. Use your editor to create a new file called `elasticsearch.conf` within the `/etc/logstash/conf.d` directory and insert the following snippet:

    ```
    output {
      elasticsearch {
        host => localhost
      }
    }
    ```

    This will take any data input into Logstash and place it into the ElasticSearch instance.

15. Finally, start the `logstash` process using the following command:

    ```
    $ sudo service logstash start
    ```

 At this point, Logstash will start and then quit; this is expected, as we have no configured input. See the next recipe to configure an input for Logstash.

See also

▶ You can find the documentation for ElasticSearch installation at `https://www.elastic.co/guide/en/elasticsearch/reference/current/setup.html`

▶ You can find the installation documents for Kibana at `https://www.elastic.co/guide/en/kibana/current/setup.html`

▶ You can find the installation documents for Logstash at `https://www.elastic.co/guide/en/logstash/current/getting-started-with-logstash.html`

Importing logs into Elasticsearch with Logstash

Logstash can function as a log forwarding agent as well as a receiving server; however, due to it's reliance on both a JVM and a relatively large memory footprint, it is unsuitable for hosts of more modest means. Instead, we can use the Logstash forwarder (formerly known as Lumberjack). The Logstash forwarder is written in Go and has a significantly smaller footprint. As a result, it also removes the need for any external dependencies, such as a JVM. Using the Logstash forwarder, you can securely forward logs from your hosts onto your ELK stack.

Getting ready

For this recipe, you will need an Ubuntu 14.04 server acting as a Logstash server and an Ubuntu 14.04 server with Nginx to act as the forwarder. Nginx has been used to supply example logs and can be swapped out with the application of your choice.

How to do it...

The following steps will show you how to use a Logstash forwarder to import logs into Elasticsearch:

1. To start, we are going to install the Logstash log forwarder. Use the following command to download the package:

   ```
   $ wget https://download.elastic.co/logstash-forwarder/binaries/
   logstash-forwarder_0.4.0_amd64.deb
   ```

2. Next, we can install the package using this command:

   ```
   $ sudo dpkg -i logstash-forwarder_0.4.0_amd64.deb
   ```

3. Now, we need to return to the Logstash server to configure certificates. To maintain the security of your messages, the Logstash forwarder will only communicate over SSL connections, so at the very least we need to generate some self-signed certificates. On your Logstash server, create a directory to hold your keys and certificates:

   ```
   $ sudo mkdir -p /etc/logstash/ssl/certs && mkdir -p /etc/logstash/
   ssl/keys
   ```

4. Now, we create the key using the following command:

   ```
   $ openssl req -x509  -batch -nodes -newkey rsa:2048 -keyout
   logforwarder.key -out logforwarder.crt -subj /CN=<< ELASTICSEARCH
   SERVER NAME >>
   ```

5. Finally, we can copy the certificates into place with this command:

```
$ sudo mv logforwarder.key /etc/logstash/ssl/keys && sudo mv
logforwarder.crt /etc/logstash/ssl/certs
```

6. You will also need to copy the certificate onto the log forwarding host; copy it into `/etc/ssl/certs/logforwarder.crt`.

7. Now, we are ready to create our configuration; in this example, we're going to configure the forwarder to forward logs from our Nginx instance to our ElasticSearch server. Open the file `/etc/logstash-forwarder.conf` in your editor and replace the contents with the following:

```
{
  "network": {
    "servers": [
      "<<ELASTICSEARCHSERVER>>:5043"
    ],
      "ssl ca": "/etc/ssl/certs/logforwarder.crt",
    "timeout": 15
  },
  "files": [
    {
      "paths": [
        "/var/log/syslog",
        "/var/log/*.log"
      ],
      "fields": {
        "type": "syslog"
      }
    },
    {
      "paths": [
        "/var/log/nginx/access.log"
      ],
      "fields": {
        "type": "nginx-access"
      }
    }
  ]
}
```

> Ensure that you replace <<ELASTICSEARCHSERVER>> with the IP
> address/name of your ElasticSearch server, ensuring that it matches the
> certificate name.

As you can see, this is straightforward JSON. This configuration will do the following:

- Forward the selected logs onto your ElasticSearch server
- Forward events from the syslog file and any file with a `.log` file extension within the `/var/logs` directory and process them as syslog files
- Forward events from the `nginx` log file located within `/var/log/nginx/access.log`

8. We have one last step we need to perform before we can receive the logs; we need to add a Logstash filter to correctly parse the incoming data. First, we create a directory to hold the pattern by issuing the following command:

```
$ sudo mkdir /opt/logstash/patterns/
```

9. Next, we can create our pattern. Using your editor, create a new file under `/opt/logstash/patterns` called `nginx` (no extension) and insert the following content:

```
NGINXACCESS %{IPORHOST:clientip} \[%{HTTPDATE:timestamp}\]
"%{WORD:verb} %{URIPATHPARAM:request} HTTP/%{NUMBER:httpversion}"
%{NUMBER:response} (?:%{NUMBER:bytes}|-) (?:"(?:%{URI:referrer}|-
)"|%{QS:referrer}) %{QS:agent}
```

This takes the incoming log and breaks it into discrete pieces of data for insertion into the ElasticSearch index.

> You can find further information on Logstash patterns at https://www.
> elastic.co/guide/en/logstash/current/plugins-filters-
> grok.html.

10. Next, we need to adjust our Logstash server to use our new pattern. Create a new file called `filter_nginx.conf` under `/etc/logstash/conf.d` and insert the following JSON:

```
filter {
  if [type] == "nginx-access" {
    grok {
      match => { "message" => "%{NGINXACCESS}" }
    }
  }
}
```

Nginx is also able to log straight to JSON, thus allowing you to simplify the preceding steps by simply importing the raw JSON log. You can find the `nginx logging` details at `https://www.nginx.com/resources/admin-guide/logging-and-monitoring/`.

11. This configuration file causes Logstash to inspect incoming data for any that match a type of `nginx-access`. If it matches, then the data is parsed via the pattern we created earlier. You can enable your new configuration by restarting Logstash using the following command:

    ```
    $ sudo service logstash restart
    ```

12. You can test that your logs are being forwarded correctly by querying the indices on your Elastic server. On the Elastic host, use the following command:

    ```
    $ curl 'localhost:9200/_cat/indices?v'
    ```

    You should receive a reply that is similar to the following screenshot:

    ```
    ● ● ●                          ⬆ mduffy — root@elastic: ~ — ssh — 92×6
    root@elastic:~# curl 'localhost:9200/_cat/indices?v'
    health status index                pri rep docs.count docs.deleted store.size pri.store.size
    yellow open   .kibana                1   1          1            0      2.5kb          2.5kb
    yellow open   logstash-2015.06.30    5   1        358            0    231.6kb        231.6kb
    root@elastic:~# 
    ```

    Notice the dated index; this is the content of the logs we've forwarded on and is ready to query.

See also

You can find the documentation for the Log forwarder at `https://github.com/elastic/logstash-forwarder`

Using Kibana queries to explore data

Once you have your data indexed into ElasticSearch, you will want to work with it to reveal anything of interest. Kibana is a fantastic tool to enable this, allowing you to query, display and report on data of interest. Kibana offers an easy-to-use GUI to explore your data, allowing both ad-hoc data exploration and the creation of stunning and detailed dashboards.

In this recipe we're going to focus on using Kibana to explore data to discover underlying patterns within an Nginx access log.

Getting ready

For this recipe you need an Ubuntu 14.04 server with Kibana and ElasticSearch installed; you should also have set up some inputs into ElasticSearch, preferably from an Nginx server.

How to do it...

The following steps will give you a very quick tour of how to locate and view data within Kibana:

1. First, point your browser at your Kibana instance (normally located at `<<kibanaserver>>:5601`). You should be able to see a page similar to the following:

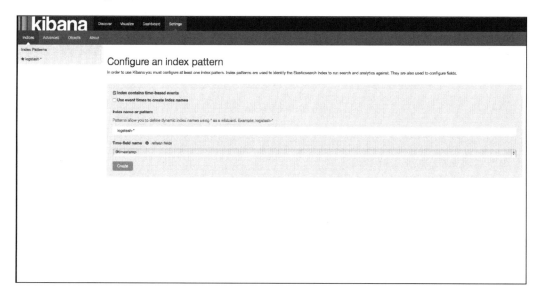

This allows you to configure your initial index pattern; this maps back to the indices available within ElasticSearch.

> If you need to see a list of available indices, you can issue this command against your ElasticSearch server: `curl 'localhost:9200/_cat/indices?v'`.

Generally speaking, if you're using Logstash to ship your logs into ElasticSearch, you should be fine accepting the default; hit the button marked **Create**.

2. The next screen allows you to select fields to analyze and should look something similar to the following screenshot:

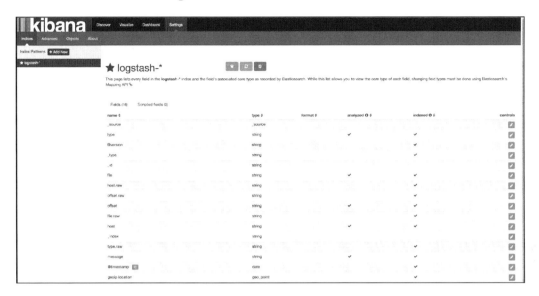

Kibana will attempt to work out the type for the field, but if it's a little wide of the mark you can use the pencil icon at the end of the row to adjust the setting. Once you're happy with your fields, you can click on the **Discover** menu item at the top.

3. The **Discover** page is where you can start to truly dig into your data. By default, it displays a graph of activity over time of all of the data that is indexed, and should look something similar to this:

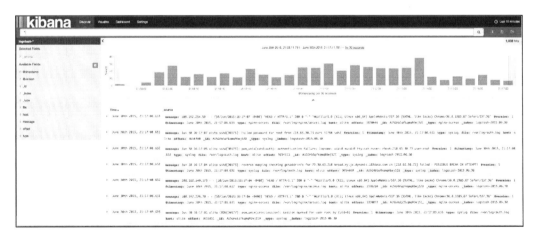

4. From here, we can start to drill into our data. At present, I have two different data sources available to me; my server's `auth.log` and my Nginx access log. Let's take a look at the Nginx access logs first. On the left-hand side of the menu, click on the item marked **file**; it should reveal a drop-down menu that looks similar to this:

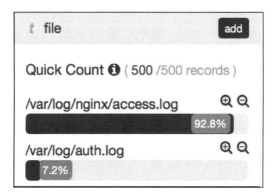

5. This menu allows you to quickly drill into the individual files that you have shipped to Kibana. It also allows you to have a look at how active the files are within the time frame. As we can easily see, my Nginx access log is by far the busiest. Let's click on the icon and drill into the data. As soon as you drill into any data, the main page updates to reflect this; for instance, my example data now looks similar to this:

6. You can already see that there is an anomalous spike of traffic in the preceding chart. There are several ways we can explore this, but by far the easiest is to click and drag over the time series we're interested in; this binds the data to the period selected:

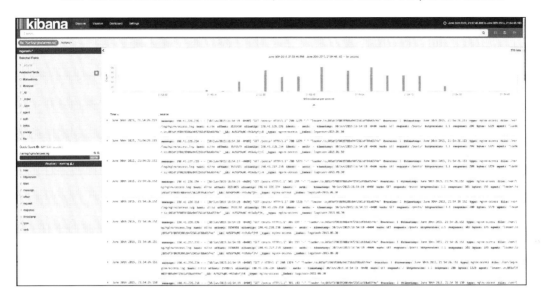

7. By zooming in, we can easily see that the traffic is coming in over a very short period; a minute in this case. We can now dig deeper into this by examining the pages that we're requesting by opening up the requests field on the left-hand menu:

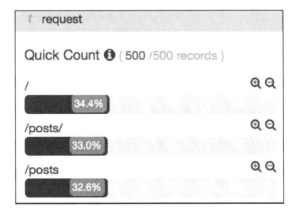

As you can see, the requests are evenly split.

8. We can use the Visualize feature within Kibana to explore the data at hand. Right now, we'll take a look at the IP addresses. Click on the **clientIP** field on the left-hand side; it should look something similar to this:

9. As you can see, it has ranked the IPs by frequency; however, we can use the visualization feature to look at the data in more detail. Click on the **Visualize** button at the bottom.

The warning is the result of the field containing analyzed data. Due to the possibly huge amount of variance available within an analyzed field, Kibana will warn you that this could be a computationally expensive operation.

10. The next screen arrays the IP's in order of the number of requests over the selected time period and will look similar to this:

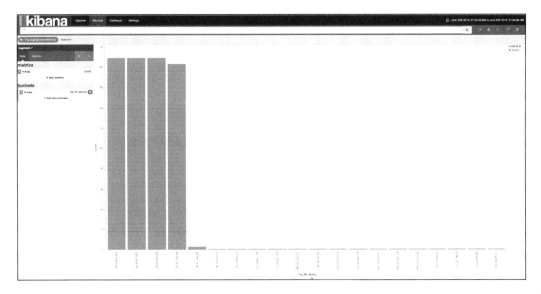

As you can see, only four IP's make up the bulk of the traffic!

11. Within the visualization we can report on this further. On the left-hand side, under buckets, click on the **Add sub-buckets** button. This opens a drop-down menu that allows you to add further data within the visualization. In this case, add the options as per the following screen shot:

12. Once you've added the options, click on the green **play** button at the top to run the query. This will order the results of the IPs by the top three requested URLs, and it should look similar to the following:

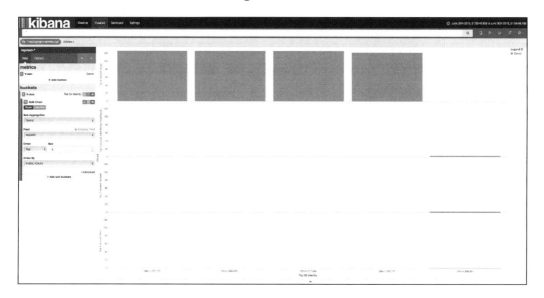

Although you can't make out the text in this image, you can see that the bulk of the requests are going to a single page; an unusual pattern.

13. As a final check, we can go back to the main page by clicking on the **Discover** button at the top and then clicking on the field on the left-hand side marked as **agent**. In my example, it looks similar to this:

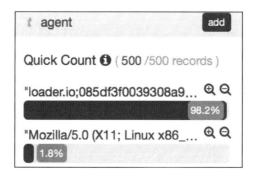

Plainly, this activity is the result of a load test and we have spotted and investigated it using Kibana.

See also

You can find the getting started guide for Kibana at `https://www.elastic.co/guide/en/kibana/current/getting-started.html`.

Using Kibana queries to examine data

The previous recipe was a whistle-stop tour of using the Kibana interface to interactively drill into and examine your data; however, some of the true power of Kibana is its ability to use the ElasticSearch query language to allow you to select elements of information for examination.

Although you can impart order to your data when you ship it using Logstash, you will probably still have a lot of unstructured data that you need to examine. Using ElasticSearch queries, you can start to construct queries to examine your data and use Kibana to display it in an easy to understand manner. This recipe will take a look at some simple ElasticSearch queries to examine security issues on a Linux host.

Getting ready

For this recipe, you will need an ELK server plus some data forwarded from an `auth.log`.

How to do it...

The following steps will show you how to search your data using queries in Kibana and how to save them as Dashboards:

1. Log onto your Kibana server and select the `files` tab from the left-hand side; it should look similar to the following screen shot:

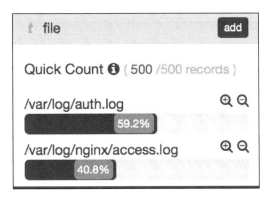

Select the plus sign next to the `auth.log` to drill further into that data.

2. The main screen should now look similar to the following:

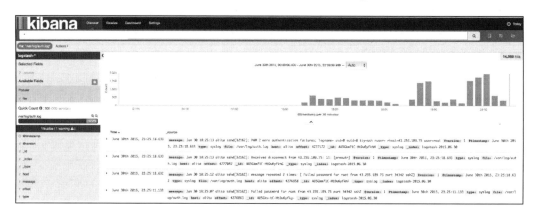

3. Although you cannot make out the text, the graph is the point of focus; this shows us the `auth` log activity over time. Now, we should start constructing our query; in this instance, I'm interested in failed logins. In the search bar in the top, enter the following:

   ```
   "Failed password"
   ```

4. You will find that Kibana is now filtering the log messages that contain that term; it will also update the graphs and data to reflect this and highlight the data. See the following screen shot for an example:

   ```
   source
   message: Jun 30 18:43:48 alita sshd[3ZZ16]: message repeated 2 times: [ Failed password for root from 43.255.189.75 port 40693 ssh2] @version: 1 @timestamp: June 30th 2015, 23:43:51.1
   33 type: syslog file: /var/log/auth.log host: alita offset: 4295669 _id: AU5GpAW1C-HtDu6yfkm0 _type: syslog _index: logstash-2015.06.30

   message: Jun 30 18:43:44 alita sshd[3ZZ16]: Failed password for root from 43.255.189.75 port 40693 ssh2 @version: 1 @timestamp: June 30th 2015, 23:43:51.13Z type: syslog file: /var
   /log/auth.log host: alita offset: 4295574 _id: AU5GGn-tC-HtDu6yfkmN _type: syslog _index: logstash-2015.06.30
   ```

5. It's certainly nice to be able to search for a term, but you can also chain together queries with operators to gain a little granularity. For instance, I want to be able to filter out the entries that are failed logins for the root user and see the non-root accounts that are being affected. In your search bar, enter the following:

   ```
   ("Failed password") NOT ("root")
   ```

   This runs the first query (find all entries with the text **Failed** password) and then use the `NOT` operator to exclude the ones that include the text `root`.

6. Let's take it further and also exclude invalid users. This allows us to see the non root users who are actually present on the box and are being targeted. Enter the following query into the search bar:

   ```
   ("Failed password") NOT ("root") NOT ("invalid user")
   ```

Hit the **run** button. In my example, my result looks similar to this:

```
Failed password for backup from 208.109.103.212 port 47550 ssh2 @version:
799 _id: AU5GS4UkC-HtDu6yfjxm _type: syslog _index: logstash-2015.06.30

Failed password for uucp from 208.109.103.212 port 45944 ssh2 @version: 1
0 _id: AU5GS2m7C-HtDu6yfjxM _type: syslog _index: logstash-2015.06.30

Failed password for uucp from 62.210.7.55 port 62775 ssh2 @version: 1 @ti
id: AU5GGgHpfkqmqR6wj5x- _type: syslog _index: logstash-2015.06.30

Failed password for nobody from 189.211.79.178 port 35616 ssh2 @version: 1
04 _id: AU5Fkzrjfkqmqr6wj46E _type: syslog _index: logstash-2015.06.30

Failed password for games from 189.211.79.178 port 35508 ssh2 @version: 1
6 _id: AU5FkwqAfkqmqR6wj452 _type: syslog _index: logstash-2015.06.30
```

As you can see, there are users such as UUCP, backup, and others who are valid users and are being targeted by some form of brute-force attack.

7. This is an interesting query and one that I'd like to be able to quickly return to. To do this, we can save the query. Click on the **disk** icon on the top left corner:

8. You will be prompted to name the saved search; go ahead and call it something meaningful. Now, whenever you want to see this query, you can load it by clicking on the **load** icon:

You can use this feature to build up a library of reports that allow members of the team who are less familiar with the query language to quickly and easily access information.

See also

You can find more details of how to use Kibana to query data at `https://www.elastic.co/guide/en/kibana/current/discover.html` and `https://www.elastic.co/guide/en/kibana/current/discover.html`.

10
Monitoring with Sensu

In this chapter, we are going to cover the following topics:

- ▸ Installing a Sensu server
- ▸ Installing a Sensu client
- ▸ Installing check prerequisites
- ▸ Finding community checks
- ▸ Adding a DNS check
- ▸ Adding a disk check
- ▸ Adding a RAM check
- ▸ Adding a process check
- ▸ Adding a CPU check
- ▸ Creating e-mail alerts
- ▸ Creating SMS alerts
- ▸ Using Ansible to install Sensu

Introduction

One of the cornerstones of DevOps engineering is the effective monitoring of resources and services, and the ability to react to them in a timely fashion. This is not unique to DevOps; monitoring has been one of the key aspects of running a system for as long as there have been systems to run.

Monitoring takes many forms and there is no such thing as a finished monitoring system. Just when you think you have everything monitored, you will find an obscure edge case that will cause issues if not correctly accounted for. On the other side, you need to ensure that your monitoring is accurate. Nothing kills a monitoring platform quicker than having to wade through a wall of false alerts. People start to ignore alerts, sooner rather than later, and you end up with an outage, which you could have seen coming but did not.

Fortunately, there are many products to choose from when it comes to monitoring and alerting, both open source and commercial, and each has its strengths and weaknesses. For many years, the de facto standard for open source monitoring was Nagios (`https://www.nagios.org`). Nagios is a hugely popular product and is used all over the world. However, it has some weaknesses. Several branches of Nagios are addressing some of these perceived weakness, with Icinga (`https://www.icinga.org`) becoming especially popular. However, some projects have gone further and have started to re-evaluate the core principles to rearrange the monitoring infrastructure.

One more promising product is Sensu (`https://sensuapp.org`). Sensu takes a different approach to many monitoring solutions and, rather than using a master/client solution, it uses a Publication/Subscription model using a message queue. This approach makes it far simpler to configure monitoring for a large number of services and is useful for environments that contain a large amount of ephemeral hosts. By allowing clients to subscribe simply and easily to a set of checks, it makes it much easier to roll out new clients; they simply start the client with the correct subscription, and start running and sending results back to the master to process.

Other than utilizing a message queue, Sensu allows for custom checks to be written relatively easily and with flexibility. This allows the responsibilities of writing checks to be split evenly among team members, both application and infrastructure developers. It should help ensure that your monitoring coverage is as broad as possible.

Sensu is an open source project that also has a commercial offering; the open source product is referred to as Sensu Core, while the commercial version is Sensu Enterprise. Sensu Enterprise offers a better issue routing system, tweaked dashboard and, perhaps most compellingly, support. However, Sensu Core is a powerful product in its own right, and can happily monitor huge amounts of clients.

This chapter will show you how to set up, configure, and roll out checks using Sensu. We will also look at how to configure Sensu to alert you via the two most important avenues: SMS and e-mail.

Installing a Sensu server

Setting up Sensu and its pre-requisites is reasonably straightforward, and it should take little time to set it up and configure some initial checks. This recipe will show you how to install Sensu Core and Uchiwa as its dashboard. Thus, giving you both a powerful and scalable Sensu server; however, it only gives you a single place to examine any issues. Using Uchiwa allows you to have multiple Sensu servers across many sites and still have a singular place to examine them in a graphical fashion.

Lastly, we will also set up SSL keys to ensure that the communication between the Sensu queue and its subscribing hosts remains confidential.

Getting ready

For this recipe, you require an Ubuntu 14.04 server to host both Sensu Core and Uchiwa.

How to do it...

The following steps will demonstrate how to install a Sensu server, RabbitMQ, and the Uchiwa panel:

1. Our first step is to install RabbitMQ, which requires Erlang to be installed. Use the following command to install Erlang:

   ```
   $ sudo apt-get update && sudo apt-get -y install erlang-nox
   ```

2. Now that we have Erlang, we are ready to install RabbitMQ. The Sensu project recommends the use of the latest upstream release of Rabbit rather than the version available for distribution. To do this, we need to first download and install the RabbitMQ package signing key:

   ```
   $ sudo wget http://www.rabbitmq.com/rabbitmq-signing-key-public.asc && sudo apt-key add rabbitmq-signing-key-public.asc
   ```

3. Next, we need to make the `apt` repository available and install the RabbitMQ package with the following two commands:

   ```
   $ echo "deb     http://www.rabbitmq.com/debian/ testing main" | sudo tee /etc/apt/sources.list.d/rabbitmq.list
   $ sudo apt-get update && sudo apt-get install rabbitmq-server
   ```

4. Now we will create the keys to secure our Sensu communication, but first we need to install the OpenSSL tools with the following command:

   ```
   $ sudo apt-get install openssl
   ```

5. Once OpenSSL is installed, we can download a tool provided by the Sensu team to generate the certificates. The script uses the OpenSSL tools to generate a set of certificates and place them into the CA, server and client directories. First we download the script using the following command:

```
$ wget http://sensuapp.org/docs/0.20/files/sensu_ssl_tool.tar &&
tar -xvf sensu_ssl_tool.tar
```

6. Once downloaded, we run the script and generate the certificates using the following command:

```
$ sudo./sensu_ssl_tools/ssl_certs.sh generate
```

7. This should produce new directories containing the Certificate Authority, client certificates, and Server certificate and key. Next, we both create the directory structure, and copy the server and Certificate Authority certificates using this command:

```
$ sudo mkdir -p /etc/rabbitmq/ssl && sudo cp sensu_ca/cacert.pem
server/cert.pem server/key.pem /etc/rabbitmq/ssl
```

8. Finally, we need to amend our RabbitMQ configuration to make use of the certificates. Create a new file called `rabbitmq.config` within `/etc/rabbitmq/` and insert the following content:

```
[
    {rabbit, [
    {ssl_listeners, [5671]},
    {ssl_options, [{cacertfile,"/etc/rabbitmq/ssl/cacert.pem"},
                   {certfile,"/etc/rabbitmq/ssl/cert.pem"},
                   {keyfile,"/etc/rabbitmq/ssl/key.pem"},
                   {verify,verify_peer},
                   {fail_if_no_peer_cert,true}]}
    ]}
].
```

9. This directs RabbitMQ to start a new listener on TCP port `5671` using the certificates we have generated to secure communication on this port. Now that we have configured the certificates, you should restart the RabbitMQ server using the following command:

```
$ sudo /etc/init.d/rabbitmq-server restart
```

10. With RabbitMQ installed and configured, we can start creating the RabbitMQ users and virtual hosts for Sensu to be used as a publishing endpoint. Let's start by creating a new RabbitMQ virtual host for Sensu with the following command:

```
$ sudo rabbitmqctl add_vhost /sensu
```

11. Next, create a RabbitMQ user with a password of your choice with the following command:

    ```
    $ sudo rabbitmqctl add_user sensu <<YOURPASSWORD>>
    ```

    Remember to replace `<<YOURPASSWORD>>` with the password of your choice.

12. Finally, we give the `sensu-user` full permission over its virtual host with this command:

    ```
    $ sudo rabbitmqctl set_permissions -p /sensu sensu ".*" ".*" ".*"
    ```

13. We're finished with RabbitMQ and now we are ready to move onto the next prerequisite, which is Redis. In this case, the version included with the Linux distribution is fine. You can install Redis using the following command:

    ```
    $ sudo apt-get install redis-server
    ```

14. Now that we have installed and configured RabbitMQ and Redis, we can install Sensu Core. First, we add the Sensu package signing key using the following command:

    ```
    $ wget -q http://repos.sensuapp.org/apt/pubkey.gpg -O- | sudo apt-key add -
    ```

15. We can then add the repository with this command:

    ```
    $ echo "deb      http://repos.sensuapp.org/apt sensu main" | sudo tee /etc/apt/sources.list.d/sensu.list
    ```

16. Finally, we install the Sensu package. This installs the server, API, and client as a bundle:

    ```
    $ sudo apt-get update && sudo apt-get install sensu
    ```

17. Now we have installed the Sensu server, we can configure it. First, copy the client certificate we created earlier in place with the following command:

    ```
    $ sudo mkdir -p /etc/sensu/ssl && sudo cp client/cert.pem client/key.pem /etc/sensu/ssl
    ```

18. Next, we configure our Sensu server's basic connectivity. Create a new file called `config.json` under the directory of `/etc/sensu` and insert the following content:

    ```
    {
      "rabbitmq": {
        "ssl": {
          "cert_chain_file": "/etc/sensu/ssl/cert.pem",
          "private_key_file": "/etc/sensu/ssl/key.pem"
        },
        "host": "localhost",
        "port": 5671,
    ```

```
        "vhost": "/sensu",
        "user": "sensu",
        "password": "<<password>>"
      },
      "redis": {
        "host": "localhost"
      },
      "api": {
        "port": 4567
      }
    }
```

Ensure that you replace <<password>> with the password you chose while setting up the Sensu RabbitMQ user.

19. Start the Sensu services using the following commands:

```
$ sudo service sensu-server start
$ sudo service sensu-api start
```

 Notice that we're not starting the Sensu client in this instance; this is to keep this recipe focused. I thoroughly encourage you to configure a client on your Sensu master and monitor it as with any other host.

20. Next, we are going to install uchiwa. Uchiwa is an elegant and easy to use dashboard for Sensu, designed to be used for information radiators, such as TVs. Install Uchiwa using the following command:

```
$ sudo apt-get install uchiwa
```

21. Now that we have installed Uchiwa, we need to configure it; edit the file /etc/sensu/uchiwa.json and ensure that it has the following content:

```
{
  "sensu": [
    {
      "name": "<<site description>>",
      "host": "<<sensuserver>>",
      "port": 4567,
      "timeout": 5
    }
  ],
```

```
"uchiwa": {
  "host": "0.0.0.0",
  "port": 3000,
  "interval": 5
}
}
```

Ensure that you replace `<<site description>>` and `<<sensuserver>>` with the correct values. The site description can be set to a description of your choice; I tend to use it to delineate geographical sites (for instance, London, DC). Ensure that the `sensu` server is set to the DNS name or IP address of your Sensu server.

22. Start the service using the following command:

```
$ sudo service uchiwa start
```

Within your browser, navigate to your Sensu server on port `3000` and you should be able to see a screen similar to the following screenshot:

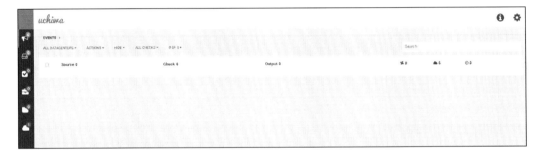

See also

▶ You can find further installation details for Sensu at `https://sensuapp.org/docs/0.20/installation-overview`

▶ You can find installation details of Uchiwa at `http://docs.uchiwa.io/en/latest/getting-started/`

Installing a Sensu client

Once you have installed the Sensu server, you need to install the Sensu client to run checks and report the data back to the server. The Sensu client subscribes to the RabbitMQ virtual host and listens for checks to be published in a subscription to which the client belongs. When a check is published, the client runs the assigned check and publishes the results back onto the RabbitMQ; from here, the Sensu server then processes the check results.

Getting ready

For this recipe, you will need an Ubuntu 14.04 client to act as the Sensu client and a Sensu server to connect to.

How to do it...

The following steps show you how to install the Sensu Core package and how to configure the Sensu client.

1. The Sensu Core package used to install the Sensu client includes the client, server, and API package. First we add the Sensu package signing key using the following command:

   ```
   $ wget -q http://repos.sensuapp.org/apt/pubkey.gpg -O- | sudo apt-
   key add -
   ```

   Then we add the repository:

   ```
   $ echo "deb    http://repos.sensuapp.org/apt sensu main" | sudo
   tee /etc/apt/sources.list.d/sensu.list
   ```

2. Finally, we can now install the Sensu package using the following command:

   ```
   $ sudo apt-get update && sudo apt-get install sensu
   ```

> If you have already read the *How to install a Sensu server* recipe, then you might have noticed that the steps are the same for both client and server. This is because the Sensu package is an omnibus package that contains everything; you only start the services you want.

3. Next, we need to copy the client key into place. You can start by creating a directory to place the certificates with this command:

   ```
   $ sudo mkdir -p /etc/sensu/ssl
   ```

4. Copy the following files from the keys you created when you created your Sensu server and into the directory you created in the step above:

client/cert.pem

client/key.pem

5. Now, we can configure the Sensu client. First, create a file in /etc/sensu called config.json and insert the following content:

```
{
  "rabbitmq": {
    "ssl": {
      "cert_chain_file": "/etc/sensu/ssl/cert.pem",
      "private_key_file": "/etc/sensu/ssl/key.pem"
    },
    "host": "<sensumaster>",
    "port": 5671,
    "vhost": "/sensu",
    "user": "sensu",
    "password": "<password>"
  },
  "redis": {
    "host": "localhost"
  },
  "api": {
    "port": 4567
  }
}
```

Note that you need to replace the values of <<sensumaster>> and <<password>> with the IP or name of your Sensu Master and Sensu password, respectively.

6. Now that we have configured the general Sensu connectivity, we can configure the client specific settings. Create a new file under /etc/sensu/conf.d called client.json and insert the following content:

```
{
  "client": {
    "name": "sensuhost",
    "address": "<ip address>,
    "subscriptions": [ "common" ]
  }
}
```

It's worth going over this slim piece of configuration. The first part of the configuration defines the name that is displayed for this host when reporting the check results; I suggest that this should be the DNS name of the client for easy identification. The `address` field allows you to define an IP address that the client reports as its originating address. The subscriptions field allows you to add subscriptions for checks. I recommend that you have a common set of checks that all hosts should respond to; these can be things, such as disk space, CPU usage, RAM usage, and so on.

> Subscriptions are a key part of using Sensu, and are a fantastic organizational tool. I generally recommend using a common subscription for the usual suspects, such as RAM and CPU checks. You can use a role description for other subscriptions, such as a subscription called `nginx_server`, or `haproxy_lb`.

7. Now that we have configured our client, we are ready to start the Sensu client service. Start it by issuing the following command:

    ```
    $ service sensu-client start
    ```

8. On your `sensu` master, log into your `uchiwa` panel and select this icon:

This takes you to the client-listing page. Once there, you should be able to see your new host listed and it should look something similar to the following screenshot:

See also

You can find further details about the client installation at `https://sensuapp.org/docs/0.20/install-sensu-client`.

Installing check prerequisites

Sensu checks are generally written using Ruby and there is broad support for the language throughout Sensu. However, this means that there are certain dependencies on Ruby for some checks.

Getting ready

For this recipe, you will require an Ubuntu 14.04 server with Sensu installed.

 This recipe requires you to install development tools to compile the native Ruby extensions that some checks require. If having development tools on hosts contravenes your security policies, I recommend that you use a tool, such as FPM (`https://github.com/jordansissel/fpm`) to build the checks on a build machine and then re-package for distribution.

How to do it...

To install the various packages, issue the following command:

```
$ sudo apt-get install -y ruby ruby-dev build-essential
```

Finding community checks

Once the Sensu client and server are installed, it's now time to add the checks to be monitored for any issue. By default, the Sensu client reports nothing; it is up to you to add any relevant checks to make it useful.

Sensu checks can be written in any language as long as it returns the correct response to the server via RabbitMQ; however, they are generally written either in Bash or more commonly in Ruby. Luckily, the Sensu community has contributed a great many open source checks to the project. These can be installed, thus saving you from having to create your own and they cover many of the common check scenarios.

Getting ready

For this recipe, you will need an Ubuntu 14.04 host to act as the Sensu check host and a Sensu server to connect to. You should also have installed the prerequisite packages as detailed in the recipe *Installing check prerequisites*.

How to do it...

You can find the Sensu community checks at `http://sensu-plugins.io/plugins/`.

Each link should take you to a Github page containing the code for that particular check, and it should have the additional documentation on the usage of the check.

See also

> ▸ You can find further details of the Sensu community checks at `http://sensu-plugins.io/plugins/`
>
> ▸ You can find details of the Sensu check format at `https://sensuapp.org/docs/latest/checks`

Adding a DNS check

Almost every application has external dependencies, such as databases, Redis caches, e-mail servers, and so on. Although it is generally reliable, DNS can occasionally cause problems and, at first glance, it can be difficult to diagnose. By adding a check that constantly checks the DNS record, you can be assured that these dependencies are available.

Getting ready

For this recipe, you will need an Ubuntu 14.04 host to act as the Sensu check-host and a Sensu server to connect to. You should also have installed the prerequisite packages as detailed in the recipe *Installing check prerequisites*.

How to do it...

Let's start by adding DNS check to track DNS records:

1. For this recipe, we're going to install the `sensu-plugins-dns`. Use the following command to install the new plugin:

   ```
   $ sudo gem install sensu-plugins-dns
   ```

2. You can test if the plugin has been installed successfully by issuing the following command:

```
$ check-dns.rb -d www.packtpub.com
```

3. You should see a response like the following:

```
DNS OK: Resolved www.packtpub.com A records
```

4. On the Sensu server, create a new file called web_check.json under the directory /etc/sensu/conf.d and insert the following content:

```
{
  "checks": {
    "check_google": {
      "command": "/usr/local/bin/check-dns.rb -d google.com",
      "interval": 60,
      "subscribers": [ "web_check" ]
    },
    "check_yahoo": {
      "command": "/usr/local/bin/check-dns.rb -d yahoo.com",
      "interval": 60,
      "subscribers": [ "web_check" ]
    },
    "check_fail": {
      "command": "/usr/local/bin/check-dns.rb -d sdfdsssf.com",
      "interval": 60,
      "subscribers": [ "web_check" ]
    }
  }
}
```

5. Once you have entered the configuration, restart the Sensu server by issuing the following command:

```
$ service sensu-server restart
```

6. Next, we need to configure our client to subscribe to the checks. Edit the client.json file located within /etc/sensu/conf.d and to reflect the following code:

```
{
  "client": {
    "name": "sensuhost",
    "address": "<<SENSUCLIENTIP>>",
    "subscriptions": [ "common","web_check" ]
  }
}
```

7. Notice the additional subscription. When you restart the client, it will subscribe to a set of checks that publish themselves for `web_check` clients to run. Restart the Sensu client by issuing the following command:

```
$ service sensu-client restart
```

8. Your checks should now be running; however, it may take a few minutes for them to show up. This is due to the checks being placed on the MQ and being checked at the interval specified (60 seconds in the above example). To check, log on to Uchiwa on your Sensu master and select the following icon on the left-hand side:

You should see the check to which we have deliberately given a nonsense address:

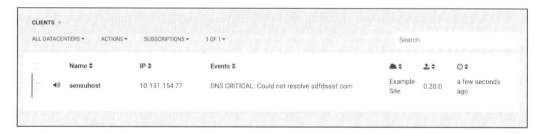

9. You can also check in `/var/log/sensu/sensu-server.log` and locate the line that resembles the following:

```
{"timestamp":"2015-07-14T16:55:14.404660-0400","level":"info",
"message":"processing event","event":{"id":"c12ebe42-62ed-454f-
a074-49c71c3c8f7a","client":{"name":"sensuhost","address":"10.1
31.154.77","subscriptions":["common","web_check"],"version":"0
.20.0","timestamp":1436907305},"check":{"command":"/usr/local/
bin/check-dns.rb -d sdfdsssf.com","interval":60,"subscribers":["w
eb_check"],"name":"check_fail","issued":1436907314,"executed":1436
907314,"duration":0.262,"output":"DNS CRITICAL: Could not resolve
sdfdsssf.com\n","status":2,"history":["2"],"total_state_change":0}
,"occurrences":1,"action":"create"}}
```

See also

You can find further details of the Sensu DNS check at `https://github.com/sensu-plugins/sensu-plugins-dns`.

Adding a disk check

Disk checks are a critical part of infrastructure monitoring. A full disk can cause processes to fail, servers to slow down, and logs to be lost. Providing alerts for disk issues in a timely manner is vital to the smooth running of any infrastructure.

This recipe shows you how to install the community disk check and add it to a subscription called **common**.

Getting ready

For this recipe, you will need both a Sensu server and at least one Sensu host. You should also have installed the prerequisite packages as detailed in the recipe *Installing check prerequisites*.

How to do it...

Let's install the community disk check:

1. First, we install the disk check `gem` using the Gem package manager:

   ```
   $ sudo gem install sensu-plugins-disk-checks
   ```

 This gem installs many additional disk based checks in addition to space usage, allowing you to check for issues such as SMART alerts, and so on. You can see the details at: `https://github.com/sensu-plugins/sensu-plugins-disk-checks`.

2. Now we can configure the check configuration. On the Sensu master, create a new file called `disk_checks.json` under the `/etc/sensu/conf.d` directory and insert the following content:

   ```
   {
     "checks": {
       "check_disk_usage": {
         "command": "/usr/local/bin/check-disk-usage.rb -w 75 -c 90",
         "interval": 60,
         "subscribers": [ "common" ]
       }
     }
   }
   ```

The configuration above makes use of the disk check plugging, and uses the -w and -c switches. These switches are relatively common amongst Nagios-style checks and allows you to set a warning and a critical threshold. In this case, I'm using a warning at 75% and a critical alert at 90%. This is very useful as it allows us to use different alert types based on the threshold; for instance, a warning could trigger an e-mail and a critical alert could send an SMS. Read the plugin documentation to fid details of what thresholds you can set and how to set them.

3. On the client side, edit the file called `client.json` within `/etc/sensu/conf.d` and ensure that the following code is present:

```
{
  "client": {
    "name": "sensuhost",
    "address": "10.131.154.77",
    "subscriptions": [ "common","web_check" ]
  }
}
```

4. To check that the check is running correctly, look in `/var/log/sensu/sensu-server` and check that a line resembling the following is present:

```
{"timestamp":"2015-07-14T17:26:42.689883-0400","level":"info","mes
sage":"publishing check request","payload":{"name":"check_disk_us
age","issued":1436909202,"command":"/usr/local/bin/check-disk-
usage.rb -w 75"},"subscribers":["common"]}
```

See also

You can find more details for the community disk checks at `https://github.com/sensu-plugins/sensu-plugins-disk-checks`.

Adding a RAM check

Having sufficient RAM available for a server is a crucial part of running a performant service. When memory resources run short, the application either runs slow, if the OS is forced to use swap space, or in extremes can cause applications to crash.

This recipe demonstrates how to use Sensu to monitor that sufficient free RAM is present on a monitored system.

Getting ready

For this recipe, you will need both a Sensu server and at least one Sensu host. You should also have installed the prerequisite packages as detailed in the recipe *Installing check prerequisites*.

How to do it...

Let's add the RAM check:

1.   We need to install the `sensu-plugins-memory-checks` gem; this installs an executable for the RAM check:

     ```
     $ sudo gem install sensu-plugins-memory-checks
     ```

2.   Now we can configure the `config` check. On the Sensu master, create a new file called `ram_checks.json` under the `/etc/sensu/conf.d` directory and insert the following content:

     ```
     {
       "checks": {
         "check_ram": {
           "command": "/usr/local/bin/check-ram.rb -w 70 -c 95",
           "interval": 60,
           "subscribers": [ "common" ]
         }
       }
     }
     ```

     Again, note the use of the -w and -c switches; these set the thresholds in percentage used that needs to trigger an alert.

3.   On the client, edit the file called `client.json` within `/etc/sensu/conf.d` and ensure that the following code is present:

     ```
     {
       "client": {
         "name": "sensuhost",
         "address": "10.131.154.77",
         "subscriptions": [ "common","web_check" ]
       }
     }
     ```

4. To determine that the check is running correctly, look in `/var/log/sensu/sensu-server` and check that a line resembling the following is present:

```
{"timestamp":"2015-07-14T17:43:28.066609-0400","level":"wa
rn","message":"config file applied changes","file":"/etc/
sensu/conf.d/check_ram.json","changes":{"checks":{"check_ram_
usage":[null,{"command":"/usr/local/bin/check-ram.rb","interval":6
0,"subscribers":["common"]}]}}}
```

See also

For further details on the Sensu memory checks, see the following page `https://github.com/sensu-plugins/sensu-plugins-memory-checks`.

Adding a process check

One important item to monitor is if a process is actually running on a system. It's little use knowing that you have plenty of disk and CPU resources, but not realizing that your apache server has fallen over. Sensu can be used to monitor the key processes that are running on your server and it can alert you if a process has gone AWOL.

This recipe shows you how to check if the `sshd` process is running on any host subscribed to the common subscriptions; however, the same technique can be used to monitor any process.

Getting ready...

For this recipe, you will need both a Sensu server and at least one Sensu host. You should also have installed the prerequisite packages as detailed in the recipe *Installing check prerequisites*.

How to do it...

This recipe will show you how to install the Sensu process check plugin and how to configure it to monitor a running process.

1. First, we install the process check gem using the Gem package manager. Use the the following command to install the plugin:

```
$ sudo gem install sensu-plugins-process-checks
```

2. Now, we can configure the check configuration. On the Sensu master, create a new file called `sshd_process_check.json` under the `/etc/sensu/conf.d` directory and insert the following content:

```
{
  "checks": {
    "check_sshd_usage": {
      "command": "/usr/local/bin/check-process.rb -p 'sshd -D'",
      "interval": 60,
      "subscribers": [ "common" ]
    }
  }
}
```

This check makes use of the `-p` switch to allow us to specify a process that we wish to monitor; this should be the full string of the running process (notice that, in the preceding example, I have added the `-D` switch that the process runs with).

3. On the client, edit the file called `client.json` within `/etc/sensu/conf.d` and ensure that the following code is present:

```
{
  "client": {
    "name": "sensuhost",
    "address": "10.131.154.77",
    "subscriptions": [ "common","web_check" ]
  }
}
```

4. To determine if the check is running correctly, look in `/var/log/sensu/sensu-server` and check that a line resembling the following is present:

```
{"timestamp":"2015-07-14T18:13:48.464091-0400","level":"info","me
ssage":"processing event","event":{"id":"f1326a4f-87c2-49a7-8b28-
70dfa3e9836b","client":{"name":"sensuhost","address":"10.131.154
.77","subscriptions":["common","web_check"],"version":"0.20.0","
timestamp":1436912025},"check":{"command":"/usr/local/bin/check-
process.rb -p 'sshd -D'","interval":60,"subscribers":["common"],
"name":"check_sshd_usage","issued":1436912028,"executed":1436912
028,"duration":0.128,"output":"CheckProcess OK: Found 1 matching
processes; cmd /sshd -D/\n","status":0,"history":["1","1","1","1",
"0"],"total_state_change":0},"occurrences":4,"action":"resolve"}}
```

See also

You can find further details of the process checks at `https://github.com/sensu-plugins/sensu-plugins-process-checks`.

Adding a CPU check

Having sufficient CPU resources is a vital part of running a performant service and it is hard to spot without sufficient monitoring. Using Sensu to alert when CPU usage is running high, you will be able to deal with slow running processes before the customer notices.

Getting ready

For this recipe, you will need both a Sensu server and at least one Sensu host. You should also have installed the prerequisite packages as detailed in the recipe *Installing check prerequisites*.

How to do it...

Let's add a CPU usage check:

1. First, we install the CPU check gem using the Gem package manager. Use the following command to install the plugin:

   ```
   $ sudo gem install sensu-plugins-cpu-checks
   ```

2. Now we can configure the check configuration. On the Sensu master, create a new file called cpu_check.json under the /etc/sensu/conf.d directory and insert the following content:

   ```
   {
     "checks": {
       "check_cpu_usage": {
         "command": "/usr/local/bin/check-cpu.rb",
         "interval": 60,
         "subscribers": [ "common" ]
       }
     }
   }
   ```

3. On the client, edit the file called client.json within /etc/sensu/conf.d and ensure that the following code is present:

   ```
   {
     "client": {
       "name": "sensuhost",
       "address": "10.131.154.77",
       "subscriptions": [ "common","web_check" ]
     }
   }
   ```

4. To determine that the check is running correctly, look in `/var/log/sensu/sensu-server` and check that a line resembling the following is present:

```
{"timestamp":"2015-07-15T16:24:26.800371-0400","level":"info"
,"message":"publishing check request","payload":{"name":"che
ck_cpu","issued":1436991866,"command":"/usr/local/bin/check-cp.
rb"},"subscribers":["common"]}
```

See also

You can find further details of the process checks at `https://github.com/sensu-plugins/sensu-plugins-cpu-checks`.

Creating e-mail alerts

Although you can view your Sensu alerts using the Uchiwa panel, it's unlikely that you will have your eyes glued to the TV at all times. Instead, you need to give Sensu the ability to alert you in a more interactive fashion, and one of the most tried and trusted methods is via e-mail. In today's world of laptops, Smartphones and tablets, it's a rare time indeed when you are not able to receive e-mails.

This recipe will show you how to configure the Sensu e-mail plugin to allow you to receive e-mails whenever an alert is triggered.

Getting ready

For this recipe, you will need a configured Sensu server and Sensu client. You should also have at least one check configured. You will also need an SMTP server that can relay mail. You should also have installed the prerequisite packages as detailed in the recipe *Installing check prerequisites*.

How to do it...

Let's create an e-mail alert:

1. First, you can use Ruby's gem to install the mail plugin using the following command:
   ```
   $ gem install sensu-plugins-mailer
   ```

2. Now, we can configure the mail plugin. Create a new file called `plugin_mailer.json` within `/etc/sensu/conf.d` and insert the following content:

```
{
  "mailer": {
        "admin_gui": "http://<sensuserver>/#/events",
        "mail_from": "<<fromaddress>>",
        "mail_to": "<<toaddress>>",
        "smtp_address": "<<smtpaddress>>",
        "smtp_username": "<<smtpusername>>",
        "smtp_password": "<<smtppassword>>",
        "smtp_port": "587",
        "smtp_domain": "<<smtpdomain>>"
  }
}
```

Ensure that you replace the values inside the angle brackets with the relevant information for your e-mail setup. The admin `gui` is simply a link to the `uchiwa` panel, so fill in the address of your Sensu server.

3. Now the mailer plugin is configured, we can create the handler.

4. You can combine the plugin and handler settings into the same file, but it's better practice to keep them separate.

5. A handler is an executable piece of code that is triggered by an event sent via a Plugin; you can think of plugins as raising alerts and handlers as dealing with how to distribute the event to end users. Sensu allows you to configure many different handlers, which allows you to be flexible in how you are alerted. You may wish to e-mail some checks, others you might want to send via SMS, and still others you might want to allow for a combination of the two; handler definitions allow you to define these. To create the `handler` definition for the mailer, create a new file called `mail.json` under the `/etc/sensu/handlers` and insert the following content:

```
{
  "handlers": {
    "mailer": {
      "type": "pipe",
      "command": "/usr/local/bin/handler-mailer.rb"
    }
  }
}
```

6. This has created a new handler called **mailer** that we can make available for our checks. The type of `pipe` is the most commonly used type of handler and outputs the contents of the Sensu event into the command. Effectively, the event is raised by a plugin, placed on the MQ, processed by the Sensu Server, and then parsed via the handler.

7. To add the handler to a check, open up a check definition and amend it to include the following code:

```
{
  "checks": {
    "check_cpu": {
      "command": "/usr/local/bin/check-cpu.rb",
      "interval": 60,
      "subscribers": [ "common" ],
      "handlers": ["mailer"]
    }
  }
}
```

8. Now, whenever an alert is triggered, you should receive an e-mail that resembles something like this:

```
DNS CRITICAL: Could not resolve sdfdsssf.com
Admin GUI: http://sensumaster.stunthmaster.com/#/events
Host: sensuhost
Timestamp: 2015-07-15 19:07:14 -0400
Address:  10.131.154.77
Check Name:  check_fail
Command:  /usr/local/bin/check-dns.rb -d sdfdsssf.com
Status:  CRITICAL
Occurrences:  1
And when the check is resolved, you should see a resolution E-mail
that looks something like this:
Resolving on request of the API
Admin GUI: http://sensumaster.stunthmaster.com/#/events
Host: sensuhost
Timestamp: 2015-07-19 19:15:12 -0400
Address:  10.131.154.77
Check Name:  check_fail
Command:  /usr/local/bin/check-dns.rb -d sdfdsssf.com
Status:  OK
Occurrences:  2976
```

By editing the `handler-mailer.rb` code, you can modify this e-mail to more suit your formatting needs.

See also

▶ You can find more details of the Sensu handlers at `https://sensuapp.org/docs/0.20/handlers`

▶ You can find more details of the e-mail handler at `https://github.com/sensu-plugins/sensu-plugins-mailer`

Creating SMS alerts

Sometimes you need alerts that are more immediate than an e-mail. When a critical service goes down, you don't want to miss it because you eschewed carrying a smartphone and your laptop wasn't near by.

SMS messaging is a fantastic way to send default alerts and is in many ways the spiritual successor to the pager. SMS has the advantage of being almost universal and it is virtually impossible in this day and age to find a cell phone that does not support it.

Unlike e-mail, you cannot run a local SMS server to send messages directly; instead, you need to sign up with an SMS gateway, which will route your messages to the various mobile phone providers. In this recipe, we're going to use Twilio (`https://www.twilio.com`). Twilio supports both Voice and SMS gateways and has an easy to use API. Like all SMS gateways, Twilio charges per message; however, trial accounts are available to test your integration.

Getting ready

For this recipe, you will need a Sensu server, Sensu client, and at least one configured check. You will also need a Mobile phone to receive your test message. You should also have installed the prerequisite packages as detailed in the recipe *Installing check prerequisites*.

How to do it...

Let's create SMS alerts:

1. First, signup for a new Twilio account by visiting `https://www.twilio.com/try-twilio`. It will ask you for some basic details, and will send you an e-mail to confirm the account. Ensure that you have confirmed your details, and that you can log in.

2. Once you have a Twilio account, you can install the Twilio Sensu plugin using the following command:

   ```
   $ sudo gem install sensu-plugins-twilio
   ```

3. Next, we will configure the plugin. As with the mailer plugin, this takes two forms: the handler configuration and the plugin configuration. Let's deal with the plugin configuration first: create a new file `/etc/sensu/conf.d/plugin_twilio.json` and insert the following content:

   ```
   {
     "twiliosms":{
       "token":"<<TWILIOTOKEN>>",
       "sid":"<<TWILIOSID>>",
       "number":"<<TWILIONUMBER>>",
   ```

```
        "recipients":{
          "+<<RECIPIENTNUMBER>>": {
            "sensu_roles":["all"],
            "sensu_checks":[],
            "sensu_level": 1
          }
        }
      }
    }
```

4. There are a few things to note with this code. First, you need to have your own Twilio API and SID at hand; if you need to find them, you can find them on this page:

   `https://www.twilio.com/user/account/settings`

   They should be available about halfway down the page and will resemble this:

5. Next we need to set up the recipient number. This is an array and can contain as many recipients as you need; however, the recipient will need to be acknowledged within the Twilio panel.

> A Twilio test account has many limitations, including a limit on the recipients.

6. Each recipient can have a different set of roles and checks that will trigger an SMS; in our example, we're leaving it as all roles to ensure that every alert will send an SMS. However, you can use this configuration item to restrict SMS alerts only to critical roles.

7. Next, we can configure the handler configuration. Create a new file called `/etc/sensu/handlers/plugin_twilio_sms.json` and add the following configuration:

```
{
  "handlers": {
    "twiliosms": {
      "type": "pipe",
      "command": "/var/lib/gems/1.9.1/gems/sensu-plugins-twilio-0.0.3/bin/handler-twiliosms.rb"
    }
  }
}
```

8. Once you have done this, save the file and restart the Sensu server with the following command:

```
$ sudo service sensu-server restart
```

The next time you have an alert, you should receive an SMS message that looks similar to the following screenshot:

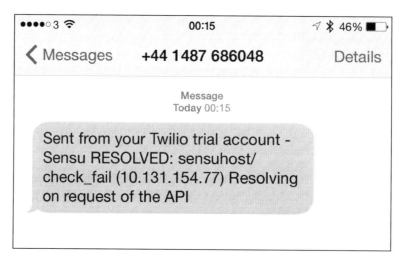

See also

▶ You can find more information about Twilio at `https://www.twilio.com`

▶ You can find further information about the Twillio plugin at `https://github.com/sensu/sensu-community-plugins/blob/master/handlers/notification/twiliosms.rb`

Using Ansible to install Sensu

When rolling out on any kind of scale, it's almost certain that you will want to use automation to perform the install, especially for the clients; this allows you to roll out the changes quickly, easily, and with minimum fuss.

As with other recipes in this book, we are going to use Ansible as our automation tool of choice and rather than write a new playbook from scratch, we're going to make use of a truly excellent role available on the Ansible galaxy (`https://galaxy.ansible.com/detail#/role/279`).

If you need a refresher on Ansible, see *Chapter 5, Automation with Ansible*.

Getting ready

For this recipe, you will need a node to run the Ansible playbook and at least two servers: one to act as the Sensu server and the other, the Sensu client. The Sensu Server node should have RabbitMQ and Redis already installed on it. You should also have installed the prerequisite packages as detailed in the recipe *Installing check prerequisites*.

 Although slightly out of scope for this recipe, you can use two other Ansible roles to automate both RabbitMQ and Redis, `https://github.com/Mayeu/ansible-playbook-rabbitmq` and `https://github.com/DavidWittman/ansible-redis`, respectively.

How to do it...

1. On the host that will act as your Ansible node, run the following command to install the Sensu role:

```
ansible-galaxy install Mayeu.sensu
```

 If you do not have Ansible installed in the default location, you can also clone the role and place it in your own structure; the code is available here: `https://github.com/Mayeu/ansible-playbook-sensu/blob/master/vagrant/site.yml`.

2. Next, let's create an inventory. I'm assuming you are using the default location for the inventory; otherwise, use the `-i` switch on the `ansible-playbook` command to specify one in the location of your choice. In the inventory, ensure that you have the following:

```
[sensu_servers]
    <<SENSUSERVERS>

[sensu_clients]
    <<SENSUCLIENTS>>
```

Where <<SENSUSERVER>> is the DNS name of your Sensu server and <<SENSU_ CLIENTS>> are the DNS names of your Sensu clients.

3. Now, we need to create a new playbook; create a new file called <<playbook>>/ sensu.yml and insert the following content:

```
- hosts: sensu_servers
  user: <<sudo_user>>
  vars:
    - sensu_install_server: true
    - sensu_install_client: false
  vars_files:
    - group_vars/sensu.yml
  roles:
    - Mayeu.sensu

- hosts: sensu_clients
  user: <<sudo_user>>
  vars:
    - sensu_install_server: false
    - sensu_install_client: true
    - sensu_client_hostname: '{{ ansible_hostname }}'
    - sensu_client_address: '{{ ansible_eth0["ipv4"]["address"]
    - sensu_client_subscription_names [common]
}}'
  vars_files:
    - group_vars/sensu.yml
  roles:
    - Mayeu.sensu
```

4. Replace `<<playbook>>` with the name of the directory you wish your playbook to reside in. Also replace the `<<sudo_user>>` with a user that has sudo permissions on the servers you are connecting to.

   As you can see, in this playbook we are defining two different plays: one for the Sensu Server and another for the Sensu clients. Note how each play references a variable file allowing us to define certain shared configuration items. We are also setting certain variables at the client level where we need differences.

5. Next, we need to create some directories to contain the files that the Ansible role will require. Use the following command to create them:

   ```
   mkdir -p <playbook>/files/sensu/extensions && mkdir -p <playbook>/
   files/sensu/handlers && mkdir -p <playbook>/files/sensu/plugins
   ```

   These folders are to hold your handlers, plugins, and if you use them, your extensions.

 You can find details of Sensu extensions at `https://sensuapp.org/docs/0.20/extensions`.

6. For instance, if you wish to add a new plugin, you will first add the plugin `ruby` file to the `<playbook>/files/sensu/plugins` directory; this will then be placed in the appropriate place on the Sensu server.

7. Next, create a folder to hold your Sensu certificates:

   ```
   mkdir -p <playbook>/files/sensu/certs
   ```

   Now, copy your certificates into the newly created folder.

 You can find the details for how to create the certificates in the recipe entitled *How to install a sensu server*.

8. Now, let's create the variables file for the common Sensu items. Create a new file under `<<playbook>>/group_vars` called `sensu.yml` and insert the following content:

   ```
   sensu_server_rabbitmq_hostname: '<<SENSUSERVERDNSNAME>>'
   sensu_server_rabbitmq_user: <<sensuMQuser>>
   sensu_server_rabbitmq_password: <<sensuMQpassword>>
   sensu_server_rabbitmq_vhost:    "sensu"
   sensu_server_api_user: <<SENSU_USER>>
   sensu_server_api_password: <<SENSU_PASSWORD>>
   ```

The values in this file define the settings for your Sensu server and cover aspects such as the MQ to connect to the vhost, username, password, and so on. You may notice that this seems to be a short list; this is because this particular role has very sensible defaults. You can find the list of defaults on the readme at `https://galaxy.ansible.com/detail#/role/279`.

9. Now we have configured our server and client, the next step is to define some checks to run on the client. First, we configure the server to send out a request for the check to the `common` subscription. Insert the following into the `<<playbook>>/group_vars/sensu.yml` file:

```
sensu_checks:
  cpu_check:
    handler: default
    command: "/usr/local/bin/check-cpu.rb"
    interval: 60
    subscribers:
      - common
```

10. You will also need to install the check-package onto the clients; you can do this by inserting the following code within the role that sets up the client. I normally recommend making this part of any common role that is used to setup all hosts:

```
name: "Install Sensu CPU Check Plugin"
gem: name='sensu-plugins-cpu-checks' state=present
```

11. Finally, we should define a handler on the Sensu server; insert the following code into the `<<playbook>>/group_vars/sensu.yml` file:

```
sensu_handlers:
  basic_mailer:
    type: pipe
    command: "mailx -s 'Sensu Alert' opsuser@opsaddress.com"
```

The preceding handler will send a simple e-mail if there is an alert, and you can use the same technique to set up as many handlers as you like.

12. Run Ansible using the following command:

```
ansible-playbook -K sensu.yml
```

This should install Sensu and Uchiwa, and configure the clients with a CPU check, plus add a simple handler.

See also

You can find details of the Sensu Ansible role at `https://github.com/Mayeu/ansible-playbook-sensu`.

11
IAAS with Amazon AWS

In this chapter, we are going to cover the following topics:

- ▶ Signing up for AWS
- ▶ Setting up IAM
- ▶ Creating your first security group
- ▶ Creating your first EC2 host
- ▶ Using Elastic Load Balancers
- ▶ Managing DNS with route53
- ▶ Using Ansible to create EC2 hosts

Introduction

The term cloud computing has diluted immensely over the years and the cloud label is being applied to any technology that interacts over the network. Originally though, it was used to describe what is now being termed as **Infrastructure-as-a-Service** (**IAAS**).

IAAS has revolutionized the approach of many companies by helping them build applications and infrastructure, and for many companies, has turned infrastructure into a utility rather than a massive internal cost center. This in turn has freed them to explore new platforms and systems without the requirement of building costly servers and data centers. At it's heart, IAAS platforms offer the ability to provision servers rapidly, but it may also offer additional features, such as load balancers, persistent storage, and other elements of a traditional data center offering; thus, allowing you to run a full-bodied infrastructure on a pay-as-you-go basis.

Amazon was one of the earliest IAAS vendors and it became the most popular very rapidly. Its features are possibly the most complete of all IAAS vendors, offering features, such as compute units, load balancers, big data tools, and orchestration facilities. Amazon boasts clients of every size, from one-man development companies, through to the giants of the industry, such as Netflix. However, there are alternative. For some, the sheer complexity of the Amazon platform can be an issue and there are many competitors available, ranging from compute focused companies, such as DigitalOcean to fully featured offerings, such as Rackspace.

There are disadvantages of using IAAS platforms and it is important that you design your architecture to suit the particular foibles of such an offering. First, IAAS platforms are heavily contended for RAM, CPU, Disk, and network, and performance is not guaranteed. Your applications should be able to balance the load across many nodes, rather than relying on single, powerful nodes to do the heavy lifting. There is also the issue of cost; generally speaking, costing large IAAS platforms can be a complex task, with elements, such as CPU and RAM being charged by the minute, disks being charged via usage, and networks being charged by the megabyte of transferred data (sometimes on differing rates depending on it being external, or inter-DC traffic). However, as long as you are aware of the shortcomings, the benefits of using an IAAS can be vast.

Signing up for AWS

Before you can use any of the features of Amazon AWS, you need to register and set up your account to be ready for use. This recipe takes you through the steps required to set up an account.

Getting ready

For this recipe, you will require a web browser, an e-mail address to sign up with. You will also need a valid credit/debit card, but this will not be charged until you start using a billable compute.

How to do it...

Before we can approach any recipe in this chapter, we need to create a new AWS account. You can create an account by navigating to `https://aws.amazon.com` and the following the steps detailed in the signup process.

> ▸ You can find the AWS getting started guide at `https://aws.amazon.com/ documentation/gettingstarted/`

> ▸ You can see pricing information at `https://aws.amazon.com/ec2/pricing/`

Setting up IAM

Security is a critical part of managing any infrastructure regardless of its origin and a key part of security is having the ability to identify and limit access to the platform. Amazon provides a tool known as **Identity and Access Management** (**IAM**) that allows you to set up fine-grained users and access rights to access your AWS infrastructure. Using IAM, you can ensure that all the relevant users can access your AWS resources. It also ensures that users are only able to access and interact with the resources in the manner of your choice.

Getting ready

For this recipe, you will need an AWS account.

How to do it...

The following steps will illustrate how to use the AWS IAM system to create a new user and assign suitable roles:

1. Log in to your AWS account and select the IAM panel by selecting the following icon:

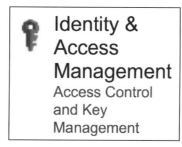

2. You will be greeted by a page that gives you a summary of your users. It will also give a recommendation checklist for a new account and it should look similar to the following screen shot:

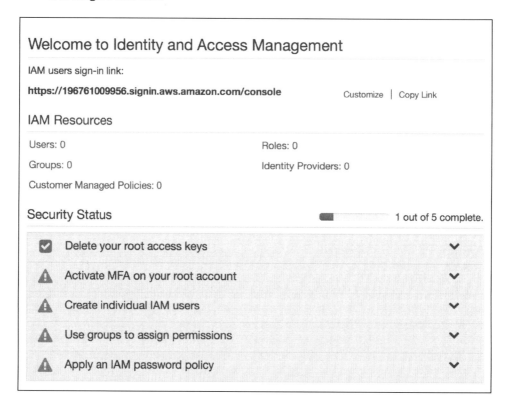

Click on the drop-down menu beside **Activate MFA on your root account** and select **Manage MFA**.

 MFA stands for **Multi Factor Authentication** and ensures that in addition to a password, you also need a device that will give you a one-time code to enter alongside it. MFA is a crucial part of keeping your AWS account secure and I highly recommend enabling it.

3. The next screen will prompt you to select a type of MFA token, either a virtual or a hardware token; both offer the same functionality but differ in form factor. If you have a smartphone, then you will be able to use one of many applications, such as Google Authenticator that offers MFA tokens; select the virtual option if you wish to use these.

4. If you select the virtual MFA option, then you should be presented with a barcode that will allow you to register your MFA device and it will resemble the following screenshot:

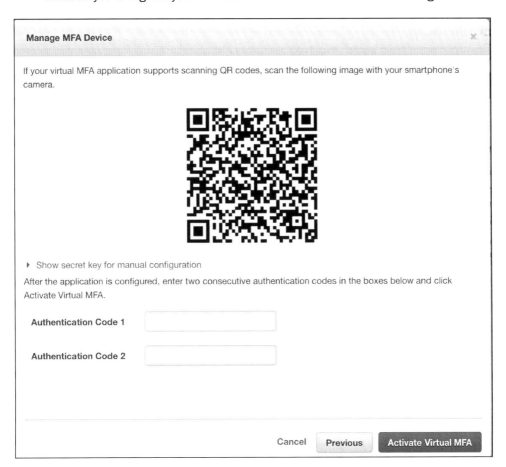

In your smartphone app, you should be able to point your camera at the screen and it will register the account and offer you the MFA tokens. Enter the first two codes when prompted and select **Activate Virtual MFA**.

5. Now that you have secured the root AWS account, it is good to create individual users to login. This gives the ability to audit and lock down users from certain activities. You can start by returning to the IAM panel and selecting **Create individual IAM users** and then **Manage users**.

    You will be presented with a list of your current users. Select **Create New Users**. In the next screen, you should be able to enter a list of usernames that you want to create:

Enter User Names:
1. test1
2. test2
3. test3
4. test4
5. |

Maximum 64 characters each

☑ **Generate an access key for each user**

Users need access keys to make secure REST or Query prot

For users who need access to the AWS Management Consol

Notice the tick box; this controls the creation of access keys to be used for the API. If you are creating users that will only interact with AWS via the web console, then you can leave this un-ticked. Once you are happy with your users, click on **Create**.

The next screen will show you a confirmation that your users have been created and, if requested, the details for the API access.

6. Now that we have created users, we can provide permissions via user-groups. Return to the IAM panel and select **Use groups to assign permissions** and click on **Manage groups**. Like the user panel, you will be presented with a list of your current groups. Click on **Create New Group**.

7. Start by assigning a name for your group and click on **Next step**. This will take you to the policy selection; these should look a little something similar to this:

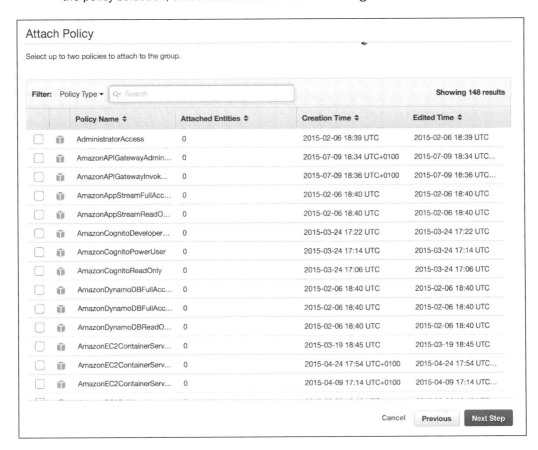

These policies allow you to control the amount of access that users in this group will have in considerable detail. Select the appropriate policy, and click on **Next Step**.

> You can see what a policy will do by reading its name; you can also find more details of IAM policies at `http://docs.aws.amazon.com/IAM/latest/UserGuide/policies_managed-vs-inline.html#aws-managed-policies`.

For this recipe, I recommend that you apply the **AdministratorAccess** role to any user that you will be following the recipes in this chapter with.

8. The next screen will allow you to review your choices; check that you are happy with them and select **Create Group**.

9. You should be returning to the `Groups` list. To add users to your new group, click on it in the list and select **Add Users to Group**. You can then select the users you wish to apply the new role to and add them.

10. Finally, you can set the overall password policy for your AWS infrastructure by returning it to the IAM panel and selecting **Apply an IAM policy**. A password policy is very important and allows you to ensure that your users set strong passwords. In combination with an MFA token, it makes the brute force cracking of user accounts as hugely unlikely. The **Password Policy** panel resembles the following screenshot:

▾ Password Policy

A password policy is a set of rules that define the type of password an IAM user can set. For more information about password policies, go to Managing Passwords in Using IAM.

Currently, this AWS account does not have a password policy. Specify a password policy below.

Minimum password length: `6`

- ☐ Require at least one uppercase letter ❶
- ☐ Require at least one lowercase letter ❶
- ☐ Require at least one number ❶
- ☐ Require at least one non-alphanumeric character ❶
- ☑ Allow users to change their own password ❶
- ☐ Enable password expiration ❶
  - Password expiration period (in days):
- ☐ Prevent password reuse ❶
  - Number of passwords to remember:
- ☐ Password expiration requires administrator reset ❶

Apply password policy   **Delete password policy**

Select the options that make the most sense for your organization; you should ensure a decent length of password and at least some guarantee of variety.

See also

You can find details of the IAM utility at `https://aws.amazon.com/documentation/iam/`

Creating your first security group

Security groups are the equivalent of a firewall and defines the type of traffic that can be directed to a host, both originating from your platform and from the outside world. Like any firewall, it's important to define the security groups correctly, as this is the first point of securing your traffic.

This recipe will show you how to define a new security group ready to be applied to new EC2 hosts to use as a basic web server.

Getting ready

For this recipe, you need an AWS account.

How to do it...

The following recipe will demonstrate how to use the EC2 security group configuration to set a secure policy.

1. Log into the AWS management console, and select the **EC2** options:

   In the EC2 panel you will find a menu on the left-hand side; select the menu entry called **Security Groups** around halfway down the menu.

2. In the **Security Groups** panel, you should find a list of security groups; by default, you should only have one, the default group. To create a new one, select the **Create Security Group** button.

3. You should be presented with a screen similar to the following:

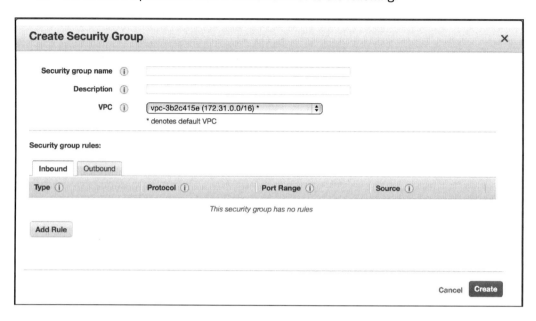

This allows you to give your new security group a name, a description, and attach it to a VPC.

A **VPC** is a **virtual private cloud**. AWS allows you to have several segregated clouds, each with its own policies and hosts. This allows separation of concern between them, for instance a development infrastructure and a production environment. It is not to be confused with availability zones, which offers geographically separated sites to aid with reliability and performance.

Once you have named your group and given it a description, click on the **Add Rule button**.

4. The next step is to create your inbound rule set; this is the traffic that you will allow to reach your instances from the outside world. Click on the button titled **Add Rule**; this will open a window that allows you to select the rules you wish to add. The dropdown list allows you to select either from a set of common types or a free-form custom type. In my example, I've added the common ports for a web server as shown in the following screenshot:

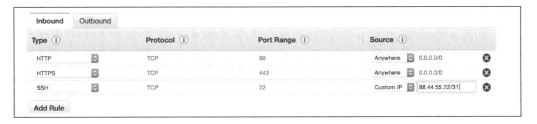

5. Note that I have also added SSH to the inbound group; this is to allow me to manage instances. It's worth noting that I have locked this rule down to a specific IP address to ensure that it can't be accessed via random port brushing by opportunistic scripted attacks.

6. Now, since we have set our inbound rules, we can now set our outbound rules. By default, these are set to allow all traffic out; this can be a valid configuration, but if possible, it is better to lock this down by removing the default outbound rule and allowing only certain protocols. In the following example, I've limited any instance using this security group to only be able to access DNS and SMTP:

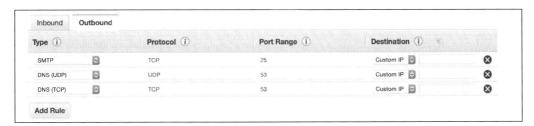

Once you have edited the rule-set to your liking, click on the **Create** button. The security group is now available for use everywhere within this VPC.

See also

You can find details of the AWS security groups at `http://docs.aws.amazon.com/ AWSEC2/latest/UserGuide/using-network-security.html`.

Creating your first EC2 host

The basic unit of an IAAS platform is a compute unit and on AWS it is comprised of EC2 (Elastic Compute) instances. An EC2 instance is a highly configurable server, which is able to cater to almost any conceivable usage; from CPU hungry analysis platforms to IO bound database instances. As noted in the introduction, you should keep in mind that these are generally contended, and you should factor that into application design.

> Within the creation process of an EC2 instance, you have the option to create a dedicated instance. This allows you to remove some of the contention constrains and allows security conscious users to ensure that they are not physically sharing equipment. This is a particular concern for users in the industries, such as the financial sector.

This recipe will show you how to create a new EC2 host running Ubuntu.

Getting ready

For this recipe, you will need an AWS account.

How to do it...

The following steps will demonstrate how to create a new Elastic Compute instance and assign a security group to it.

1. Login to the AWS management panel and select the EC2 panel using the following icon:

2. The EC2 panel gives you a top-level overview of the EC2 resources you are using and gives you a quick view of the health of your region.

> Keep in mind, this view is just for a single region. If you are using multiple regions, then you will need to use the drop down in the top right of the screen to select that particular region. It can be easy to forget that an instance is running if it's not in your default region.

It is also where you can launch new Instances. Click on the button marked **Launch Instance** to start a new EC2 compute instance.

3. The first step is to select the type of **Amazon Machine Image** (**AMI**) that you wish to create. This essentially boils down to selecting the operating system/distribution that you prefer and covers the most popular Linux distributions and even Window.

 If you select a commercial distribution, such as RedHat or Windows; it attracts a higher cost due to licensing. This is reflected in the hourly running cost of the instance.

Select your preferred distribution and click on the button marked **Select** next to it.

 It's worth noting that you can create your own AMI's from launched instances. This allows you to create your own AMI, complete with tools that you require rather than the generic images offered.

4. The next choice is the instance type. As you can see in the following screenshot, this is essentially your choice of virtual hardware and storage type and varies from the micro instances made-up of a single processor and 1GB of memory, to the compute optimized instances made up of 36 processors and 60GB of RAM.

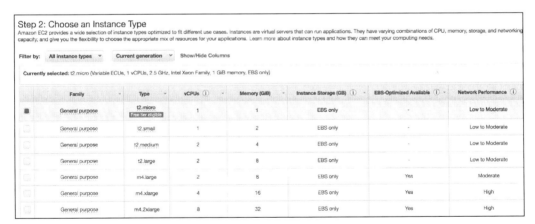

5. Select the instance type that fits your intended usage and budget.

EC2 pricing can become extremely complex and it's worth reading up on the various costs at `https://aws.amazon.com/ec2/pricing/`. There are calculators available on the pricing portal that will allow you to come to an indicative price for your AWS infrastructure.

6. You can click on the **Review and Launch** button at this point. This will launch the instance with a default security group and the default VPC; however, for this example, click the button marked **Configure Instance Details** to set more options.

7. The next screen will allow you to configure the details of your instance, as you can see in the following screenshot:

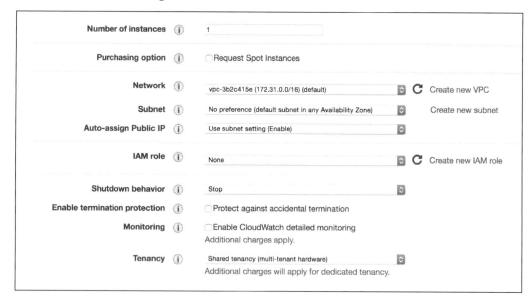

This includes elements, such as the number of instances, network, and subnet if you have multiple VPC's defined. One element to consider is if you want this instance to be publicly available; if you do, you can select the option marked **Auto-assign Public IP**. This will give this instance a publicly available IP address from Amazon's pool and make the instance available to the wider Internet.

8. You can also receive detailed monitoring using Amazon's monitoring product, Cloudwatch; you can leave this un-ticked and still receive the basic Cloudwatch package. However, if you require any level of detail about the instance usage, the commercial Cloudwatch package is probably of interest.

9. By setting the **Tenancy** option, you can run it on an isolated hardware; thus, ensuring that you are not sharing the compute unit with other clients; this can be useful if you have security policies that demand a certain level of isolation. Be aware though, that this option attracts a higher hourly fee.

10. Once you are happy with your selections, click on **Add Storage**.

11. The storage page allows you choose both the size of your **EBS** (**Elastic Block Store**) volumes and the type and performance.

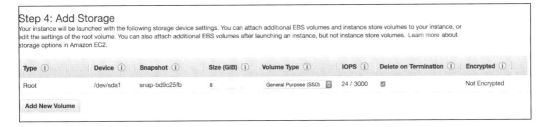

Of particular note in this panel is the volume type option; here, you can select from a general purpose SSD, guaranteed IOP's SSD, and platter based magnetic storage. Each of these has a trade-off in terms of cost and performance and you should select the one most suitable for your usage. You can also select what happens to your data when you terminate your EC2 instance; by default, it is deleted along with the instance. However, you can use this panel to save certain partitions so that they are kept when the instance is terminated.

12. Once you have created the appropriate storage for your image, select **Tag Instance**.

13. Within the tag instance page, you can add free form metadata in the form of key value pairs. This allows you to set a tag to denote the environment this instance is for, department, or any other relevant information. See the following screenshot for examples of tagging:

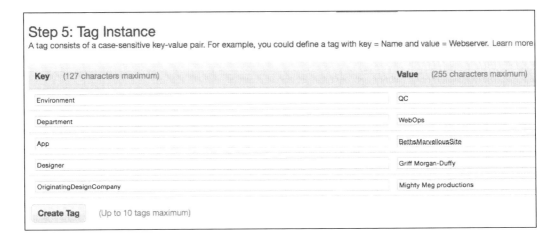

Once you've added tags, click on the button marked **Configure Security Group**.

14. The security group page allows you to add the security group details for your new instances. By default, you can create a new security group, or alternatively, you can select a pre-existing group.

 From my experience, it is better to create your own security groups up front rather than creating them on a per instance basis. This helps to keep a cohesive policy in place and avoids configuration drift and replication.

If you have an existing security group, you can select **Select an existing security group** and a list of the existing groups will be displayed. Similar to the following screenshot:

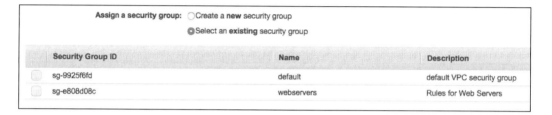

	Security Group ID	Name	Description
Assign a security group: ◯ Create a **new** security group ◉ Select an **existing** security group			
	sg-9925f6fd	default	default VPC security group
	sg-e808d08c	webservers	Rules for Web Servers

Make a note that you can create a new security group based on an existing one by selecting the **Copy to new** option. This is useful when you have an existing complex policy that requires a simple tweak for the new instance.

15. Once you are happy with your selections, click on **Review and Launch**.

16. The next page allows you to review your instance details and gives you the option to edit any elements that don't look quite right. Once you're happy, you can select launch.

17. If you haven't uploaded an SSH key pair you will be prompted to create one in the following screenshot:

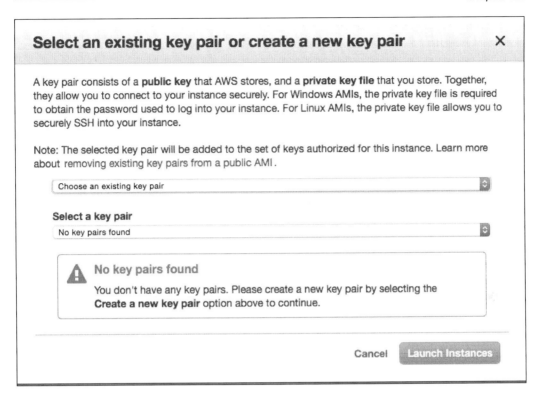

Select an existing key pair or create a new key pair   ✕

A key pair consists of a **public key** that AWS stores, and a **private key file** that you store. Together, they allow you to connect to your instance securely. For Windows AMIs, the private key file is required to obtain the password used to log into your instance. For Linux AMIs, the private key file allows you to securely SSH into your instance.

Note: The selected key pair will be added to the set of keys authorized for this instance. Learn more about removing existing key pairs from a public AMI.

> Choose an existing key pair

Select a key pair

> No key pairs found

> ⚠ **No key pairs found**
>
> You don't have any key pairs. Please create a new key pair by selecting the **Create a new key pair** option above to continue.

Cancel   **Launch Instances**

18. You also have the option to proceed without using a Key pair; however, I do not recommend this unless you are using a custom AMI with pre-existing secure authentication methods built in.

19. Once you have created and downloaded your key pair, click on **Launch instance**.

 THIS IS THE ONLY TIME YOU CAN DOWNLOAD THE KEYS. Be sure that you have copied them down, as there is absolutely no way to re-download them afterwards.

You will be shown a page that shows the EC2 instance being set up and you will return to the EC2 panel. Your new instance should be listed alongside its Public IP and you should now be able to log in using the key pair you downloaded in the previous step.

See also

You can find the documentation for EC2 at `https://aws.amazon.com/documentation/ec2/`.

Using Elastic Load Balancers

One of the key elements of running applications on an IAAS platform is to ensure that work can be balanced between many nodes. This offers an increased resiliency, but also allows you to offset one of the weaknesses of an IAAS platform, performance issues caused by contention. Unless you have a compelling reason not to, you should use load balancing for any production instance of an application.

This recipe shows that you how to set up an Elastic Load balancer group that directs web traffic between two different nodes.

Getting ready

For this recipe, you will require an AWS account and at least a single EC2 instance.

How to do it...

The following steps show you how to create a new EC2 Elastic Load Balancer and assign both balanced ports and an EC2 to host it:

1. Start by logging into your AWS management panel and select the EC2 link.

2. In the EC2 management panel, locate the link titled Load Balancers in the left-hand menu and click on it.

3. The next page gives you a summary of your Load Balancers. If this is your first time in this panel, it should be blank. Click on the blue button at the top of the screen marked **Create Load Balancer** to create a new Load Balancer.

4. The next page allows you to set certain basic elements of your load balancer. In this example, I am going to create a load balancer to balance common web traffic (HTTP and HTTPS). You can start by giving the load balancer a name that will allow you to identify it. Next, you can select the VPC you wish to create the load balancer in and select if this is an internal only load balancer

Internal load balancers are extremely useful to balance load between your applications internally, and is especially crucial when designing architectures, such as a Micro Service based app.

5. You can also perform advanced VPC configurations at this point, allowing you to select specific VPCs to load balance to if you require granularity over the configuration.

6. Next, we have the listener configuration. This is where you select the ports you wish to load balance.

> Notice that you can select the load balancer and instance port to be different; this is exceptionally useful when you cannot make the application listen on port 80 directly; for instance, with applications that run inside Tomcat containers.

As you can see in the following screenshot, I have kept it simple and added both HTTP and HTTPS to be load balanced:

Load Balancer Protocol	Load Balancer Port	Instance Protocol	Instance Port
HTTP	80	HTTP	80
HTTPS (Secure HTTP)	443	HTTP	443
Add			

Once your happy with your choices, click on the button titled '**Assign Security Groups**

7. Much like creating an EC2 instance, assigning security groups allows you to set the pre-existing security group you wish to use or alternatively to set up new ones. If you create a new group, it should use the initial listener configuration to create a template.

8. Once you have created/selected a group that you are happy with; click on **Configure Security Settings**.

9. If you have selected a listener to be HTTPS then you will be directed to the next page, **Configure Security Settings**, otherwise you will have to click through a warning that notes that you have no secure listener.

> It is now expected that a website should be usable over HTTPS, and indeed, it is becoming increasingly common for sites to only offer HTTPS connections, and Google will penalize the site in it's page ranking if they do not offer HTTPS.

This page allows you to upload an SSL certificate, which will allow the load balancer to terminate the SSL connections for you, saving you the need to configure individual servers to handle an SSL termination. If you have previously uploaded a certificate, then you can select it here; otherwise, you can paste the details into this form:

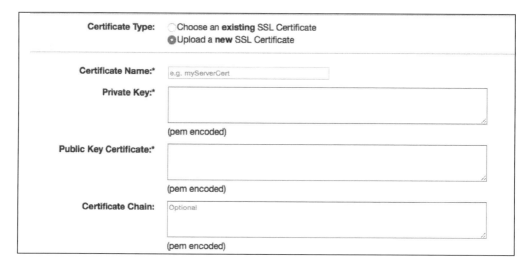

Once you have entered your certificate details, click on the button marked as **Configure Health Check**.

10. In the next screen, you can set the health check that will be regularly sent to the instances that the load balancer is sending traffic to. This allows the load balancer to remove instances that are no longer capable of serving requests or are no longer performant. The health check comprises of either a HTTP or HTTPS request for a nominated health page, or can use a simple TCP or SSL check on a certain port.

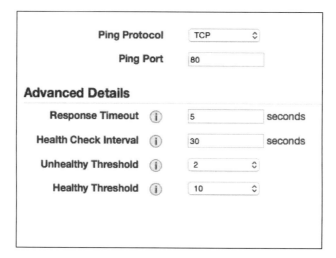

As you can see in the preceding screenshot, you can also set a reasonable set of granularity to the checks; thus, allowing you to tweak how slowly a node should respond to be considered unhealthy and how often to call the health check itself. Once you are happy with your choices, click on the button marked **Add EC2 Instances.**

11. The next screen will show you a list of your EC2 instances and will allow you to select the members for your load balancer group. Select each of the instances that you wish to partake in the load-balanced group. If you are using multiple availability zones, you can also set options to allow you to balance across them, allowing you to spread traffic geographically.

12. Once you have selected the EC2 instances that you wish to include in the load balancer, click on the button marked as **Add Tags**.

13. The next screen allows you to set tags against the load balancer; as with EC2 instances, this allows you to add key value pairs and helps you to identify your load balancer within a busy AWS infrastructure.

    Add any tags you believe are relevant and click on the blue button marked **Review and Create**

14. The next screen will show you a summary of the load balancer you are about to create and it will offer you the opportunity to amend any details. Review them and when you are happy, click on the button marked **Create load balancer**. The load balancer will be created and you will be passed back to the **Load Balancer management** screen.

15. The Load Balancer management screen should list your new load balancer and it should look something similar to the following screenshot:

Note the DNS name; you should use a CNAME DNS record to point your records that you wish to be load balanced.

 Do not be tempted to use an A record; the IP address of the Elastic Load Balancers can and will shift.

16. You should now be able to direct traffic at your new load balancer and have it balanced across your selected EC2 instances.

See also

You can find further details of Elastic Load Balancing at `https://docs.aws.amazon.com/ ElasticLoadBalancing/latest/DeveloperGuide/elastic-load-balancing. html`.

Managing DNS with route53

Domain Name Services (**DNS**) underpins the Internet and a reliable and performant DNS service is crucial to running a web service of any kind. It's a surprisingly neglected area of performance monitoring and a poorly configured or poorly performing DNS server can have a very large impact on the health of your application.

AWS Route53 is a highly scalable DNS server, which has advanced features allowing for geo-routing, Apex CNAME records, and so on. It is also highly performant with DNS servers in most major geographical areas, allowing for a minimum network hops to resolution.

This recipe will show you how to set up a new DNS zone and how to add new records.

Getting ready...

For this recipe, you need an active AWS account. You will also need a registered domain name that you wish to use.

How to do it...

This recipe will show you how to take an existing domain and manage its DNS records using Amazon Route53:

1. Log into your AWS management console and select the **Route 53** panel by clicking on the following icon:

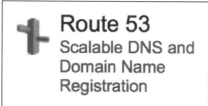

This will take you into the Route53 panel and if this is your first time, you will be greeted with the following introductory screen:

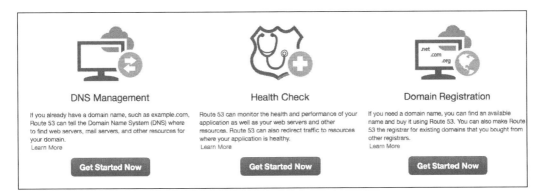

 For this recipe, I'm going to assume that you already have a domain to manage; if this is not the case, then you can select the domain registration and register them via AWS.

2. Click on the button titled **Get Started Now** underneath the DNS management header; this will take you to the DNS management panel. The management panel allows you to see at a glance the DNS zones that you are managing via Route53. Click on the blue button marked **Create Hosted Zone** to create a new zone.

    This should open a panel allowing you to input your Zone name and resembles the following screenshot:

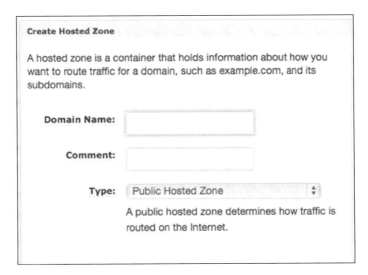

This allows you to enter your zone name (for instance, example.com), and select the scope. By default, it is created as a public DNS zone and will make the zone available to all public clients; however, you can create zones that are only available to instances hosted within AWS. This is useful in building your internal network and keeping its records hidden from public view.

Input your domain name into the input and click on the blue button titled **Create**.

3. Once you have entered your domain name, you will be taken to the record set management screen. This allows you to enter the records that describe your infrastructure and any permissible DNS record type.

 You can find a good rundown of DNS record types at https://support.google.com/a/answer/48090?hl=en.

By default, the Zone will be populated with the name server records, and should look like this:

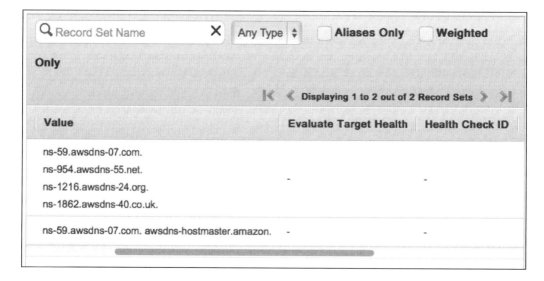

4. To create a new record, click on the blue button marked **Create Record Set**.

5. The record set creation screen allows you to enter your DNS record; for instance, creating an A record would look something like this:

6. Route53 is like many DNS systems in that you enter a record name, select the DNS type, and enter a relevant value and TTL (Time to live). Where Route53 differs is its routing policy. Routing policies allow you to add additional flexibility to your DNS infrastructure, allowing you to add features, such as Geographical DNS, allowing different countries to resolve to different IP's.

Enter the desired record type and click 'create' to create your new record. Once you click on create, your record will be created, propagated, and made available to the public.

See also

You can find further details of Route53 at `https://aws.amazon.com/documentation/route53/`.

Using Ansible to create EC2 hosts

Using an IAAS platform ensures that you automate early and often; due to the cost model of AWS, it's more efficient to be as on demand or elastic as possible. By using automation, you can automate the deployment of an application across its entire lifecycle, from the creation of a host to deployment of an application and finally, the destruction of the host. This also allows you to stand up to new environments easily, as there is no need to provision new hardware, networks, or any other such activities.

This recipe will demonstrate how to use Ansible to create a new EC2 host.

Getting ready

For this recipe, you will need an active AWS account and an Ansible client

How to do it...

The following recipe demonstrates how to use a very simple Ansible playbook to automatically create an EC2 instance:

1. First, create a directory to hold your Ansible code using the following command:

    mkdir ansibleec2

2. Next, we create our inventory. Create a new file called ec2inventory and insert the following content:

    ```
    [ec2]
    localhost
    ```

    Note that you are simply asking Ansible to run commands on the same host on which the Ansible playbook is run; this is because you are essentially using your own host to run commands against Amazon's EC2 API rather than interactively working directly with AWS.

3. Now we have an inventory, we can use Ansible to create our EC2 instance. Create a new file called ec2.yml and add the following code:

    ```
    - hosts: ec2
      connection: local
      tasks:
        - name: 'Create EC2 instance'
          ec2:
              aws_access_key: AKIAICW3HOQKY6LMCD4A
              aws_secret_key: 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
    ```

```
key_name: test
region: us-west-2
group: webserver
instance_type: t2.micro
image: ami-5189a661
wait: yes
wait_timeout: 50
monitoring: yes
vpc_subnet_id: subnet-89770eec
assign_public_ip: yes
```

This code is relatively straightforward and is an example of using a playbook outside of a role. First, it ensures that it uses the localhost entry listed in the inventory and also uses a local connection rather than the usual SSH. Next, we define our list of tasks, in this case calling the Ansible EC2 module and giving it several parameters. These are generally self-explanatory and map directly back to the options you could use in the GUI. One interesting parameter is the wait parameter; this ensures that Ansible will only return once the host is created, rather than assuming that all is well.

4. Run the playbook using the following command:

```
ansible-playbook -i ec2inventory ec2.yml
```

This will create a new EC2 instance and start its running.

 Its also worth pointing out that in production use you will want to either pass the AWS credentials as an environment variable or encrypt them using Ansible vault. You can find the details at `http://docs.ansible.com/ansible/guide_aws.html#authentication`.

See also

You can find further details of the EC2 Ansible module at `http://docs.ansible.com/ansible/ec2_module.html`.

12

Application Performance Monitoring with New Relic

In this chapter, we are going to cover the following topics:

- ▶ Signing up for a New Relic account
- ▶ Installing the New Relic Java agent
- ▶ Using the performance overview
- ▶ Locating performance bottlenecks with Transaction Traces
- ▶ Observing database performance with New Relic
- ▶ Release performance monitoring with New Relic
- ▶ Server Monitoring with New Relic

Introduction

Monitoring is a key part of running any system, from the smallest to the largest; however, monitoring takes many forms. We covered application monitoring in *Chapter 10, Monitoring with Sensu* and those recipes demonstrated how to set up monitoring for application faults. Fault monitoring is only one part of the picture; however, for a true reflection of your application's health, you need to know how well it is performing, how effectively it can communicate with it's dependencies (Databases, external API's, and so on), and if there are particular elements that are not performing as you expect.

This monitoring niche can be filled with an **Application Performance Monitoring tool (APM)**. APM solutions offer the ability to drill into your application, exposing performance and reliability issues with considerable detail. Generally speaking, they use some form of agent that allows the APM tool to insert hooks into the running code at runtime, allowing it access to method calls, network calls, and so on. It may also offer additional tools, such as more 'traditional' server monitoring, external site monitoring, and so on.

The key to a good APM tool is the ability to present this myriad form of data in an accessible form and allow proactive reporting and alerting to be set up against it. Most, if not all APM tools on the market today offer web consoles that allow you to drill into the data in a fairly intuitive fashion; this is important, as it can offer a meeting place for Developers, stake holders, and infrastructure staff to examine issues, without needing to learn many different esoteric tools.

The APM market place is growing and at the time of writing, there are several competitors, but by far, the most popular tools are AppDynamics and New Relic; both offer a broad set of features allowing detailed monitoring of application performance and both offer a SAAS platform (although AppDynamics also offers on premises options). Both AppDynamics and New Relic are commercial tools, albeit ones that offer free limited accounts. At present, the open source community has yet to create a tool that can compete on features; however, that looks to be changing, with several projects showing promise.

In this chapter, we are going to briefly look at New Relic. New Relic is easy to use, offers a free (if limited account), and a trial of its full package. To cover the product in detail requires a book in itself; so, I have focused on some of the key elements, with recipes that demonstrate how to pinpoint common application bottlenecks.

Signing up for a New Relic account

Before we can use New Relic, we need to create an account. This is straightforward and by default, it will offer you a trial of the full enterprise product. After the trial expiration, the account will revert to a free limited account. The free account misses many of the options; thus, allowing for detailed monitoring; however, it still allows for an excellent top-level view of your application.

Getting ready

For this recipe, you will need a web browser.

How to do it...

Let's start up with signing up with New Relic account:

1. Open the following URL in your browser:

   `https://newrelic.com/signup`

2. You should see a screen similar to the following:

This single page form is all you need to fill in order to create your account. Ensure that the e-mail address you use is valid, as you will need to confirm the sign up.

3. Once your account has been created, you will be taken to the initial sign in page; this will show you a banner of the New Relic application stack:

New Relic. **APM**	New Relic. **BROWSER**	New Relic. **MOBILE**	New Relic. **SERVERS**	New Relic. **INSIGHTS**	New Relic. **SYNTHETICS**
Our flagship product helps you monitor the performance and availability of your web applications.	Browser specific data so you can understand your software's performance from an end-user's perspective.	Quickly pinpoint performance problems in your mobile apps operating in complex productions environments.	Find health issues to things like CPU utilization, memory utilization, disk I/O utilization, and disk capacity.	Query application business metrics, performance data, and customer behaviors at lightning speed.	Test and find issues with your software's business critical functionality before real users do.

These links allow you to access the various products that New Relic offers, from the APM product, to mobile app monitoring, Real User Monitoring from the browser, data exploration, and external site monitoring.

See also

You can find further details on the signup process at `https://docs.newrelic.com/docs/accounts-partnerships/accounts/account-setup/create-your-new-relic-account`.

Installing the New Relic Java agent

To gather statistics, New Relic uses an agent that views transactions as they pass through the application. This is then recorded and sent onto New Relic. The Java agent is suitable for use with any Java based application, both inside and outside of a container. In this recipe, we will demonstrate how to setup the New Relic agent within a Tomcat container.

Getting ready

For this recipe, you will need a New Relic account and an application that runs within a Tomcat container.

How to do it...

Let's install the New Relic Java component:

1. Log into your New Relic Account and click on the profile menu in the top-right corner. From the drop-down, select the item title **Account Settings**. On the right-hand side of the next screen, you will find a list of available agents. Click on the **Java release** to download it.

You'll notice that there is a separate download for the Java 8 installer; keep this in mind when downloading the agent. There are also links to 'established' releases. These are the versions that have the most established user base. Use this one if you are cautious.

2. Copy the `zip` file containing the Java agent onto the server that you wish to monitor and `unzip` it using the following command:

```
$ unzip -d /opt <pathto_newrelic.zip>
```

Where `<newrelic.zip>` is the versioned `zip` file. This will unpack the New Relic agent into the `/opt` directory.

3. With your favorite editor, open up the `setenv.sh` file within your Tomcat application, this will be located within the bin directory of your Tomcat installation. If one does not exist, create it and edit it to resemble the following:

```
JAVA_OPTS="$JAVA_OPTS -javaagent:/opt/newrelic/newrelic.jar"
```

 This is based on a vanilla install of Tomcat; if you already have your `JAVA_OPTS` set, ensure that you add the `-javaagent` option in the correct place.

4. Restart your application. After start-up, pause for around five minutes for New Relic to start logging data and then log into your account. Click on the **APM** menu and you should see a screen similar to the following:

5. Click on the **My Application**, and you should see the following screen:

Your application is now set up and is recording performance metrics.

By default, all data is transmitted to a New Relic using SSL and you can obfuscate certain data elements to ensure that sensitive information is not stored within their platform. See `https://docs.newrelic.com/docs/accounts-partnerships/accounts/security/security` for details of what you can secure.

See also

Further details of the Java agent can be found at `https://docs.newrelic.com/docs/agents/java-agent`.

Using the performance overview

New Relic offers a huge amount of information in a readable format; this allows you to see at a glance if your application and dependencies are performing, as you would expect. This data is readily available on the performance overview screen and gives you a window into the detail that New Relic holds about your application. This recipe briefly touches on the major parts of the overview screen and highlights elements that can reveal issues.

Getting ready

For this recipe, you need a New Relic account and an application reporting data.

How to do it...

Now let's go through the performance overview:

1. Log into your New Relic account and select the **APM** tab; you will be presented with a list of applications that are currently reporting to New Relic. Select the app you wish to examine; this will take you onto the summary screen for that application.

2. The first part to focus on is the main graph and should look a little something like this:

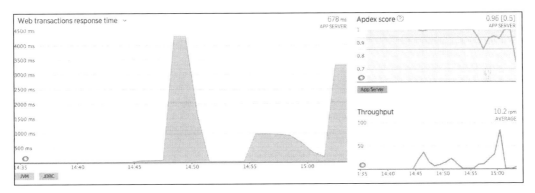

This chart summarizes the following areas:

- Response times of the application split by its components (in this case, the JVM or application code and database).

- The throughput of the application in requests per minute

- The Apdex rating of the application

Apdex is a method of taking the measurements that New Relic gathers and presenting them in a single easy to use metric. The Apdex measures user satisfaction, allows you to set an overall goal (the site should respond in n seconds), which can then be used to extrapolate how many of your users are satisfied, tolerating, and frustrated. More details can be found here: http://www.apdex.org.

The response time chart is stacked and will include the following:

- ❏ JVM (App) response time
- ❏ Database response time
- ❏ External resources response time

3. Clicking the legend will allow you to strip the elements out; thus, allowing you to focus on a badly behaving component. You can also drag on the chart to zoom in on a particular time period and this will cause any other view you visit to reflect the time selected.

4. Also, note that the chart is split between web and non-web transactions. You can change the view by clicking on the drop-down menu on the top-left of the chart, it should resemble the following screenshot:

> Web transactions response time ⌄

5. Underneath the charts, you can see a list of transactions in the selected time period, a chart of the current Error rate, and a complete list of the Recent Events. It should look something like this:

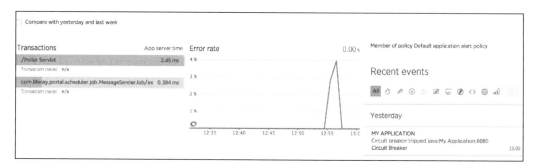

6. Look first at the **Transactions** list:

Transactions	App server time
/com.liferay.portlet.wiki.action.EditPageA	7.61 sec
Transaction traces: 7.6 s	
/com.liferay.portlet.wiki.action.ViewNode	4.17 sec
Transaction traces: 8.3 s	
/com.liferay.portlet.login.action.LoginActi	2,310 ms
Transaction traces: n/a	
/com.liferay.portal.action.LayoutAction	1,810 ms
Transaction traces: 8.8 s 4.8 s	
/html/portal/layout/view/portlet.jsp	996 ms
Transaction traces: 2.3 s	

This is a list of the top transactions that the platform has processed in the time period, and the average response time. These can be clicked on, and are linked to the more detailed transaction list, and allows you to see exactly where the time is being spent in these processes.

7. Next, we have the **Error rate** chart.

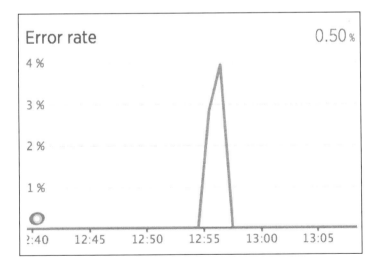

8. Any time an error is logged within the application that generates one of the following response codes, New Relic logs it:

      ❑   400 Bad Request

      ❑   401 Unauthorized

      ❑   403 Forbidden

      ❑   502 Bad Gateway

      ❑   503 Service Unavailable

> It is possible within the New Relic settings to exclude certain errors; this can be useful if they are expected, and can stop alerts being generated.

9. Next, we have the **Recent events** list:

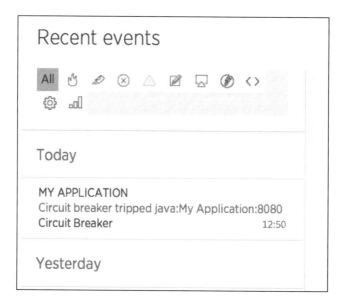

Any time a significant event happens; New Relic will record it and display it here. Significant events can be anything from serious application errors, to deployments, to warnings, and offers you a quick way to check if an event has occurred you were unaware of.

10. Finally, we have the server list:

1 server						
Server name	Apdex	Resp. time	Throughput	Error Rate	CPU usage	Memory
liferay 1 app instance	$0.88_{0.5}$	576 ms	3 rpm	0.50 %	21 %	1.3 GB

New Relic records details of every server hosting the application in the current time span and offers a brief summary of its throughput, responsiveness, and resource usage. This is linked to the New Relic server monitoring and if the monitoring agent is installed, it allows you to view server-monitoring statistics during this period.

See also

You can find further details of the summary screen at `https://docs.newrelic.com/docs/apm/applications-menu/monitoring/apm-overview-dashboard`.

Locating performance bottlenecks with Transaction Traces

New Relic can dig deep into the reasons as to why an application may not be performing well by performing a Transaction Trace. Transaction Tracing allows for a huge level of details, allowing you to see why a certain transaction is running slow, right down to the individual method calls.

Transaction Tracing is initiated when New Relic notices and records certain transactions that are breaching the Apdex rating. At this point, it starts to sample these transactions, recording in detail what the transaction is doing.

Using the Transaction Traces, you can easily spot where code is less than optimum, highlighting inefficient SQL queries, long running elements of code, and slow external services.

Getting ready

For this recipe, you will require a New Relic account (paid) and an application with the New Relic agent installed.

How to do it...

1. Log into the New Relic portal and click on the **APM** in the top menu. From the left-hand menu on the next screen, select **Transactions**.

2. You should see a screen similar to the following:

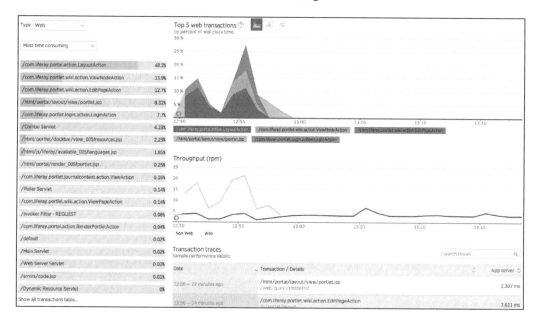

Notice the table on the bottom left-hand side of the screen; this is a list of Transaction Traces. Select one by clicking on the link.

3. When you click on the **Trace**, it opens a new overlaid window with the **Trace details** and it should resemble something like this:

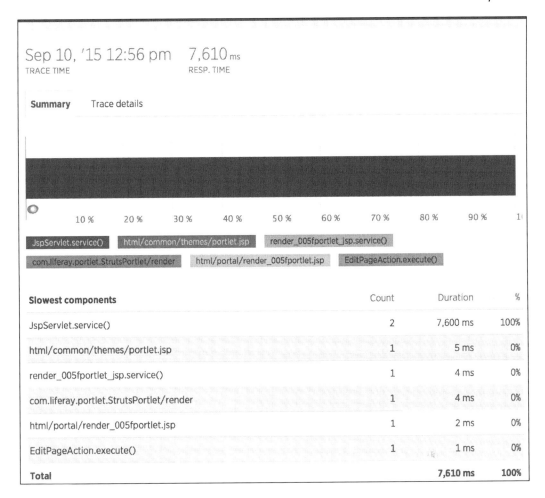

Sep 10, '15 12:56 pm   7,610 ms
TRACE TIME   RESP. TIME

Summary   Trace details

Slowest components	Count	Duration	%
JspServlet.service()	2	7,600 ms	100%
html/common/themes/portlet.jsp	1	5 ms	0%
render_005fportlet_jsp.service()	1	4 ms	0%
com.liferay.portlet.StrutsPortlet/render	1	4 ms	0%
html/portal/render_005fportlet.jsp	1	2 ms	0%
EditPageAction.execute()	1	1 ms	0%
Total		**7,610 ms**	**100%**

This is a break down of the wall clock time of this particular trace, including a graph demonstrating where the time was spent. The list of components lists the slowest elements of this transaction, and most importantly, how many times it was called. This can be useful if you are looping through and calling resources unnecessarily, such as multiple SQL queries that could be collapsed into a single and more efficient query.

4. Click on the tab titled **Trace Details**. This should show a screen similar to the following:

Sep 10, '15 12:56 pm   7,610 ms
TRACE TIME   RESP. TIME

Summary   **Trace details**

Expand performance problems   Collapse all

Duration (ms)	Duration (%)	Segment	Drilldown	Timestamp
7,610	100.00%	**render_005fportlet_jsp.service()**	🔍	0.000 s
2.0	0.03%	html/portal/render_005fportlet.jsp	🔍	0.000 s
0	0.00%	com.liferay.portlet.InvokerPortletImpl/render	🔍	0.002 s
7,610	99.92%	˅ com.liferay.portlet.StrutsPortlet/render	🔍	0.002 s
1.0	0.01%	˃ EditPageAction.execute()		0.006 s
7,600	99.86%	˅ InvokerFilter.doFilter()	🔍	0.007 s
7,600	99.86%	˅ JspServlet.service()	🔍	0.007 s
7,600	99.84%	˅ portlet_jsp.service()	🔍	0.007 s
7,600	99.84%	˅ html/common/themes/portlet.jsp	🔍	0.007 s
0	0.00%	˃ page_jsp.service()		0.008 s
0	0.00%	˃ page_jsp.service()		0.008 s
7,600	99.78%	˅ InvokerFilter.doFilter()	🔍	0.008 s
7,600	**99.78%**	JspServlet.service()	🔍	0.008 s

5. This is a list of the methods that the transaction called and the wall clock time that each method took. Notice that New Relic has highlighted the element of code that is problematic. We can drill into this by clicking on the magnifying glass icon; this will then expand the method to show the stack trace, allowing you to examine in greater detail what this piece of code was doing; it should look something like this:

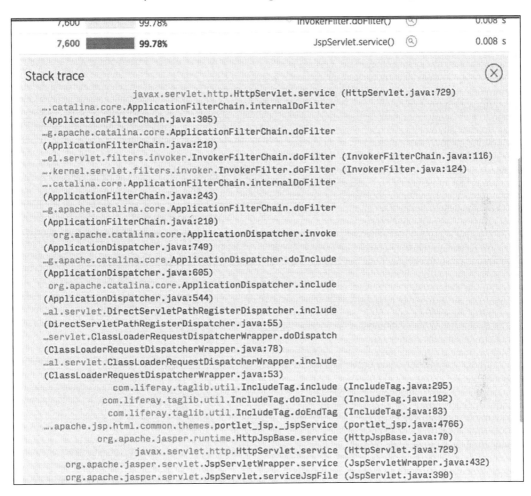

See also

You can find further details of Transaction Tracing at `https://docs.newrelic.com/docs/apm/transactions/transaction-traces/transaction-traces`.

Observing database performance with New Relic

Many, if not most, modern applications are backed by a SQL database, generally providing a persistent data storage. The performance of this data store is critical to the overall application performance and yet it can be somewhat opaque to view.

New Relic tracks database calls, allowing you to see both the overall performance of the database and the details of where the database calls originate within the application and where it may be running slowly.

Getting ready

For this recipe, you will need a New Relic account (trial or paid), an application deployed with the New Relic agent, and a database that the application connects to (and a JDBC compatible database should work).

How to do it...

1. Log into your New Relic account and click on the menu item titled **APM**. From the next screen, select the link on the left-hand sidebar titled **Databases**. This should present you with a screen that looks similar to the following screenshot:

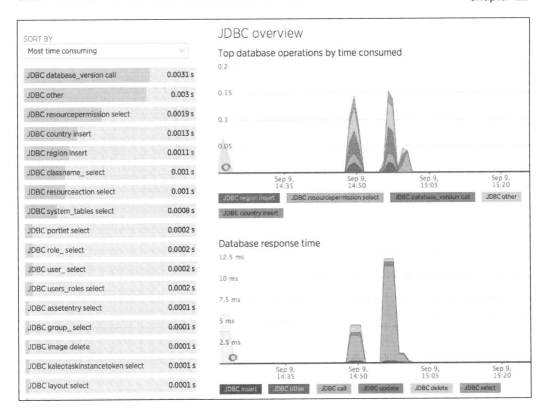

2. This is a list of every database call made during the selected time period and it graphs the duration of the top calls and response time of the database operations and finally a throughput of the database.

3. You can easily sort between the most time consuming and the slowest response time throughput by clicking on the Sort by menu at the top of the transaction list. This enables you to quickly zero in on interesting data on these three axis.

4. When you find a transaction that interests you, click on it in the list. This will open the detailed transaction view and should resemble the following screenshot:

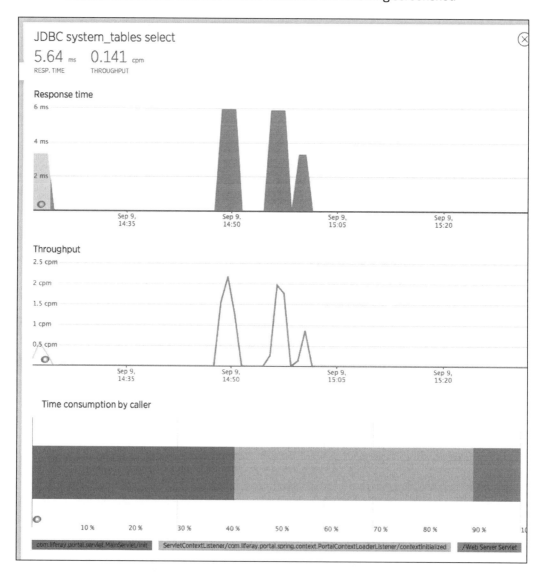

This gives you a breakdown of that particular transaction and highlights the response over time alongside throughput. Of particular interest is the bottom graph; this illustrates the most common transactions that are calling this an SQL query, charted by the overall time spent being called by that particular transaction. These are linked to the transaction view; thus, allowing you to see detailed information about that particular transaction.

See also

You can find further details of the New Relic SQL monitoring at `https://docs.newrelic.com/docs/apm/applications-menu/monitoring/databases-slow-queries-dashboard`

Release performance monitoring with New Relic

One of the most important events to track in any monitoring is a release; this can be anything from a software release, through to server upgrades and anything in between. New Relic allows you to add these as reportable elements, allowing you to perform before and after performance reporting. Using the release monitoring you can take the guesswork out of the effectiveness of a release and this allows you to use empirical data to judge if a release was good.

New Relic offers an API to record a release, allowing you to integrate your automated release tools, configuration management, and others. Using the New Relic API, you should be able to ensure that any automated process can register the release.

In this recipe, we will examine using the New Relic REST API to trigger a deployment notification using a simple curl from the command line.

Getting ready

For this recipe, you will need a New Relic account (free/trial/paid) and an application with the New Relic agent installed.

How to do it...

1. First, we need to enable the API access. Log onto your New Relic account and click on the profile menu located in the menu on the top-left. From the drop down menu, select the entry titled **Account settings** and in the next screen, click on the link in the left-hand sidebar titled **Data sharing**.

2. In the data-sharing screen, you will be offered the option to create a new **REST API Key**. Click on this link and a new API key will be generated and API access to the account will be granted.

3. From your command line, use the following command to record a release against your application:

```
curl -H "x-api-key:<APIKEY>" \
-d "deployment[application_id]=<APPLICATION ID>" \
-d "deployment[description]=<DEPLOYMENT DESCRIPTION>" \
```

```
-d "deployment[revision]=<NEW APP VERSION>" \
-d "deployment[changelog]=<LIST OF CHANGES>" \
-d "deployment[user]=Michael Duffy" https://api.newrelic.com/
deployments.xml
```

Ensure that you replace the elements between the angle brackets with your own items.

You can find the **Application ID** within the deployments tab, underneath the link titled **Show instructions**.

4. If all goes well, you should receive an XML reply containing a summary of elements prior to release; it will resemble something along these lines:

```
<?xml version="1.0" encoding="UTF-8"?>
<deployment>
  <account-id type="integer">1078425</account-id>
  <agent-id type="integer">8699096</agent-id>
  <avg-apdex-f type="integer" nil="true"></avg-apdex-f>
  <avg-apdex-s type="integer" nil="true"></avg-apdex-s>
  <avg-apdex-t type="integer" nil="true"></avg-apdex-t>
  <avg-apdex-threshold type="float" nil="true"></avg-apdex-
threshold>
  <avg-cpu type="float">0</avg-cpu>
  <avg-db type="float">0</avg-db>
  <avg-enduser-apdex-f type="integer" nil="true"></avg-enduser-
apdex-f>
  <avg-enduser-apdex-s type="integer" nil="true"></avg-enduser-
apdex-s>
  <avg-enduser-apdex-t type="integer" nil="true"></avg-enduser-
apdex-t>
  <avg-enduser-apdex-threshold type="integer" nil="true"></avg-
enduser-apdex-threshold>
  <avg-enduser-rt type="float">0.0</avg-enduser-rt>
  <avg-enduser-throughput type="float">0.0</avg-enduser-
throughput>
  <avg-errors type="float">0.0</avg-errors>
  <avg-memory type="float">1359.3242187499998</avg-memory>
  <avg-rt type="float">0.0</avg-rt>
  <avg-throughput type="float">0.0</avg-throughput>
  <changelog>I added many interesting things to the code.</
changelog>
  <description>A shiny deployment</description>
  <end-time type="datetime" nil="true"></end-time>
  <id type="integer">8908958</id>
```

```
<revision>1f1f1</revision>
<timestamp type="datetime">2015-09-10T13:59:28-07:00</timestamp>
<user>Michael Duffy</user>
</deployment>
```

5. Log into your New Relic account and click on the item titled **APM** from the top menu. From the left-hand menu on the next screen, click on the item marked Deployments under the events heading.

6. The next screen offers a list of deployments and a brief summary of the **Apdex score**, **Response time and throughput**. If you click on one of the deployments, you should see a screen similar to the following:

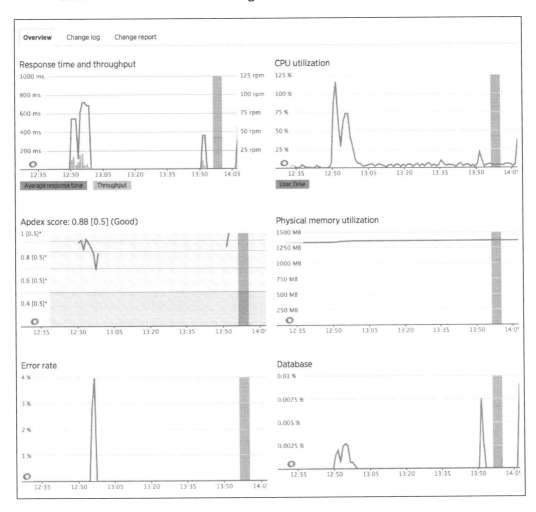

This details the performance prior to the release and after, with the grey bar marking the point of release.

See also

You can find further details of release monitoring at `https://docs.newrelic.com/docs/ release-notes/agent-release-notes/java-release-notes`.

Server Monitoring with New Relic

New Relic is made up of several different products and combined allow you to see end-to-end performance metrics of every part of your application. For instance, if the APM-panel tells you, there are performance issues; one of the first things you should do is look at the performance of the underlying server.

New Relic offers a simple, yet easy to use server monitoring tool, allowing you to monitor your servers alongside your applications. Although lacking some of the sophistication of other monitoring packages, it has the advantage that it is closely tied to APM monitoring. If you are looking at a particular time span in the APM, you can check the server monitoring and have it automatically adjust the time-range to match your app. New Relic can also map apps to servers, allowing you see at a glance, which app is running on which server.

Finally, at the time of writing, Server Monitoring is a free component and you can add as many servers as you like; they do not need to have applications that are monitored within the APM. This allows you to monitor your app servers, but also dependencies, such as database servers and file servers within the same place.

Getting ready

For this recipe, you will require an Ubuntu 14.04 server and a New Relic account.

How to do it...

1. On the host on which you wish to install the New Relic server monitoring, run the following command:

   ```
   $ sudo echo deb http://apt.newrelic.com/debian/ newrelic non-free
   >> /etc/apt/sources.list.d/newrelic.list && wget -O- https://
   download.newrelic.com/548C16BF.gpg | apt-key add -
   ```

2. This adds the New Relic package repository and adds the signing key. Next, run `apt-get update` using the following command:

   ```
   $ sudo apt-get update
   ```

3. You can install the New Relic server monitoring package using the following command:

```
apt-get install newrelic-sysmond
```

4. Although the package is installed, you still need to configure it to send data to your New Relic account. To do this, use the following command:

```
$ sudo nrsysmond-config --set license_key=<LICENSE>
```

Replace `<LICENSE>` with your New Relic account license. You can find this by clicking on the profile menu on the top-right of the New Relic panel and by clicking on **Account Settings**. On the next screen, you should find a panel on the right-hand side that resembles the following screenshot:

Account information

Name
Stunt Hamster ltd_2 🖉

Subscription
Web Lite
Mobile Lite
Insights None
Browser Lite
Synthetics Lite

Billing CC Email
— 🖉

License key
09ceca111dc7a9df6a96495a1115510a2ec24505

5. Finally, you can start the New Relic server monitor by issuing the following command:

```
$ sudo service newrelic-sysmond start
```

6. You should wait for around five minutes for initial data to be propagated to New Relic, but once you have, you can log into your New Relic account and click on servers. You should be able to see the server that you added to the list, and if you click on it, you should see something similar to the following screenshot:

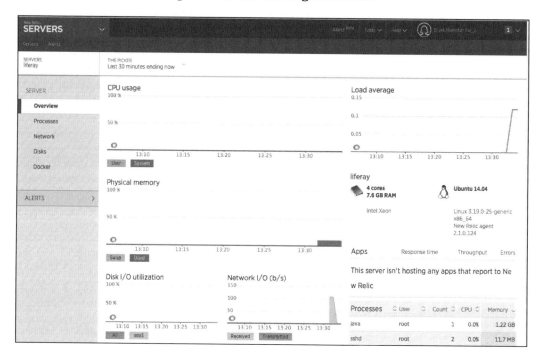

From here, you can explore details of the process running on the server, network, and disk and, if you use it, Docker usage.

See also

You can find more details of the New Relic server monitoring solution at `http://newrelic.com/server-monitoring`.

Index

D

dashboards
  creating, with Grafana 191-195
data
  exploring, with InfluxDB data
      explorer 184-187
database performance
  observing, with New Relic 296-298
disaster recovery (DR) 40
disk check
  adding 237, 238
**Distributed Version Control Software
      (DVCS) 2**
DNS check
  adding 234-236
  URL 237
DNS record types
  reference 276
Docker
  about 118
  installing 119
Docker containers
  building, Jenkins used 159-163
Dockerfile
  creating 124-128
Domain Name Services (DNS)
  managing, with route53 274-277
Do not repeat yourself (DRY) 30
DSL (Domain Specific Language) 79
**Dynamic Host Configuration Protocol
      (DHCP) server 46**

E

EC2 Ansible module
  URL 279
EC2 host
  about 264
  creating 264-269
  creating, with Ansible 278, 279
  URL 269
Elastic Block Store (EBS) 267
Elastic Load Balancers
  about 270
  URL 274
  using 270-273

Elasticsearch
  installing 204-207
  logs importing, with Logstash 208-211
  URL 207
e-mail alerts
  creating 243-245
e-mail handler
  reference 245
esxcli command
  reference 73
ESXi
  configuring 60
  installing 59-62
  references 60
  SSH access, allowing to 66-68
  URL 59
ESXi command line
  used, for destroying guests 73, 74
  used, for starting guests 73, 74
  used, for stopping guests 73, 74
events
  logging, with InfluxDB REST API 180-182
existing Git repository
  cloning 19
**Extra Packages for Enterprise Linux
      (EPEL) 28**

F

FPM
  URL 233
freeform commands
  executing, with Ansible 34

G

Git branch
  creating 23, 24
git checkout -b command 24
Git client
  configuring 15
  installing 15
git merge command 24
Git plugin
  installing 146-150
Git remote
  changes, pushing to 21, 22

Thank you for buying
DevOps Automation Cookbook

About Packt Publishing

Packt, pronounced 'packed', published its first book, *Mastering phpMyAdmin for Effective MySQL Management*, in April 2004, and subsequently continued to specialize in publishing highly focused books on specific technologies and solutions.

Our books and publications share the experiences of your fellow IT professionals in adapting and customizing today's systems, applications, and frameworks. Our solution-based books give you the knowledge and power to customize the software and technologies you're using to get the job done. Packt books are more specific and less general than the IT books you have seen in the past. Our unique business model allows us to bring you more focused information, giving you more of what you need to know, and less of what you don't.

Packt is a modern yet unique publishing company that focuses on producing quality, cutting-edge books for communities of developers, administrators, and newbies alike. For more information, please visit our website at www.packtpub.com.

About Packt Open Source

In 2010, Packt launched two new brands, Packt Open Source and Packt Enterprise, in order to continue its focus on specialization. This book is part of the Packt open source brand, home to books published on software built around open source licenses, and offering information to anybody from advanced developers to budding web designers. The Open Source brand also runs Packt's open source Royalty Scheme, by which Packt gives a royalty to each open source project about whose software a book is sold.

Writing for Packt

We welcome all inquiries from people who are interested in authoring. Book proposals should be sent to author@packtpub.com. If your book idea is still at an early stage and you would like to discuss it first before writing a formal book proposal, then please contact us; one of our commissioning editors will get in touch with you.

We're not just looking for published authors; if you have strong technical skills but no writing experience, our experienced editors can help you develop a writing career, or simply get some additional reward for your expertise.

Continuous Delivery and DevOps – A Quickstart Guide

Second Edition

ISBN: 978-1-78439-931-3   Paperback: 196 pages

Deliver quality software regularly and painlessly by adopting CD and DevOps

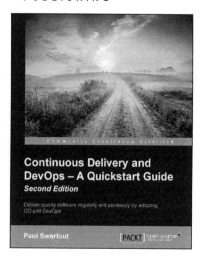

1. Use DevOps and the Continuous Delivery approach to identify the underlying problems that can stifle the delivery of quality software and overcome them.

2. Learn how Continuous Delivery and DevOps work together with other agile tools.

3. A guide full of illustrations and best practices to help you consistently ship quality software.

Implementing OpenShift

ISBN: 978-1-78216-472-2   Paperback: 116 pages

A fast-paced, practical guide for using OpenShift to deploy your own open source Platform-as-a-Service

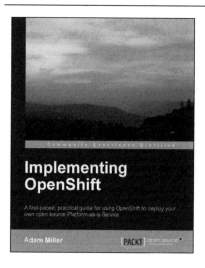

1. Discover what the cloud is, tear through the marketing jargon, and go right to the tech.

2. Understand what makes an open source Platform-as-a-Service work by learning about OpenShift architecture.

3. Deploy your own OpenShift Platform-as-a-Service cloud using DevOps orchestration and configuration management.

Please check **www.PacktPub.com** for information on our titles

Printed in Great Britain
by Amazon.co.uk, Ltd.,
Marston Gate.